The Pain & The Glory

"My dear friend Smetana.
May God gather him in His bosom.
He has earned eternal glory and rest.
He was indeed a true genius"

FRANZ LISZT
May, 1884

Bedrich Smetana

Fr.

The Life of
SMETANA

The Pain & The Glory

Written by
LIAM NOLAN

*from the Story
and Research of*
J. BERNARD HUTTON

GEORGE G. HARRAP & CO. LTD
London • Toronto • Wellington • Sydney

First published in Great Britain 1968
by GEORGE G. HARRAP & CO. LTD
182 High Holborn, London, W.C.1

© *J. Bernard Hutton & Liam Nolan* 1968
Copyright. All rights reserved

SBN 245 59215 6

Composed in Linotype Georgian and printed by
Willmer Brothers Limited, Birkenhead, England
Made in Great Britain

For Walter G. Harrap

whose last book this was
with affection and gratitude

The first time I heard music by Smetana was in 1917, when I was only six years old. I was taken to a concert at which the main item was Smetana's *Ma Vlast—My Country*—and I remember the music moving me so deeply that I started crying. For days afterwards I was humming and whistling the *leitmotiv* from *Vltava*, pestering my mother to take me to another concert so that I could hear the music again.

A year or so later a travelling theatre company came to Chrast and, among other things, staged *The Bartered Bride*. We went to see it, and again I was fascinated by the music. It gave me an overwhelming feeling of contentment. At that time I had already had a year's tuition in violin-playing, and my favourite compositions were Smetana's. Without ever tiring I would stand for hours trying to master them.

After we moved to Berlin in 1920 many house concerts were held in our apartment, and although Wagner, Beethoven, Mozart, Liszt, Schubert, and other composers were frequently played, Smetana's music was always in demand. And every time I heard his compositions I experienced the same feelings, the same enthusiasm. As time went on I got to know more of them, and the more I knew the more fascinated I was. I was intrigued by the composer and read everything about him that was available, little though this was.

Later, when I returned to Prague in 1933, I took every opportunity of seeing the Smetana operas produced at the Czech National Theatre. I spent hours at the Smetana Museum in Prague, visited his birthplace in Litomysl, and learnt all I could about this extraordinary man. When I came to England I represented the Smetana Society in the United Kingdom.

Thirty years ago I made up my mind to write the complete story of Smetana some day. A number of books had been published about the composer, but none of them gave the full story of the man and his music. But I kept on postponing work on the book—either because there was something else I had to write or because I discovered that I still needed to study more facts from contemporary records.

After the Second World War I spent a great deal of time at the Smetana Museum, at various Czech archives and libraries, and collected everything I could about Smetana, both published and unpublished. But when I returned to England I again had to postpone writing the Smetana book because there was always urgent work to be done, other books to be written.

At long last I sat down and started preparatory work on the book. But suddenly the fear arose in my mind that I might not be able to write an objective, impartial book about the man to whom I felt so drawn. Being a Czech and an admirer of Smetana, might I not present too coloured a picture? One day I spoke about my project and my worries to my friend and fellow-writer Liam Nolan. And, as I briefly outlined the Smetana story to him, I saw that he was interested. He offered to write the book from the material I had collected and prepared. I jumped at this opportunity because I knew he would bring a balance to it that would have been difficult for me to achieve.

So it came about that this book was written.

J. BERNARD HUTTON

One day in 1965 Joe Hutton began to talk to me about Bedrich Smetana, and as he talked there was the light of what some people would call fanaticism, but which I prefer to think was love, in his eyes.

For thirty years, it seemed, Joe had been living with the idea of trying to get the story of his great compatriot down on paper. But, as he explained, there were always difficulties of some sort or another. He had already collected a great mass of background material, and it had accumulated in his various homes, daring him to begin, building up in him the frustration that any writer feels when unable to tackle something on which he dearly wants to make a start.

Now it so happened that I was in love with as much of Smetana's music as I knew, though I am bound to admit that this did not extend beyond *The Bartered Bride* and the six symphonic poems, *Ma Vlast*—for me there has never been a piece of music which captures so accurately and exquisitely the picture of a river that Smetana paints with his *Vltava*—so when Joe Hutton began to tell me snippets of the life of the composer, I said I would like to attempt the task of writing the story of the man who had created such beauty. It soon became a labour of love.

I think it important to emphasize that the book is not, nor was it ever intended to be, a work that set out to explore the technicalities and techniques of Smetana's music. Nor does it make any claim to provide a full historical background to the country in which he lived most of his life, the area now known as Czechoslovakia. It is, in short, a biography about a man and the people who surrounded him and influenced his life.

LIAM NOLAN

BOOK

[1]

CHAPTER

[1]

IT MADE A GOOD STORY, whether or not you took it seriously. Placed where it was, on the front page of the newspaper of the Czech town of Litomysl, not many of the local inhabitants missed it.

One of the brewery workers slapped the page and said to his workmate, "Did you read this? About the manager's wife?"

His friend looked up. "Is the baby here already? Surely it's not due—"

"No, it hasn't even been born yet, but if this is to be believed the woman is a prophet!"

"A prophet?"

"That's what I said." He took the paper, cleared his throat, looked around to make sure no-one in authority was eavesdropping, then began to read out aloud: "Mrs Barbora Smetana, wife of brewery manager Frantisek Smetana, claims to have had a remarkable dream in which an Angel revealed to her some startling details about the baby she is expecting early in March.

"This newspaper heard about Mrs Smetana's claim from one of the lady's neighbours, and we sent a reporter to talk to the pregnant woman. She said that it was true she had had a dream in which she saw an Angel. 'The Angel assured me that I would give birth to a son,' Mrs Smetana said, 'and that he would grow up to become a great musician.'

"Mrs Smetana (née Lynka) has already given birth to two

daughters; there are five other girls in the family from the husband's two previous marriages.

"Mrs Smetana told our reporter that on the night following her dream of an Angel, she had another dream. 'In it I dreamt that a son was born to me,' she said, 'and I saw him become one of the greatest men of our Czech nation.'"

The man put the paper down and snorted derisively. "I always knew Frantisek Smetana had ideas of grandeur," he said, "but when even his *wife* . . ."

It was February 1824, and most of the townspeople talked about the story for a day or so. Then it was forgotten. After all, women expecting babies imagined all sorts of things.

But Frantisek didn't forget. He believed his wife's story. He wanted a son. He wanted the boy to become famous, because then he too would be famous, as the father of an extraordinary son. Fame and social position meant a great deal to Frantisek Smetana.

The pre-Lenten festivities were in full swing on the night of Monday, March 1st, and Barbora Smetana, heavy and swollen with child, danced with as much vigour as the best of them.

"She is extraordinary!"

"Amazing!"

"She should be at home—this is no place for such exhibitionism from a woman in her condition."

If Barbora heard the comments she didn't show any sign of their effect upon her. It was long past midnight when she and Frantisek went home.

On the Tuesday morning Barbora remained in bed. No, she told Frantisek, she didn't think the baby was coming yet, but it had been a late and hectic night and she thought she would lie on and rest for an hour or so.

Relieved, Frantisek kissed his wife and went about his work, overseeing the jobs in and around the brewery. He was crossing the yard when he caught sight of one of the maids, skirts lifted to avoid tripping, running towards him out of breath.

"Sir! Sir! Sir!" she was calling.

He went towards the girl, anxiety now building up inside him. He grabbed her wrists fiercely and said, "Quiet now, *quiet,* girl! What is it? What's wrong? Tell me, girl, *tell* me!" His voice was becoming high and harsh with alarm.

The girl took a desperate breath and then blurted: "The baby, sir, the baby—it's here, and it's a boy!"

Just for an instant Frantisek Smetana stood, rooted, silent, dumfounded. Then he threw his head back and let out a great joyous roar. "A boy!" he bellowed. "A boy! Do you hear that, everyone? I've got a boy, a son!"

And he suddenly grabbed the startled maid by fingers and waist and went into a wild, whirling dance with her around the yard, shouting and yelling with happiness.

Then, as suddenly as he had started, he stopped, turned away from the panting girl, and ran across the yard and into the house to see his wife and brand-new son.

Barbora's face was white and drawn and her hair in disarray when he went, timidly now, into the room. A huge grandmother of a woman was wiping the sweat off the mother's forehead, and, wrapped like a miniature mummy, Frantisek Smetana's baby boy was squealing his first protests at the world.

Frantisek looked at the child. True, the baby was just like all the others when they'd been born. But it wasn't the same— this one was a boy, and that was a wonderful thing.

He went then and sat on the edge of the bed and took Barbora's hand in his. He looked at her face, so tired-looking with those enormous eyes close to tears. But the tears were of happiness and effort.

"So your dream was true, my love," he said.

"The first part of it, yes," she replied, and smiled. "Are you happy?"

"You know I'm happy," he answered. "And very, very proud. Thank you for my son."

And then he laughed and stood up. He went out into the corridor, threw open the window, and stuck his head out.

"You can all stop work," he shouted. "Do you hear me? Go inside and tell them, Josef. Tell them I, Frantisek Smetana, have had a son. Tell them they can stop work for the day. And you can, all of you, drink all you can hold. The good God has sent me a boy, and it is fitting that we should celebrate."

The singing and dancing in and around Count Valdstejn's brewery at Litomysl went on late into the night of March 2nd, 1824.

Frantisek was a man who, all his life, had craved respectability. The son of a carpenter (and youngest of six children), he had spent a childhood of singular unhappiness, and at an early age became obsessed with the idea of hauling himself up the social ladder, away from the strata of society inhabited by mere tradesmen. He became restless, was permanently on the look-out for contacts who might help him to leave the working class. To some extent he was a tortured man.

After an apprenticeship served in a brewery he left home and moved from job to job. Each time he moved he went to a region in which he was unknown. And each time he got a slightly better job.

When Bedrich was born Frantisek had (apart from accumulating three marriages) achieved at least part of his life's desire. As manager of the brewery on Count Valdstejn's estate some of the trappings of respectability were already his, and those which he hadn't yet attained he meant to fight for.

However, the arrival of the new baby worked like a soothing balm on the brewery manager. He took to sitting and looking at his son as though amazed that this little human being was his own flesh and blood. He became softer, less consumed by ambition. At times he would take out his violin and, in the quietness of the afternoon, play to the child. He adored the look of astonished pleasure that crept over the tiny face, and he knew instinctively that his own playing of the instrument was somehow better on these occasions than it had ever been.

The boy walked at an early age, and before very long the sight of his curly-headed figure waddling around the brewery yard was familiar to workmen and visitors alike. By the time Bedrich was four years old he was the darling of his elder sisters. They fought among themselves for the privilege of looking after him and being seen with him. The oldest girl, Albina, seemed to be the child's favourite, and he would go to her more readily than to anyone else save his mother and father.

In character and behaviour he was different from all the others. He frequently wandered off on his own and would be found later staring at a flower, fondling it with the utmost gentleness, or walking slowly, as though in wonder, through the trees.

And yet he was not just a dreamer. He was as mischievous and 'normal' as any of the children. Nor was he precocious in speech, though he had a well-developed sense of mimicry, a dubious talent when it caused embarrassment to his blushing parents.

One night Frantisek, who had been away from the house all day on business, was sitting by the stove talking to Barbora.

"And what has my son and heir been doing today?" he asked.

"Oh, that *boy*, Frantisek!" Barbora said in mock horror. "There is some imp of mischief in him. You know that man Balous who comes from the other side of Litomysl?"

"Tonik Balous? The fat one?"

"The very one. Well, at about eleven o'clock this morning when I was in the bedroom cleaning, I heard a lot of laughter coming from outside. I went to the window to find out who was so amused, and why. I could see a crowd of the brewery men gathered together and rocking with laughter, and there, right in the centre of the circle, was Master Bedrich! He'd found that old hunting-hat of yours and was wearing it, and somehow or other he'd got hold of my rouge and spread it all over his face! He had one of the pups stuffed up his smock to make him look fat, and was slapping his thigh and throwing his head back and shouting 'Ho! Ho! Ho!'—just like old Balous! And, of course, the men were encouraging him. What with the pup struggling to get out, and the noise of the men, we never heard the cart coming into the yard until it was right behind us. And then I turned—and watching the whole performance was old Balous himself!"

Frantisek, who had been laughing throughout the story, stopped and said, seriously, "Balous? What did he do? He's one of our best customers."

"That's what was in my mind," Barbora said. "I went down to pick up Bedrich and scold him, but Balous got there first,

B

picked the boy up, laughed louder than any of us, and gave him five ducats!"

"Five ducats?" Frantisek said. *"Balous?"*

"Yes, he said it was the funniest thing he'd ever seen."

"Well, well. So our son has earned his first pay."

"Yes, Frantisek, but what if Balous had taken it the wrong way?"

"Stop, Barbora! He didn't. Let us be thankful. But that boy—what a boy!"

They laughed together for a long time. Presently Frantisek became aware that Barbora was sitting very still, her head cocked slightly, straining as if to hear.

"What is it?" Frantisek asked.

Barbora held up a finger. "Ssh!" she whispered. "Listen."

He couldn't hear anything. She stood up and went quietly to open the door.

"Now?" she whispered.

A child's voice came quite clearly into the room.

"Bedrich?" Frantisek asked, his eyebrows rising.

"Yes."

"Singing?"

"Yes, but do you hear *what* he's singing?"

Frantisek listened again for a few seconds, and suddenly his face lit up with amazed delight. "That's a Mozart sonata..."

"I know. It's the Sonata in E-minor," Barbora said. "Our Bedrich! You played that for him on Sunday for the first time, didn't you?"

"Yes," Frantisek said, "at dinner-time or just before."

He'd played it twice, and then the child had come over to him and plucked at the violin strings, laughing at the magic sound his pudgy fingers had made. The boy had actually picked up the tune in two short hearings.

The proud parents went to the room where Bedrich was lying, eiderdown kicked away, feet stuck vertically into the air. He didn't hear his mother and father coming into the room, and they stood there motionless, listening to him, before Frantisek eventually ran across and picked the child up and almost smothered him with kisses.

CHAPTER

[2]

IT WAS A FORTNIGHT AFTER the nocturnal singing of the Mozart sonata that Frantisek Smetana came in at lunch-time and said to his wife, "Barbora, how many pieces has the boy learnt in the last ten days—since I started playing to him every evening?"

Barbora began to count on her fingers.

"Well," she said, "he can sing seven off by heart, and he knows most of two others."

"Quite so," Frantisek replied. "Actually I thought he'd picked up only six, but if you say seven, so much the better."

He sat himself at the table, rubbing his hands at some secret decision which he hadn't yet communicated to her, but which was obviously giving him some keen anticipatory pleasure. His wife didn't rise to the bait. This was a game they often played, he tossing out bits of information and hints, trying to entice her to ask what he was talking about, she fiercely resisting the temptation, trying in turn to force him to say, "Well, aren't you going to ask me?"

This time she was succeeding very well at her part of the game.

"Yes," he said loudly and clapped his hands again. "Absolutely! That's what I'll do. Mm-mm."

She ignored it.

He, thinking she hadn't perhaps heard what he'd said, repeated it for her benefit when she came close to the table. All Barbora said was, "Good."

But she knew her husband well, knew his vanities, knew the point at which she was expected to give in. And so now, after a little more acting, she capitulated.

"Now," she asked, "what great revelation have you for me about Bedrich?"

"Ah, yes, Bedrich," he said. "Well—I've decided to teach him to play the violin."

She sat down heavily. Surely Frantisek wasn't serious.

"But he's only four years old," she said. "He's too young, Frantisek."

"Yes, he is young, but not too young. Are you against it?"

"Frantisek, is this a joke, or do you mean what you are saying?" she asked.

How was it that women never seemed to be able to tell when he was serious and when he was joking? "Of course I mean it."

"Oh, no," Barbora exclaimed, "it would be too much for the child—you mustn't try."

"But why, Barbora, tell me why?"

"Because it would tax his little brain too much." All her maternal instincts prodded her into a defence of Bedrich. "You can't force a child of his age. It could do all sorts of damage that we might never even know about until it was too late."

He could feel his impatience rising.

"Do you take me for a fool?" he asked, conscious of the edge in his voice.

"No, of course not, but—"

"Well, hear me out, woman!" he cut in. "I'm not going to force him at all. I have no intention of doing anything of the kind. But if the boy has a talent for music, why not give him a chance? Why not let us see if this keen musical ear which we both know he possesses is part of the beginning of something richer and grander? Can't you see what I'm getting at?"

"Are you sure it's for the child's sake you want to do this?"

"What do you mean?" Frantisek snapped. He knew what she meant, but he was angry that she had penetrated through to his real reason for wanting Bedrich to try to play the violin.

He could see from her manner that trying to win through by bluster would be useless. Barbora had a will of her own and could be just as adamant as he. He would have to change his tactics. He put his pipe down on the small table beside his chair, hauled himself upright, and went across to where his wife was sitting rigidly, her face set in lines of determination.

"Barbora, my love," he began, using a softer voice, "I wouldn't want to do anything that would harm our little son. All I want to do is show him how to hold the instrument, how to use the bow and to make different notes by fingering. That's all. Nothing more. I promise you."

"You won't get angry with him, make him practise?"

"No, no, of course I won't, I assure you."

She sat, not looking at him. Finally he put an arm around her shoulders.

"Well?" he asked.

After a while she looked up and said, "Very well, then."

He kissed her lightly on the forehead. "You'll have nothing to worry about. If he likes it and can manage it it will be up to him whether he wants to practise. I promise you I'll not force him to do anything he doesn't want to or is unable to do. And now, my love, I must be away or Count Valdstejn will be wondering why his manager is not working."

When he came in that evening, and before he ate his meal, he called Bedrich to him and sat the boy on his lap.

"Would you like to hear some more music, my son?" he asked.

"Yes, Papa," the boy said shyly.

"And what would you like Papa to play for you?"

The boy thought for a moment, his forehead puckering in concentration. "A dance, Papa."

"A folk-dance, eh? The one I played last night?"

The boy nodded.

"Very well, then. Down you get, and go and ask your mother for my violin. But be careful. You won't drop it?"

It was the first time he had trusted the boy to carry the violin in its bulky case, and he smiled with pride as Bedrich crossed the room carefully, his face again frowning with concentration and effort.

Frantisek made an elaborate show of thanking him, saying how strong a boy he was, and then lifted him up into a big chair where the tiny figure was swamped by the height and depth of the piece of furniture. When Frantisek lifted the instrument, tuned it, and began to play, young Bedrich's face took on a look of delight. Nor was this lost on the father. Surely now was the time to start the boy? Frantisek played a second piece, and then took the violin away from under his chin and laid it and the bow side by side on the table. Bedrich's disappointment that the recital was at an end could be read in his face.

Some of the older children had come in while Frantisek was playing, but Barbora had hushed them and sent them off into another room. She was standing now by the door, watching, and nervously twitching the ends of her white apron between her fingers. She knew what was coming, and she hated being there to see; at the same time she felt unable to leave.

Frantisek glanced over his shoulder once at her and noticed how tense she looked, but he banished the thought from his mind and turned again to the child.

He spoke softly. "Did you like that music?"

"Yes, it was—" The boy searched for words. "It was— so beautiful." He had never used such a large word before, and he articulated it carefully. Frantisek felt a lump coming into his throat.

"And would you like to be able to play music like that?"

"Oh, yes, yes," the boy answered, excitement lighting up his whole face.

Frantisek looked around once more at Barbora, then went on, "Would you like Papa to teach you?"

This time Bedrich couldn't even talk. He nodded vigorously, hopped down from the chair, and stood before his father, waiting.

Frantisek ruffled his son's curls, lifted the violin and bow, and gave Bedrich his first lesson on how to hold the instrument, how to use the bow, and how to get different notes by shifting the positions of the fingers. Then he placed the violin in position under the childish chin, held the other end of the instrument himself to support its weight, and handed the bow to Bedrich.

For the first time in his young life Bedrich Smetana made music.

Barbora Smetana needn't have worried about her son being forced to learn the violin. He took to the task of learning straight away, and now, instead of spending all his daylight hours romping with his playmates, he passed long periods by himself trying to coax new and more ambitious sounds from the instrument. Hardly an evening passed when he hadn't learnt some extra fragment to play for Frantisek. And his father would sit listening keenly, rarely able to refrain from praising the child whose fingers sped over the strings and who used the bow with such growing fluency.

In the beginning the older children joined in their brother's praise, and boasted of his accomplishments to other children. But as Bedrich began to spend more and more time practising, and paid less and less attention to the chores he was given, resentment grew. After all, if they were told to do something —help with cleaning rooms, washing dishes, or running errands —they did as they were told. If they didn't obey they were severely chastised. Bedrich, it seemed, often elected to ignore these commands, or to say, "Yes, I'll do it in a minute." It was always "in a minute". In the end someone else invariably had to do his chores, while he practised music.

The only one who never seemed to mind was the eldest girl, Albina. To her Bedrich was an angel who could do no wrong. She was the only one with whom he never fell out.

By the time he was five Bedrich could sight-read music, and his father was talking of him as "our little Mozart". Many people in Litomysl had heard of his violin-playing and came to the Smetana household to hear him. The word 'prodigy' began to be used, sparingly at first, but with increasing frequency as more people exclaimed in wonder at the boy's talent. Their amazement was all the greater when they learnt that no professional tutor had given young Smetana so much as a single lesson. Apart from occasional pointers from his father, the boy was entirely self-taught. It was enough to turn any parent's head.

For his own fifty-second birthday on October 26th, 1829,

Frantisek Smetana decided to have a musical evening at his home. Barbora spent three days getting the house prepared, polishing all the windows, cleaning the silverware, brushing every speck of dust and dirt out of the house. She bought the best of food and wines, new silk ribbons for the girls' hair, and a new black-velvet suit and buckled shoes for Bedrich. It was important that the occasion be impressive, for many of Frantisek's most influential friends would be coming, and they would have to be shown that he was a man whose wife knew how to keep house and family in style. Such an occasion might open new social doors to him.

On the morning of his birthday Frantisek went around the house with Barbora making sure everything was perfect, complimenting her as they went from room to room.

Then he called the children in, stiffly accepting their "Happy Birthdays", and lectured them on what their behaviour and manners should be, enjoining Albina to keep them all in order.

When the guests began to arrive Frantisek and Barbora greeted them, desperately anxious to impress; the children curtsied in well-drilled sequence; the maids poured drinks and handed them round.

Several of Frantisek's closer friends inquired, "How is the boy prodigy?" and, "Is this the new Mozart?" Bedrich blushed. His father flushed with ill-disguised pride.

When everyone had arrived and the customary introductions and speeches had been made, Frantisek bade all present to be seated, and called on his three musician friends to take their places.

"As you know," he said to the guests, "this is to be a musical evening, and I am grateful to all of you for coming. It is a great joy to my wife, Barbora"—he bowed graciously towards her—"and to myself that you have honoured us by your presence—and by your presents!" He laughed, and his guests took their cue and joined in. "We shall have some dance music presently, and I hope to see all of you take the floor with your beautiful ladies. However, before the gaiety begins I think there is time for music of a—shall I say—*higher* order? We are a race of music-lovers, are we not? My three friends here on my right have done me the honour of consenting to help me in presenting to you a quartet by Haydn."

There was a ripple of applause and anticipation.

"So, if you are ready, we shall begin."

He turned to his wife and bowed to her, whereupon she crossed over and handed him his violin and bow. The murmur of sound died down.

Then he held up the instrument and dramatically said, "However, ladies and gentlemen, I am not going to play the first violin part as arranged."

Again there was a rising murmur among the guests, and several cries of "Why not, Frantisek? Oh, you *must*."

He waited for a moment, then said, "Because, ladies and gentlemen, I am going to ask, instead, Master Bedrich Smetana, aged five, to take my place!"

At this there was a concerted shout of surprise which turned quickly to applause as the small black-clad figure crossed the room, solemnly took the violin and bow from his father, bowed, and sat with the other three musicians.

There was a hum of expectation in the room as the three men and the child adjusted their instruments, and then, with a nod of the head from the boy, they started to play.

At the end of the performance everyone, including the musicians, stood and applauded the child. He had relapsed into childish innocence again now, embarrassed by these cheering, clapping adults. But they kept up their shouting of "Bravo! Bravo!" And at the end he went to bed with his ears ringing and his hands sore from being shaken.

In the days that followed many of the people who had been at the birthday-party came to Frantisek Smetana and advised him to send Bedrich to an acknowledged music-teacher.

"Certainly it will cost you money," Balous said, "but the boy is an outstanding performer already, considering his age. I don't wish to underrate your own ability as a teacher, but, after all, you haven't got the time to devote to both the boy and your duties."

People who wouldn't normally enter his home except on direct invitation, or to settle some business matter, were arriving daily to talk of the boy's promise and talent. It was only when Barbora began to pester him about whether he was going to take the advice that he gave the issue any serious thought. Doubts as to whether he could afford the cost of lessons were quickly banished when he thought of the further social kudos that would come his way if Bedrich made the progress all his advisers seemed certain he would.

So one morning, when the snow was lying crisp and pure on the fields and the air was sharp and clear, Mr and Mrs Frantisek Smetana and their five-year-old son presented themselves at the house of Jan Chmelik, music-teacher. The boy, bundled up in scarves and furs and woollens, knew what the journey to this part of Litomysl meant. His father had told him that Jan Chmelik was the best music-teacher in the town, and that from now on Bedrich was to have the benefit of Mr Chmelik's tuition.

"Thank you, Papa," Bedrich had said. "I shall be a good violinist for you some day."

"You already are, but I want you to be a *great* one," Frantisek answered. "And also a fine pianist."

"I can't play the piano, Papa, you know that," the boy replied, surprised at what his father had just said.

"I am aware of that, but you shall learn."

This was a side of his father Bedrich hadn't noticed before —the unwavering, slightly mean-looking Frantisek who meant to get his money's worth from Jan Chmelik's music lessons.

However, Bedrich too had a will, young as he was, and he was determined not to have any more to do with the piano than he could manage. He looked straight back at his father and said, "I do not like the piano. I shall not learn to play it."

Frantisek Smetana glowered at the boy. "You will do as I tell you," he said, roughly.

The change in his father Bedrich found not so much frightening as disillusioning. Was this the same gentle papa who used to play the violin to him in the evenings? His mind couldn't grapple with the transformation. Instead, he concentrated on the issue between him and his father. To emphasize his determination he stamped his foot hard on the ground and shouted, "I will *not* learn the piano!"

Frantisek's patience snapped. As he stepped towards the

defiant Bedrich his two hands shot out and grabbed the boy's ears. He twisted angrily, viciously.

"Now, *kneel down!*" Frantisek roared.

The five-year-old, howling with agony from ears that felt as if they were being torn from his head, fell to his knees.

"Frantisek!"

Barbora had come running at the sound of the child's screams.

"Frantisek! Frantisek, for God's sake, what are you doing?"

"Keep quiet, woman—I'll deal with this my way."

"Stop it! Stop it! You're hurting him," she yelled, and began to tear at her husband's arms.

"Mama! Mama! Mama!" Bedrich screamed.

Frantisek released one of the boy's ears and caught his wife's wrist in a fist strengthened by over forty years of hard work. He yanked the arm up and down until Barbora stopped shouting. The boy was screaming with fright; his father pushed him away, letting his ear go. "Kneel," he roared. "*Kneel!* And stop your noise or I'll give you something to cry for. Now, you"—he swung Barbora round to face him—"remember who I am. Remember I am the man of this house, his father. What *I* say *he* does. And if he gives me impertinence, then by God he'll suffer. Do you understand?"

He shook her.

"Now go and get ready," he shouted, and he pushed her from him across the room.

Suddenly he felt ashamed. He walked over to the window and stayed looking out across the yard where the criss-crossing footprints in the snow were already turning to brown slush. Finally, when he felt more composed, he walked back to Bedrich and lifted the child off his knees and stood him on a chair. He gazed at the tear-streaked face and felt even more ashamed. He took out his handkerchief and wiped Bedrich's eyes.

"There now," he said. "That's better, isn't it?"

The boy didn't speak.

"You angered Papa. Papa doesn't like getting angry, but, you see, he—I lost my temper. Papa hates getting angry, especially with you and Mama. You won't make him angry any more, will you?"

The boy shook his head, his eyes filling again.

"All right, let's forget it then, shall we?" He pulled the boy to his chest and held him there. After a while he said, without looking at Bedrich, "I want you to go now and ask Mama to wash your face, and when you're ready we'll go to see Jan Chmelik, who will teach you the violin and the piano. And you'll work hard at both, won't you?"

He felt the boy's head moving. He pushed Bedrich away from him and said, "Say 'Yes, Papa.'"

"Yes, Papa."

That had been an hour ago. Any second now the front door of this town house in Litomysl would swing inwards and he'd meet Jan Chmelik for the first time. What sort of man would he be? Angry, like Papa had been before coming here?

The door opened, and they were invited inside by a plain-faced, fat, middle-aged maid who ushered them into a pleasant sitting-room in which music scores littered the central table. Somewhere someone was practising scales, and Bedrich listened for a harsh voice to cut across the piano sounds, but none came. When mistakes were made all he heard was a soft voice. He could make out no words, but the tone indicated encouragement rather than anger.

He let go of his mother's hand and crossed to one of the windows. He watched a tree's snow melting and dropping in crystal globules like tiny transparent pears. At that moment he felt completely isolated and cut off from both his parents. He blew his breath on to the window and, where the glass became hazy, traced the B of his name with a forefinger. The door opened behind him, but he took no notice until his mother called, "Bedrich!"

He turned then and saw the man who had come in.

He was a polite man who bowed twice and said quietly, "I am Jan Chmelik."

Bedrich's first thought when he saw and heard the man was that he was going to like Jan Chmelik.

"I have heard that you play the violin rather well for such a little fellow," Chmelik said after Bedrich's parents had left. "But it is always better to judge for oneself, you understand."

He took a violin from its case, an exquisite instrument which he handled with love, and put it gently on a chair in front of Bedrich.

"I am going to tell you something you won't really understand," he said to the boy. "That violin was made by a man who was taught by Amati of Cremona. It is a superlative musical instrument, but in the hands of a bungler it would sound no more beautiful than the squeals of a pig. Prove to me you are not a bungler."

Bedrich stepped back.

"Come on, boy. Why do you hesitate?"

Bedrich had heard of Stradivari and the Amati family before. His father had told him.

"No, sir, I couldn't," he said.

Chmelik walked towards him, then turned and picked up the violin himself. He placed it in position, and in a second the rich gold vibrance of its sound filled the room. Bedrich had never heard such richness.

Jan Chmelik lowered the instrument and walked with it towards Bedrich. "See," he said, holding it out, "it is nothing to be afraid of. It won't bite you. Take it."

The boy reluctantly did so.

"Play it," Chmelik said, softly and persuasively.

After a moment of doubt Bedrich slowly raised the violin, lifted the bow, and began to play. His nervousness left him as the full, mellow notes sang out from the sound-box. He became lost in the music, and it was only when he got to the end of the piece and Jan Chmelik clapped three or four times that he came back to reality.

"Thank you, Bedrich," the music-teacher said. "You are not yet an artist. But you are far—very far—from a bungler. Now, my boy, your father tells me I must also attempt to instil into you the principles of pianoforte. Do you play that as well as you play the violin?"

"No, sir," Bedrich answered. "I do not play it at all."

"I see. So in one department I must try to perfect your technique, while in the other I have to start right from the beginning. So, let us begin at the beginning."

The boy came for his lessons several times a week from then

on, and after a very short time he found that his initial resistance to the piano diminished. Indeed, he was drawn more
and more to the instrument until it reached the stage where
the violin lost most of its attraction for him.

Jan Chmelik noted the change. At first he felt uneasy about
it. How would he explain to the father that the child was
abandoning one instrument in favour of another? And what
if Bedrich's skill at the piano fell short of his gifts as a
violinist? Frantisek Smetana was no easy man to deal with,
and the quiet music-teacher had no inclination to incur the
brewery manager's wrath.

But Chmelik's unhappy concern vanished when he became
aware of the extraordinary degree of Bedrich's improvement.
The lad was insatiable when it came to exercises. He was all
the time asking for new and more difficult ones. Time and
again Jan Chmelik stood on one side to observe, unnoticed,
the way his pupil tackled the practice pieces. The child's concentration was of fierce intensity; he bit his lip to bleeding-
point more than once as he focused his full will on mastering
some new keyboard task. When success came Jan Chmelik was
witness to facial expressions of such innocent triumph that he
found himself bereft of words.

Frantisek and Barbora learnt of the new development before
many weeks passed, and when Jan Chmelik confirmed to the
parents that their son was indeed something out of the ordinary, Frantisek took every opportunity to spread the word.
Barbora retold many times the dream she had had about her
unborn child. The dream was now taking on uncanny reality.

The talk spread through Litomysl, and this time, since it
was backed by the views of the music-teacher, it reached and
impressed a far wider audience. Men and women who had
never heard the Smetana child play, who had never even seen
him, spoke of him and boasted about him to visitors to the
town.

Frantisek Smetana was looked at differently. After all, he
was the father of a remarkable child. From time to time Count
Valdstejn sent for his brewery manager to hear how Bedrich
was progressing under Chmelik.

*　　*　　*

One evening early in September 1830, when the first post-summer chill was beginning to hint of autumn, Barbora and Frantisek were sitting talking while Albina, the eldest child, was sewing. From along the road came the sounds of approaching horses, and Frantisek went to the window out of curiosity. Within a few seconds he saw the carriage lights approaching, and as they passed the window Barbora wondered aloud, "Someone coming here?"

"Obviously," Frantisek retorted. "Quickly, give me my jacket."

He shrugged into the garment, pulled and smoothed the wrinkles, patted his hair, and, just in time, did up his shoes. Then the doorbell rang.

"Take that sewing out of here, girl, hurry!" he ordered Albina, and after pausing a moment to see that the room was fit to receive a visitor he went to the front door and opened it.

The bearded man who stood there was old, but had about him an air of distinction. "Are you Frantisek Smetana?"

"I am, sir."

"The father of Bedrich Smetana?"

"Indeed, sir." A swelling of pride.

"Then it is with you I wish to speak," the stranger said.

"I should be delighted to converse with you, sir," Frantisek replied, secretly delighted at his own pomposity. "Would you care to step into my humble abode?" he inquired, stepping aside.

The other took off his hat with a natural grace and stepped inside.

When he had introduced his wife and settled the stranger in a chair Frantisek asked the man what he had called about. He did it deferentially, because in the light of the room he could see the stranger more clearly, and it was obvious that the man was by nature both a gentleman and a person of some importance.

"I have come to you with a special request, a proposition," the stranger began. "I have not come entirely of my own accord, but to represent my committee."

Frantisek was frankly puzzled, and directed a series of

querying glances at Barbora. But she merely shrugged her shoulders.

"And your committee—may I ask what committee it is?" Frantisek inquired.

"Oh, yes, of course! Did I not tell you? Please forgive me," the old man said. "Yes, I am the chairman of the Festival Committee—the committee organizing the celebrations for the Emperor's birthday next month."

Frantisek knew of Litomysl's proposed celebrations, and knew that the town would be *en fête.*

"We are a musical town," the man was saying, "I do not have to tell you that, and my committee has spent many hours trying to decide what the highlight of our presentation should be."

Frantisek could feel the stirrings of excitement in him. Was the man really going to suggest what he thought?

"We have many good musicians in the town," the man continued. "We could put on a fine recital. Jan Chmelik could gather together a talented orchestra that would be the envy of towns and villages for miles around. We respect Jan Chmelik."

Frantisek was impatient now. Why had the old fool come? To say what a great fellow Jan Chmelik was?

"I know Jan Chmelik well," he said. "I also respect him."

"Then we are at one," the stranger said.

"Yes."

"That's good."

"It's excellent, marvellous, but what is this all about?" Frantisek said.

"Patience, my friend. As I said, we respect Jan Chmelik, and when he made a suggestion to us we took note of it and considered it, and made a decision on it. The decision concerns you, or rather your son, because on Jan Chmelik's recommendation we should like to feature Bedrich as the main soloist."

Frantisek whirled. This was much more than he'd dreamt of. "The main *soloist?*" he almost shouted.

"Yes."

"Are you sure?"

"Quite, quite sure," the old man said impatiently. "But we need your permission, of course. May we have it?"

Barbora, sitting with her hand to her mouth in astonishment, stood up and said, "Of course! Can't they, Frantisek?"

"Yes, yes, yes, naturally. And the date? I've forgotten the date of His Highness's birth in my excitement."

"The 4th of October," the man said.

The hall at Litomysl was packed to the doors on the night of October 4th, 1830.

There would have been a large attendance anyway, but the numbers were swollen beyond imagination when the sensational announcement was made that a six-year-old boy was to play the overture to Auber's *La Muette de Portici.*

Little Bedrich was scared. Supposing he forgot?

"Couldn't we go home, Albina?" he said to his sister. "I'm frightened."

Albina knew other people looked on her little brother as a prodigy, but to her he was first and foremost a child who also played the piano. You tended to forget his extreme youth when you listened to the music that poured from him, but when he wasn't playing, and you looked and saw the six-year-old body and the eyes of a child, it came almost as a shock.

At the moment his simple "I'm frightened" moved Albina. If she let him see it Bedrich would be disturbed. Albina didn't want to upset him. She brushed his hair back and said, "I don't know what you're frightened about, darling. You've played this overture a hundred times, surely, in the past three weeks, and I've never heard you making a mistake."

"But there are so many people..."

"Try to forget them. Try to imagine you are in Jan Chmelik's music room, or at home, and that I'm the only one listening." She tilted his face up. "Will you play just for me?"

When he was presented to the audience he remembered what Albina had told him, but the noise of the clapping was coming at him like waves of thunder, and he felt as if he were being physically buffeted. Among the faces he saw his father and mother, his sisters, Count Valdstejn, Jan Chmelik; he turned in panic to where he had left Albina, and when she smiled and waved to him he felt calm again and walked to the piano.

As soon as he struck the opening notes fear went away from

c

him and he neither heard nor saw anything until once again the audience's applause assaulted his ears, and someone lifted him high in the air for everyone to see.

When the town's élite crowded around Frantisek Smetana and his wife to shake their hands and voice their congratulations, a quiet-voiced man came to Bedrich and pressed both his hands. He held them in silence as he gazed at the child. Then he walked away. There was nothing else he could teach Bedrich Smetana, and Jan Chmelik knew it.

CHAPTER

[3]

IMMEDIATELY AFTER HIS FIRST public appearance in Litomysl the six-year-old Bedrich Smetana became the darling of
the town's music-lovers. He was invited to most of the aristo-
cratic houses, a development which gave much pleasure to his
parents, to Frantisek in particular.

One such occasion saw Count Antonin's mother—a severe
and haughty woman—so overcome by the boy's playing that
for a moment she forgot her regality and rushed to him,
saying, "Please, please, let me kiss your wonderful fingers!"
She took the bewildered child's hands and pressed them to her
lips.

Pleased and flattered as Frantisek was, he remained a realist.
He knew Bedrich was at an age when he should be starting to
learn subjects other than music, and talk of school began to
be heard with growing frequency in the Smetana household.
Barbora, ever the protector, was apprehensive about the child's
reactions. But, again, she need not have worried. Bedrich himself was eager to start. He had all a child's enthusiasm for this
new experience, and wanted to leave the house every morning
just like his sisters did. He couldn't conceive what this school
business was all about, but like most boys of his age he wanted
to find out for himself.

On the day that he started he left the house full of excitement, and even when his mother said goodbye to him at the
classroom he seemed quite unconcerned.

In the evening when his father came in from his day's work

Bedrich chatted excitedly about the teacher, and the things he had seen and heard and done. And then, before going to bed, he sat at the piano for an hour and practised.

Within a few weeks, however, Barbora noticed a change coming over Bedrich. It became daily more difficult to get the boy ready to leave on time, and one morning he got into a temper and created a scene. Barbora eased him out of his fit of anger, and eventually he fell asleep in her arms.

She sat cradling him, upset at the state into which he had worked himself. Once or twice he moved restlessly and whimpered, and when he woke up, calm again but puzzled, she smiled down at him.

"Don't you like school?" she asked. He shook his head.

"Why?" she said softly, running her fingers through his hair and brushing it back off his forehead.

"There's no time..." he began, but didn't know how to go on. "My music is... and the school time..." He stopped again. He didn't have the words to explain what he was feeling, what the school was doing to him. His understanding was too limited; his vocabulary didn't encompass the word frustration.

But with a mother's insight Barbora suddenly knew, and inside her something cried out in sympathy for her child. He was experiencing his first bout of artistic frustration and didn't know what it was all about. School and the time he had to spend there were cutting short the periods he could give to his first love—music. This was all he cared about, but he couldn't express it in words.

The best his mother could offer was patience and understanding, and these she gave him in full measure. That day she kept him at home and tried to explain to him that school was necessary, that Papa would insist that he went regularly to learn. Then she left him alone at the piano.

That evening she talked to Frantisek about the morning's events.

"We shall just have to be firm with him," Frantisek said.

"I understand all that, my dear," Barbora replied. "But at the same time, he does love his music."

"Bedrich has *got* to go to school, music or no music. In fact,

if his music is going to cause this sort of upset, I would have no hesitation about stopping it altogether. I mean that, Barbora. We do have responsibilities to the child, you know, and as far as I am concerned the main responsibility is to see that he doesn't grow up a gifted musician but an ignoramus otherwise. I'm going to see that the boy qualifies at something. He's going to have a better start than his father—than I had. He's not going to scramble around for years trying to learn some poorly paid trade. We have the means to see to that. And anyway, what would people say—"

"It's always *people*, isn't it, Frantisek? Why don't you think and act for yourself?"

This drove him into a fury, and he had to fight hard with himself not to do something violent. He stamped out of the room, and into the chill atmosphere of the night air.

When he went back into the room he said, "Regardless of what you say, regardless of your jibes, Bedrich *will* go to school, and he had better learn something there. That's my last word on it. I don't want to talk about the matter any more."

Barbora looked at her husband's tight mouth. Perhaps it was useless saying anything else. Perhaps for the sake of peace she should hold her tongue. But then she thought, no, why should I remain silent?

"There is just one thing which perhaps you haven't thought about," she began. "Did it ever occur to you that Bedrich could make his living from music?"

Frantisek's head jerked round to look at his wife. "A professional musician! A son of mine a professional musician—a wandering good-for-nothing? Never!"

"I didn't mean that kind of musician. Can't you be reasonable, even for a minute?"

He threw his jacket across the room and walked out again, shouting as he went, "I don't care what you meant. I said no, and that's final."

Apart from asking, the next evening, whether Bedrich had been to school, he didn't talk to Barbora for three days.

The boy was conscious of the strained atmosphere, but it

didn't help him to like school. He went every day from then on, dully going through the routine he hated.

In the summer that Bedrich was seven his father got a new job, taking over the brewery at Jindrichuv Hradec. For Frantisek it meant more money, more social standing, a bigger house; for Bedrich it meant heartbreak. He had loved Litomysl, and during the long summer days he frequently lost himself in little fantasies about the happy times in the town they had left. The ache he felt at the loss caused him to cry when alone.

The inevitable compensation came in the form of a musical discovery—the rest of Mozart's music.

The castle of Jindrichuv Hradec was just one of the Society houses to which the young prodigy was invited, and the family inhabiting the great building at the time was intensely musical—to the extent that the town's finest violinist, Frantisek Ikavec, was fully employed there as principal musician, teacher, and conductor.

At the time the Smetanas moved to the town Mozart's was the music enjoying a vogue at the castle. The first occasion on which Bedrich heard it played by an orchestra his eyes lit up. He had never heard such music.

When Frantisek Ikavec heard the boy play he offered at once to take him as a pupil. And so the boredom of school and the pining for Litomysl were more than made up for in the boy's life as Ikavec introduced him to more compositions from the pen of the great master.

Bedrich worshipped Ikavec despite the teacher's occasional harsh outbursts. Frantisek Ikavek took his music very seriously. He was impatient over mistakes, many times taking his new pupil to task, and he would never let him go home from a lesson until he was sure the boy had mastered it. Many an afternoon he kept young Smetana long after hours.

"I want you to be much more than *just a pianist*," he used to say. "I want you to be a real musician. There is a difference, boy. A very big and real difference."

Just how much of a taskmaster he was in this respect can be gauged from the fact that the boy who loved practising frequently returned home crying from the pains in his fingers.

But despite this, Bedrich loved Frantisek Ikavec, because the teacher himself so obviously cared about the boy.

Once, after a series of particularly arduous lessons, Ikavec surprised him by saying, "No practice today, my boy. I want you to try something else."

He told Bedrich to go and stand by the window. He himself took out the violin. "Now listen very carefully to this," he said, and played a few bars of a melody Bedrich hadn't heard before. "Do you like that?" he asked.

"It's very beautiful, sir," Bedrich replied.

"Yes, it is. Listen to it again."

Once more Ikavec played the snatch of melody.

"Do you still like it?" he asked.

"Even more than the first time."

"Have you got it in your head?"

"Yes, sir, I think so."

"Could you play it for me?"

"Yes, I think so," Bedrich answered, and started to move towards the piano.

"No, stay where you are," Ikavec commanded.

Puzzled, Bedrich went back to the window where he had been standing.

"Now," Ikavec said, "sing it for me."

"*Sing* it, sir?"

"That's what I said."

"But I don't know any words for it."

"That doesn't matter. Sing without words."

Bedrich looked at his music-teacher wondering if this was some sort of funny trick, but Frantisek Ikavec seemed perfectly serious.

"Go on, boy, do as I tell you."

Bedrich closed his eyes for a moment to recall the melody, then, without hesitation, sang the piece through.

"Just as I thought," Ikavec said. "Try this." He played a scale, and Bedrich sang it. "And this." Again Bedrich sang it, his pure soprano filling the room.

"That will do for now," Ikavek said, putting down his violin. "Do you go to church with your parents?" he asked.

"Yes, sir, every Sunday."

"Very well. In five Sundays from now you will not go with your parents."

The boy was by now completely baffled by the actions and words of his music-teacher. Didn't the man realize that Papa insisted on everyone in the family going to church as a group *every* Sunday?

"I shall have to go, sir," he said. "Unless I'm sick. Papa takes us. He wouldn't allow us to miss a Sunday."

"You won't miss it, Bedrich. You shall be there. But not with your parents. You shall be in the choir, and you shall sing the soprano solo," Ikavec explained.

"But I can't sing, sir," Bedrich objected.

"I shall teach you. You have a voice, and it's true, and your pitch is near perfect. Let's have our first lesson, eh?"

The church was crowded, the altar a mass of flowers and polished candlesticks, among which the rich vestments stood out in a splendour of their own.

When Bedrich Smetana's youthful soprano voice soared out in its chilling purity, most of the congregation turned to see who the singer was. He was too small to be seen, so most of them turned back towards the altar and wondered that a human being could make such a glorious sound issue from his throat.

In the sunshine later on Frantisek Smetana was once more the centre of a congratulatory throng of people.

". . . and what was the date, Smetana? *Smetana!*"

The teacher had been talking on history for nearly twenty minutes when he noticed that Bedrich wasn't even listening. So he popped this question at the dreaming boy suddenly, asking him to repeat the last date mentioned.

"Are you asleep, boy?" the master asked acidly.

"Er . . . no, no, sir," Bedrich replied sheepishly, embarrassed now that all eyes in the classroom were turned on him. The teacher repeated his question. Bedrich looked blankly at the master. He searched his mind desperately, trying to conjure up what had been said. Nothing came to him.

"I . . . I forget, sir."

"You can't remember?"

"No, sir."

"Well, of course, that's understandable, isn't it?" The biting sarcasm in the voice cut home, and Bedrich didn't reply. "I mean, it's such a long time since I said the date, isn't it?"

Bedrich felt as if his face had been boiled.

The master went on, "It must be all of—let me see—a *minute* since I mentioned the date! And you weren't asleep, you say?"

"No, sir, truly, I wasn't asleep."

The master looked away from him, and looked around at the rest of the class.

"Now then, if you weren't asleep, what were you doing?"

"Thinking, sir."

"Ah, so your mind does work! And what, if I may be so bold as to ask, were you *thinking* about? What great thoughts were occupying that noble mind of yours?"

How could Bedrich tell him? How, he wondered, could he tell this man what had been going through his head—the airs, the melodies, the harmonies of Mozart, the church music, the admiration for men who could set down on paper the compositions that came from inside them? How could he explain the daring thought that had come into his own head, the idea of trying to compose, the snatch of tune he had worked out mentally, changed, added to, finally settled upon, and had sat trying to commit to memory? How could he tell all this before a roomful of grinning scholars?

"I was—I was thinking about music, sir," Bedrich said lamely.

"You were thinking about music," the master repeated. "Very well then, Master Smetana, when the rest of the school goes home for the day you'll stay behind and think about history for a change. Is that clear?"

"Yes, sir."

"Sit down, Smetana, sit down before I—sit down."

In fact he wasn't kept behind when the rest of the students left for the day. The teacher relented. He wasn't blind to young Smetana's preoccupation; it was just that annoyance had got the upper hand on the spur of the moment, and as the day wore on he realized that his temper and sarcasm had made him a lesser person for taking it out on someone as gifted and sensitive as this boy. He sent Bedrich home with a caution, and told him to try to pay more attention in the future.

When he arrived home Bedrich didn't start practising straight away as was his usual custom. Instead, he took some paper and a pen and ink and went into the drawing-room, where he sat at the table and started to write down the notes of the tune that had got him into trouble earlier in the day. He had had no formal tuition in the art of composition, but he still wanted to put down on paper a piece of music that was his and his alone. It didn't come as easily as he had imagined, and several times, after taking his jottings to the piano and playing through as much as he had written, he crossed out passages and went back to the table to rewrite.

Barbora came once and asked him what he was about, but he was evasive and said, "Please, Mama, wait until a little later."

Eventually, when all was done, he wrote, "By Bedrich Smetana" on the top in the way all the great composers did. He sat for some minutes, intoxicated by his own achievement. Finally, shivering with excitement, he took the sheets across to the piano, arranged them carefully on the music-stand, sat down on the stool, and called, "Mama!"

When Barbora came in he said, "Mama, please sit down over there and listen."

She settled herself in the armchair and said, "I'm ready, darling."

He played the small composition through to the end, then turned expectantly to his mother. "Do you like it?" he asked.

"Yes, my love, it's very nice."

"Do you know who wrote it?" he asked.

"Is it something Frantisek Ikavec taught you?"

"No." A smile of impish delight stole across his face.

"Something Papa played?"

"No, Mama."

"Have I heard it before?"

"No, Mama, never. No-one has ever heard it before."

"Do you mean—?"

"Yes, Mama, I wrote it. I composed it."

Barbora could hardly believe it. She stood up and came across to the piano and looked at the sheets.

"My little eight-year-old composer," she said. "You are very, very clever."

His father, when he heard about it, and then heard the piece, was also very pleased.

"You're a clever little man," he said.

"Thank you, Papa," the child said, grateful for Frantisek's praise. "I'm going to write many more pieces, and they'll be better and better."

"Yes, yes, I hope so, my son. But, Bedrich."

"Yes, Papa."

"You must pay more attention to your school subjects. It's all very well writing musical compositions and becoming a good instrumentalist, but the reports you have been getting and the results in your examinations are not good. You know my feelings about these matters."

"Yes, sir."

"Heed them. Don't make me angry."

"No, Papa." Had the teacher already told Papa about that matter of the history lesson? "I shall pay more attention in the future."

"Good. I want you to become a fine lawyer. Now, play the piece for me again."

The boy did, and at the end his father actually clapped.

However, despite the child's good intentions, he found the study of mathematics, geography, history, and all the other subjects in the school no more attractive, no easier. He was constantly in minor trouble for being slower than his class-mates. His attention always seemed to be wandering away to music and things musical. Try as he might, concentration on school lessons appeared to be impossible.

In the autumn of 1833 he came to the end of his elementary schooling, and again the results he had achieved gave rise to a severe lecture from his father. Bedrich listened, humiliated by his father's angry accusations, and disappointed that he had caused him this obvious displeasure.

There followed a year of unhappy scholastic slogging at high school for Bedrich, and at the end of it, once more, results that were very far from brilliant. Each time during lessons that thoughts of music edged through the periphery of his concentration he consciously tried to eject them. The eternal conflict left his mind insensitive to the absorption of facts pertaining to school examinations. But at least he was trying, and (more important) was seen to be trying. Frantisek's reactions at the end of the year were thus purged of anger. All that was left was disappointment of the bitterest sort.

But Frantisek had other things on his mind to leaven even this, for the brewery manager had decided to be a brewery manager no longer. Respect and eminence, it seemed to him, could never be more than partially won by a person who was a mere employee. Real status was the preserve of the independent. Frantisek would become independent. The status would follow.

He resigned from the brewery at Jindrichuv Hradec and moved his family to the farm he had bought at Ruzkovy Lhotice.

CHAPTER

[4]

AT THE AGE OF TWELVE, after spending a year at the grammar school at Jihlava, Bedrich went to the high school in Nemecky Brod. The year was 1836, and at his new place of learning he was exposed for the first time to the hard facts of political domination. In the beginning the talk of love of mother country meant little to him. It was too abstract. Love was a feeling one had for people; you loved your parents, your sisters, your uncles. "I love you, Albina," made sense to him, because it expressed the warmth of his feelings towards the smiling girl who was his eldest sister.

And then the concept broadened. It took in what he felt for animals and flowers, for the life he remembered at Litomysl, above all for the joy he got from music. But these were all things and places which had a strong personal connection. How did people expand it to embrace a whole country? A country was vast and impersonal; it was all the mountains and roads and skies and rivers and fields and villages, towns, and cities he'd never seen, and much much more besides. How could you *love* all that? He didn't know, so he just listened.

What he heard brought back echoes of things he had heard his father and other men saying from time to time. Because he was puzzled he listened avidly, and a picture began to emerge of two lands lying side by side: Austria, strong in military power and hungry for supremacy, and his own country, oppressed and unhappy, individualistic but impotent. He heard young men and old talking of these things with passion in their eyes and in their voices, teachers who referred to Austria with venom while they sought to instil into their young charges the burning feeling they called patriotism.

This awakening of interest was hastened by the sheer enthusiasm and ebullience of Karel Havlicek.

Havlicek was one of those youths who, without conscious efforts of their own, establish themselves as natural leaders at an early age. He was a good-looking, free-speaking boy with an abundance of easy charm to whom others, both younger and older than himself, looked for guidance. He settled arguments, set trends in matters of dress and thought, and was an accomplished scholar without having to work too hard at his books.

A few days after his arrival at the school Bedrich came across Karel Havlicek almost by accident. In normal circumstances a new boy would have little to do with students three years his senior. Karel Havlicek had already passed his fifteenth birthday.

Bedrich, feeling just a little lonely, was walking past groups of boys gathered together outside the main school building when he heard a voice saying, "... and the programme will be made up of works by Schubert, Weber, and Rossini." The names of the composers arrested his thoughts, and he drifted unobtrusively to the edge of the group from which the voice came.

"What about tickets, Karel?" someone asked.

"My dear Lev, has there ever been any trouble about tickets before?" the boy addressed as Karel replied.

Bedrich went up on tiptoe to catch a glimpse of him.

"No, true enough," the boy called Lev said. "But this time isn't exactly like other times. This is a gala concert."

"If it puts your mind at ease, I've already arranged for them," Karel Havlicek said. "Planning, my boy, that's all it takes. Right, names please."

The boys in the group called out their names one by one.

"Sterba."

"Honzl."

"Nesvadba."

"Dvorsky—can I have two please, Karel?"

When the last of the boys had called out his name Bedrich took a deep breath and said, "Smetana—Bedrich Smetana."

Those on the edge of the group turned immediately to look at him. One of them said, "Ho! We've got an outsider in our midst!"

Bedrich, blushing, wished he hadn't opened his mouth.

"What were you doing skulking around there?" one of the boys said, advancing threateningly towards him.

Bedrich started to back away, wondering if he should run for it, but just as he was about to turn, Karel Havlicek shouldered his way through from the middle and said loudly, "Shut up, Zelezny, Smetana is a friend of mine."

He came up to Bedrich and in the most natural way imaginable put an arm about him.

It was the turn of the others now to look embarrassed, and they fell back awkwardly.

"All right, away now, you fellows; Bedrich and I have confidential matters to discuss," Havlicek continued, and led the bewildered Bedrich Smetana to a quiet corner. When he was satisfied they were alone the older boy put out his hand and said, "I'm Karel Havlicek. I don't think we've met before."

Bedrich was both grateful and surprised at this boy's tact. He shook hands and said, "Thank you for what you did."

"Think nothing of it," Karel Havlicek said. "So your name is Bedrich Smetana?"

"Yes."

"You're not from this area, are you?"

"No, I've only been at the school a few days, and I should apologize really for butting in on your meeting like that."

"Oh, there isn't any need to apologize," Karel said. "But as a matter of interest, just why did you, as you put it, butt in?"

Bedrich told him how he had been walking past and heard the names of the composers.

"Ah, so you're interested in the arts?"

"In music, yes. I love music."

"Do you play anything?"

"Piano and violin," Bedrich replied.

"*Two* instruments!" Karel said with gusto. "That's *very* good."

From that moment on their friendship deepened. Bedrich found Karel Havlicek a most admirable companion, and often stood back and watched the older boy's ability in whipping up enthusiasm for the schemes which seemed to bubble out of him. Nor did Havlicek ever reveal to the rest of the group that the day he claimed that Bedrich was a friend was the first time he had set eyes on him. The fifteen-year-old had tact as well as authority, and his diplomacy was something Bedrich looked upon with the greatest admiration.

After the concert Karel and Bedrich walked together on the way back to the school. The others were chatting among themselves as they strolled along in two's and three's.

Havlicek asked the youngster about his impressions of the music they had heard during the previous two hours, and once the shyness had gone, Bedrich, reacting to the luxury of being respectfully listened to, spoke unreservedly about the subject nearest to his heart. Not once did Karel Havlicek interrupt. They reached the school, said their goodnights to the remainder of the party as it dispersed, and Bedrich went on talking. They stood in the stillness of the black night, one listening, the other, all inhibitions forgotten, discussing the merits of the performances, the intentions of the composers, the beauty that could be contained in sound.

Suddenly Bedrich stopped, and in an instant felt overwhelmed by awkwardness. He had just realized it was close to midnight, and he had been talking almost non-stop for an hour and a half.

"Forgive me, Karel," he said, fidgeting in the darkness, "I must be a frightful bore."

"Far from it. If I thought you were I'd have stopped you long ago."

Havlicek liked this boy Smetana. Funny, he thought, I don't think of him as younger than myself any more. And what a feeling he has for music!

"I've learnt more about you tonight," he said, "than I have about most of the others in the last three years."

"Oh, dear!" Bedrich began. "Karel."

"Yes?"

"Look, I hope you don't mind me saying this, but I've also

learnt a lot from you in the short time we've known each other."

"I don't mind you saying anything. Freedom is a great thing. But what on earth could you have learnt from me?"

"Well, that one word, for example—freedom. It never meant anything to me. It was ... just a word. But you've given it meaning for me. I can't talk as well as you, or think as well as you, you understand, but listening to you I've grown to know that a people, a country, its artists, should be free; to do their own things, go their own way. For that I'm grateful for a start."

"Oh, Bedrich, you're a kind person, but there's no need to be grateful to me. The knowledge would have come to you anyway, sooner or later."

"Maybe, but thanks to you it came sooner. You see, everyone learns from you. Now, don't laugh—it's true. I've seen it. You seem to do so much, to be *able* to do so much. How is it?"

There was silence between them for a little while. Instinctively they moved towards each other and clasped each other's arms in a gesture of companionship, and then went their separate ways.

Bedrich was freely accepted into the company of Karel's other friends, and drifted naturally towards the musical element. With Frantisek Buttula, another fifteen-year-old, and two others, he formed a quartet, and once more turned to composing. The first time he combined with three others to play something he had written gave him a repetition of the sensations (but increased, because others were involved) he had experienced on the day he had played his first composition for his mother.

Would he ever become a true artist? He was sitting turning over the thought in his mind one Sunday as he gazed across a field near the school. It was the quiet time before lunch, and bees were buzzing lazily in the warm sunlight. Somewhere in the distance a church bell was calling the faithful. He could hear a stream singing as it wound its way over pebbles and rocks. And then a white butterfly came and flew in its erratic, beautiful way from behind him, out and across the field until

D

he could see it no more. And he thought, this is my country, my own, and I love it. Some day ... some day ...

"Dreamer!"

The loudness and the suddenness of the shout startled him, and his heart raced. He turned, and there behind him was Karel.

Karel was quick to see the effect of the shout on Bedrich and was profuse in his apologies, but Bedrich laughed it off.

"I didn't mean to disturb any beautiful thoughts," Karel said, "but there's to be some dancing in a near-by village this afternoon, and I thought some of us might go. What do you think?"

Bedrich couldn't dance.

"It's time for you to learn," Karel said.

"How?" Bedrich asked.

"I'll teach you."

"There?"

"Here!"

"When?"

"Now. Stand up. First of all, get the weight off your feet on to your toes—like this."

Bedrich's first efforts to perform even the most elementary steps were hilarious, but Havlicek was patient and a good teacher, and Bedrich had an inbuilt sense of rhythm. By the time lunch was ready he had mastered one dance, and could make a passable effort at another.

That afternoon, among the village girls and boys, he danced for the first time, and his friends from the school were surprised at the speed at which he took to this new pastime. While they occasionally rested, he never did. It was as if the folk-music had got into his blood and drove him on.

There was a quality about this folk-music which intrigued and gladdened his spirits, and as the melodies were repeated he found himself humming the tunes in bursts of unfettered happiness. His good humour transmitted itself, and the country girls who were his partners threw back their heads and laughed with him.

When it was time to go he was reluctant to leave.

"Couldn't we stay a little longer?" he said.

"No, we've got to go," Frantisek Buttula answered. "We must get back, or there'll be trouble."

"Trouble? What does it matter?" Bedrich said, and made for the dance-floor again.

Karel Havlicek ran after him and caught him by the sleeve. "Come on, Bedrich. Are you crazy?" He had to haul Bedrich back.

"I was enjoying myself, that's all. I could stay here all night."

"I dare say," Karel said. "I've been watching you. I had no idea you were such a one for the girls."

"Oh, it's not that," Bedrich replied. "It's the music and the atmosphere and everything. It's marvellous."

"And the girls," Buttula added.

"*No!*" Bedrich said.

"Goodbye, Bedrich," one of the girls called, and three or four others joined in, one even shouting, "When will you be coming again, Bedrich?"

But in fact it was the music, the lively folk-dances, which had really attracted Bedrich, and all the way back he hummed the tunes, in between asking when they could go dancing again. One evening he amazed Buttula and the two other members of the quartet by handing them sheets on which he had painstakingly written down as many of the dance-tunes as he could remember.

"You want us to play this stuff?" Buttula asked incredulously.

"What's wrong with it?" Bedrich wanted to know.

"But I thought you were a lover of good music."

"I'm a lover of music," Bedrich retorted. "And I didn't notice you enjoying your dancing any the less for the music."

"But you've got it out of context, young Smetana," Buttula said pompously.

Bedrich didn't like being addressed as "young Smetana," and he flushed angrily.

"What I mean is," Buttula continued, "that all it is is dance-music."

"It's *folk*-dance music," Bedrich corrected him. "I've been hearing a lot about national pride from you fellows since I came here. Is it all just affectation after all?"

"What do you mean?" It was Buttula who felt angry now. "I consider that an impertinence."

"I consider it an impertinence that you look down your nose at your national music," Bedrich said. "You go on and on about national pride. Well, this happens to be part of our national heritage. Now, do you want to try to play it or not?"

The other two had been listening without comment, looking from Frantisek Buttula to this youngster who spoke with such heat.

One of them now said, "I think Bedrich is right, Frantisek. If you don't want to join in, then at least let us try it."

"Oh, all right," Buttula said with little grace. "Though I can't imagine why anyone should get so worked up over so little."

He took his sheet of music and sat down.

An hour later, when they were putting their instruments away, he came across to Bedrich and said, "Thanks for putting me in my place. I enjoyed that more than I can tell you, and I apologize for the way I acted at the beginning. You've made me realize something I'd never thought about before."

They broke up in the best of spirits, and frequently thereafter went to dances, learnt the tunes, and received a lot of enjoyment from playing them in their leisure hours.

On his farm Frantisek Smetana was a more contented man as far as his son was concerned. The boy at last was brushing the cobwebs from his brain, and reports from the school were highly encouraging.

"Firmness in all things, Barbora," Frantisek said to his wife. "The boy needed severity. You can see that now, can't you?"

Barbora had long since given up arguing with Frantisek. The older he grew, the more irritable and garrulous he became; and besides, she was tired. It was so much easier to take the line of least resistance, so much more conducive to a peaceful existence to agree, or at least to appear to agree, with his views.

She was pleased that Bedrich was doing well at school, but she frequently spent sleepless nights wondering if the extra efforts he was making meant that her dreams of a famous musician for a son were being destroyed.

There were other worries. The farm was not making money. Crops were poor and selling prices low, and there remained the harshly demonstrable fact that a man not born to the land found it difficult in his declining years to make the best use of it.

Frantisek was painfully aware of all this, but he was not in despair. He was pinning his hopes firmly on Bedrich. The boy would study law and become a brilliant professional man whose wealth would be the saviour of the Smetana family's respectability.

As for Bedrich, his own ambitions were running on divergent lines from those of his father, though this was no easy thing to admit openly. He still loved his father, and wanted to please him, but tucked away inside him was the burning desire to play and write music superlatively. The awful drawback at Nemecky Brod was that he had no music-teacher. Sometimes, when he thought about the valuable time being wasted because of this lack, he sank into depressions from which he found it a matter of desperate difficulty to extricate himself.

One afternoon he walked by himself in the rain through the woods near the school. The rest of the boys had gone into the town. Not feeling like joining them, he had excused himself, and gone out along the road in the opposite direction. When the rain started to fall he headed for the woods with some vague notion of sheltering. But once among the trees he carried on walking. The rain was cold and made him shiver, but somehow it didn't matter. Lost in his misery, he tramped on, his feet quickly becoming soaked and muddy. Once a branch sprang back and caught him a lacerating cut across the neck, but apart from putting his fingers up to the spot, and then looking distinterestedly at the blood on his hand, he took scant notice.

With no notion of time, he somehow arrived back at the spot from where he had started, and, getting back on to the road again, he trudged towards the school. His feet were drawn towards the room which held the piano, and he went in. He sat at the piano and, drenched to the skin though he was, began to play. All the desolation that he felt poured into the playing, and presently he was sitting at the keyboard with tears streaming down his face.

He didn't hear the door opening and closing quietly, nor did he know that a figure had tiptoed into the room and made for a corner where the shadow was deepest.

Professor Karel Sindelar sat and listened. He had heard the music through an open window and came to investigate. He knew as soon as he entered the room that he was hearing something out of the ordinary. There was a quality of the unearthly about this small, shadowy figure being able to create sounds like this; something terribly personal about what the music was saying. So, scarcely daring to breathe, the master sat in frozen immobility.

When the boy at last stopped playing—it was almost pitch-dark in the room—and put his arms on the keyboard with a discordant crash of sound, and laid his head on his arms, the Professor felt like an intruder. He wanted to go to this youth and congratulate him, say something, anything, to him. But, instead, he remained as silent and still as possible and hoped the boy would go without noticing him.

After a few minutes Bedrich moved, closed the piano, and went slowly towards the door without looking to left or right. Just for an instant the Professor saw the dark outline of the head showing black against the outside gloom, and in that instant he recognized the mystery pianist as Bedrich Smetana. Professor Sindelar went back to his living-room presently, feeling strangely disturbed but at the same time enriched by his experience.

When Frantisek Buttula, Karel Havlicek, and the rest of the older boys came to say good-bye to Bedrich—they had gone as far as they could in the high school and would soon be starting advanced studies in Prague—he could hardly speak for loneliness. They were the best friends he'd had, and they were leaving. They tried to cheer him up by promising to write often, but it was no use. He stood in the roadway as the carriage that took them away passed out of sight, and their going was like a physical tearing off of part of himself.

The letters he got from Havlicek and Buttula disturbed him greatly, and only increased his longing to join them in the great city. Havlicek's letters in particular, with their descriptions of the exciting cultural life in Prague, made him feel more than ever cut off in Nemecky Brod. The inevitable result was that he tentatively hinted to his father that it would be far better if he could continue his studies in Prague. Frantisek ignored the hint. Bedrich tried again, this time more emphatically.

"He says here that Nemecky Brod is too slow and too rustic," Frantisek remarked to Barbora as he read through his son's latest letter. "The boy has it firmly fixed in his head that I should send him to Prague. He is so stubborn." Presently he looked up and said, "I suppose he hasn't any idea what it's costing me to keep him at Nemecky Brod. Well, woman, have you any ideas about the subject?"

"I was just thinking what a pity it is to continue paying money if it is being wasted." She wondered if she dare go on, then made up her mind. "After all, we could keep him at home and use the money for other things." She knew by the way he immediately arched his eyebrows that he had acceptd the bait.

"Have him home here to grow up a buffoon!" he half shouted. "My God, woman, there are times when I despair of your intelligence." He made his old derisory snorting sound. "He'll stick to his books, and if it lands me in penury I'll send him to Prague."

So in the autumn of 1839 Bedrich arrived in Prague, and viewed it with unbounded awe and fascination. It held so much promise; this huge place with its majestic river, its great streets and towering buildings, its bustle of life, released in him feelings of tumultuous excitement.

Frantisek Buttula had a flat which Karel Havlicek was sharing, and the celebrations for Bedrich's arrival carried on so late, and with such loudness, that the old man who owned the house came in his long white nightshirt and pounded the door, demanding that the din should cease. But even then they giggled and laughed and sang songs until the early hours of the morning. The pearly light of dawn was turning the river Vltava into a broad ribbon of beaten tin, and the spires of the city into elegant black fingers pointing to the sky of a new day when finally they dropped off to sleep, but not before Bedrich had stood at the window gazing out at this morning fairyland.

CHAPTER
[5]

WHEN BEDRICH WOKE UP it was early afternoon, and it was raining. But when Havlicek and Buttula suggested they take a cab to the school Bedrich said he would prefer to walk. He ignored their protests. He wanted to see the city, to drink in its sights from the very beginning. So the three of them set out, the newcomer straggling along behind open-mouthed, stopping often to gaze up at the high, grey buildings down whose sides the rain-water was streaming.

He was unworried by the discomfort—indeed, he was unaware of it. He asked a hundred questions. What was this street? What was that building? Where were the recitals held? Would they be passing any of the concert halls?

"You'll have plenty of time to see Prague," Karel said at one stage. "And anyway you're seeing it at its worst now. Come on, let's go the rest of the way by cab."

"No, Karel, you don't understand," Bedrich retorted. "I want to see it now. I don't want to be whisked through the streets. I've been *dreaming* of this place."

"But it's horrible in the rain," Buttula said.

"Not Prague," Bedrich replied. "Look at that river, doesn't its majesty stir you?" He gestured at the buildings. "Look at those columns, those arches—magnificent."

It was a very bedraggled trio that finally rang the bell of the great door at Josef Jungmann's school. The first thing that Bedrich inquired about when Karel and Frantisek left was the whereabouts of the music-room. Just as soon as he had changed into dry clothing he went and played the piano, and was half-way through a piece of Franz Liszt when he noticed that about a dozen students had come and grouped themselves around the instrument to listen. Strange, he felt no nerves. Inhibitions didn't bother him, and, conscious of this new confidence, he played the piece out to its conclusion and delightedly accepted the round of applause from the assembled boys.

Life now became for him a surge of fascinating experiences. He worked at his studies, but only enough to get by. All his spare time he spent with Buttula and Havlicek, drinking in the cafés, visiting the places of interest, imbibing everything that was new to a country boy—and that, in Prague, was almost everything.

Josef Jungmann liked his new pupil. Certainly he entertained a certain amount of concern about the time the boy spent outside the school, but it conformed with the normal pattern of behaviour of boys who came to Prague from the country. No doubt young Smetana would soon become satiated with the novelties of the city, and settle down.

Bedrich didn't reach satiation. He only had to go into the city to feel he was in the centre of a vortex from which he had no wish to escape. There were many occasions when he just walked on his own through the streets and across the squares, or up on to the heights from which he could look down and marvel at the panorama spread out before him. He was fifteen years old and in love with Prague.

He went to concert after concert, becoming totally immersed in the sounds he was hearing, and oblivious of the company he was in. He neither heard nor spoke to anyone during a recital, but sat with his jaw cupped in his hands, his eyes alight and his heart full. Buttula and Havlicek chided him for living in a dream world, but he cared nothing for their ribbing. They couldn't get through to him in the way they wanted—to irritate him and put him on the defensive. He knew what they were up to, but could feel astonishingly detached, and, in a sense, almost impregnable.

Josef Jungmann couldn't fault him on his schoolwork. He was making adequate progress, a seemingly solid student who was neither brilliant nor dull. He had heard this new boy playing the piano, had seen the young face changing from ecstasy to ferocity, had seen the lips pursing and relaxing, the eyebrows shooting to meet each other, and then softening and retreating, the bead of sweat starting at the temple, and leaving its glistening trail down the cheek as it ran to the jawbone. So he was patient whenever Bedrich turned in work that did less than justice to the imagination and intelligence Jungmann knew him to possess.

Buttula's apartment had become Bedrich's musical headquarters. He went there on his own in the evenings and practised the piano, and within weeks of his arrival in Prague had again formed a quartet.

He was sitting now at the window looking out at the street lights. The darkness had come down early on this March afternoon, and the icy east wind was whipping papers along the pavement.

When Frantisek and Karel came in they were both blowing on their hands.

"Is it as cold as it looks?" Bedrich asked.

For answer, Buttula crossed the room to him and held the back of his hand to Bedrich's cheek. The fingers felt icy, and Bedrich drew away.

"I think it's too cold to go out again tonight, eh, Frantisek?" Havlicek said.

Bedrich was throwing a shovelful of coal on the fire, and immediately straightened up. "But you said, you *promised*—"

"Yes, that was last week, my dear fellow," Havlicek cut him short. "We weren't to know this east wind was going to—"

"Damn the east wind!" Bedrich snapped. He went to get his coat, and as he walked to where it was lying across a chair he said, "Do you know what you two are—a couple of imbeciles."

Buttula couldn't contain his laughter any longer, and it burst from his lips in a loud sputter. "He was only *fooling*."

"I don't think Franz Liszt is a person to fool about," Bedrich said.

"No, no, we weren't fooling about Franz Liszt," Havlicek protested. "Don't you see? We put on this act because we knew how much tonight's concert meant to you."

Music was not for him part of the currency of practical jokes, but Bedrich smiled. He didn't feel particularly amused, but he was expected to laugh at the joke. "And you're still coming to hear Liszt?" he made sure.

"Of course."

"There's no pianist in the world like him, you know," Bedrich went on. "He's performed feats on the piano which were thought to be impossible."

"Yes, I know."

"Beethoven, when he heard him as a child, picked him up and kissed him. *Beethoven!*"

On the way to the recital they spoke little. What conversation there was passed between Havlicek and Buttula, and it was brittle and stilted. Bedrich was not speaking at all, and they both saw his silence as evidence of his pain.

In actual fact, however, Bedrich had forgotten the incident. They were no sooner out in the street than his mind emptied of everything save thoughts of where they were going and what lay ahead of them; his heart was beating fast; he could feel that emptiness in his belly that always came when he reached a high pitch of anticipation. Franz Liszt raced through his brain. To think they were going to hear the great man in person. It seemed a sort of sacrilege to contemplate trying to relate the sound he himself made, anaemic amateur that he was, with those the great Hungarian would make in— how long?—an hour from now.

There wasn't a vacant seat when Franz Liszt, twenty-nine and at the height of his fame, appeared to the first eruption of idolatrous applause.

From that point on Bedrich sat hunched forward in homage, his blood stirred, his soul touched by beauty. When the applause came he didn't move. It was as if his body didn't exist. He was just a mass of feeling, an emotion without physical substance.

The maestro played many encores that night. Bedrich Smetana was the only one in the vast audience who neither clapped nor called for more. What was applause when you were in the presence of something not of this world?

He looked up when he felt the touch on his head.

"Are you coming, Bedrich?" Karel Havlicek asked.

Bedrich barely heard the voice. His brain didn't take in the words.

"The concert's over," Havlicek whispered in his ear. "We'll see you outside."

The hall was emptying, but Bedrich didn't know. When everyone had gone he was still sitting there, a solitary figure.

The man who came and said, "Come on, young man—we're waiting to lock up," had a rough voice which bit into the silence and slashed across Bedrich's trance.

"I'm sorry," he mumbled and got to his feet. "I didn't ... Where has ... I'm sorry."

He shuffled out, feeling a little foolish and bewildered, and angry too at the crudeness of the sounds of banging doors.

He was as quiet going home as he had been coming.

Before Franz Liszt left Bohemia's capital Bedrich Smetana heard him four more times. On each occasion the boy became successively more stunned by the quality and virtuosity of the Hungarian who was a bare thirteen years older than himself.

He tried to unravel the responses the Liszt performances aroused in him, but their complexity defeated him. At one moment his sense of hopelessness would swamp every other thought in his head; then, racing through him in an unstoppable flood, would come ambition and desire to be like Liszt, or to make the effort to climb even a minute way up to those ethereal heights. And then, transcending all else, would come what he could only think of as a river of liquid beauty (this from the memory of what he'd heard) in which he lay supine, wanting for ever to be thus washed.

In his diary he wrote: *Liszt in Prague. Five of his concerts. Very wonderful days.*

What he didn't tell Havlicek or Buttula was that on the day Franz Liszt left the city he had hung around for four hours waiting to catch a glimpse of the great man, four hours during which he had felt in turns guilty, hunted, useless, and sorrowful.

What they found out for themselves was that Bedrich had once again withdrawn into himself. The quartet became a trio—he didn't want to join in. Nor did he want to accompany them on the trips he himself had instigated—to Barvirsky Island to hear the military-band concerts. So they met less frequently, and when they did it was to play the compositions he had written for them—pieces like the *Polka for Quartet*, *Osman Polka* and *Overture for Quartet* ("following Mozart's Method"). But apart from just being numerically short, they were without his moving spirit, and the meetings were distinctly lacking in purpose. Within weeks the musical sessions petered out.

Bedrich took to wandering along the Vltava, disinclined to do anything but drift where his feet took him. He slouched through streets without noticing where he was, where he'd been, or where he was going. His thought processes seemed to have been suspended in a limbo lying between despair and ecstasy. He walked with the piano-playing of Liszt in his head, and no inclination to exert himself.

At those classes which he attended at Jungmann's school he was present in body only. He didn't write home; he didn't even read a letter Albina had written him.

It was on a clear day in April, on the 13th, that he found himself half-way to the top of the Vysehrad. The weather was mild, and he had taken off his jacket and slung it over his shoulder. It was late afternoon. He spread his jacket on a spot where the grass was thin and short, and soft moss made an inviting cushion to sit on. Song-birds, as if conscious that summer was nearly in, were opening their throats and vying with each other in sweetness. For a time Bedrich lay back, unheeding; then he was hearing them, and it was as if he was coming back to life.

He sat up and sent a great laugh of relief out into the afternoon. Then he stood up and looked away down on the city of Prague. He could see with great clarity the details of the buildings. A city of spires and gables, it looked at its most beautiful with the April sun highlighting the greens of the domes, and the reds of the roof-gables. He began to walk towards Hradcany, and when he got there he could see the river waters being parted where they ran against the sharp-prowed edges of the piers on the Charles Bridge; the sun was playing games of intricate shadow patterns on the Cathedral of St Vitus. He sat for a while, his jacket on the ground beside him. He knew by the fact that he felt alive to the beauties of the day and the place that his suffering was over.

He walked down into the city, whistling as he went, his heart light and brimming with gladness. He knew what he had to do. It would not be easy, but he was not afraid.

He stood for a moment outside the heavy oak door of Josef Jungmann's room before knocking. There was no tremor of apprehension in him. He just wanted to run over again in his mind precisely what it was he was going to say to the headmaster. Then, after he had straightened the lapels of his jacket and patted his hair, he rapped on the panelling. He heard Jungmann calling, "Come in."

The thing about Josef Jungmann's distinguished-elderly-scholar appearance was that it always made students painfully aware of just how callow and gauche they must have looked to him. He was seated behind his desk, writing, when Bedrich entered.

Jungmann knew who was there. In the moment that the door opened inwards he had caught a glimpse of Bedrich and had seen enough to tell him that young Smetana was far from overawed, was feeling very calm, and had something of importance to say. Still, the proprieties had to be observed, the game played out to the full.

Judging his timing with precision, Jungmann kept his head down until the last possible second, then laid his pen aside and looked straight at the boy.

"Smetana," he said. Nothing more. He said it as if it was a lesson-heading. He might have been saying "Algebra." He came forward in his chair and gazed levelly (quizzically, Bedrich thought) at the boy. "Smetana, I have the distinct impression that you are about to explain something to me. Would I be right?"

"Yes, sir, I—"

"You're going to tell me why you've been paying about as much attention as a corpse in the classroom. Very well, Smetana, I am listening."

If he imagined that the histrionics would impress the boy he was mistaken.

"Nobody will have to worry any more, sir," Bedrich said. "I am leaving school."

"What?"

"I'm leaving school."

Jungmann faced Bedrich. "You're leaving school?"

"Yes, sir."

"Sit down." Jungmann hooked his foot around a chair and hauled it towards Bedrich, who sat down. The headmaster's voice, when he spoke, was free from loftiness. It was quiet and almost confidential. "You really do mean it too, Bedrich, don't you?"

"Yes, sir, I do."

"This is a very big decision to make. You're only sixteen."

"Yes, sir."

"When did you decide?"

"Today, sir, on the Vysehrad."

"Yes, go on."

"Well sir, the decision only ... I'm not quite sure how to put it." He thought for a moment, then went on, "What I'm trying to say is that I've decided to leave school because I believe my life should be given over to music."

"Your *whole* life?"

"Yes, sir."

Jungmann could feel in his bones the essential rightness of it. But as long as the slimmest doubt existed he recognized it as his duty to explore it. "Do you not think this decision is somewhat premature?" he asked.

"If you mean hasty, no, sir, I don't." Bedrich was astonished at his own composure.

"What I meant was," Jungmann said, "aren't you deciding on something before the proper time for such a decision to be made? And I'm also wondering whether you are in fact the person to decide."

Bedrich pursed his lips.

"Now, don't let us become irritable," Jungmann continued. "You know your father's wishes as regards your career?"

"Yes, he wishes me to become a lawyer."

"Quite so. If you applied yourself more seriously I have no

doubt you could make an excellent career for yourself in that field."

Bedrich dropped his eyes to his feet. What was the purpose in going on with this?

Jungmann sensed that the boy was beginning to cut him off, and before the situation became irretrievable he said, "As it happens, I understand."

Bedrich looked up at him, doubt registering on his face.

"Yes, I do," Jungmann said, "and I sympathize. I wonder, though, about your father."

"Thank you, sir, so do I," Bedrich said, and stood up, knowing instinctively the dialogue was at an end.

Jungmann came around the desk, his hand extended. He shook Bedrich's, and then did, for him, an unusual thing. He embraced the boy, and said, "I have *heard* ... I have *heard*. Good luck, Bedrich. May God bless you."

He left Jungmann's school with a warmer regard for the headmaster than he'd had at any time during his stay there.

CHAPTER

[6]

KAREL HAVLICEK WAS immersing himself in the nationalist movement, and his fierce pride in his own country was finding expression at political meetings and in the fiery articles he wrote for circulation among young men of similar beliefs. When Bedrich came to the flat being shared by Buttula and Havlicek it was the latter who opened the door to him. He had been working for three hours on a new tract, and his eyes felt gritty from staring at paper and words. His brain was tired, and it was with relief, therefore, that he greeted Bedrich.

As Bedrich walked past him into the room Karel noticed the bags.

"What are you doing with those?" he asked. "Are you leaving us?"

"Joining you, I hope," Bedrich replied.

Havlicek looked at this strange boy. There was no clue on his face. And it was clear there was going to be little gained from probing him further. "What did you mean by saying you are joining us, you hope?" he said.

"I've left school," Bedrich said matter-of-factly. "I know you haven't got much room and that there is no spare bed, but believe me I'll be no trouble, I'll sleep on cushions, and I'll tidy up every morning."

"And during the day—what will you do?"

"I'll practise the piano and compose and study music."

"You make it sound remarkably simple."

"But it is, Karel, it is."

E

He was so ingenuous that the practical Havlicek didn't have
it in him to prick the bubble of innocence. "Don't misunder-
stand me, you can share whatever we eat—that is, always
assuming Frantisek would have no objection to your moving
in with us, and I can't see that he would have—but what
would you do for money?"

"I've thought of that, Karel," Bedrich said, the words pouring out of him. "I'll get some little jobs. It will be easy enough,
I'll sell programmes at the concerts, help them with putting
up posters, run errands, anything. And I won't need much
money. I don't eat much. I'll be all right."

"All right," Havlicek said with a sigh. "We can at least give
it a try."

Buttula, of course, agreed to have him, and on the very next
day Bedrich was up and out of the flat before the two older
boys were awake.

He went down to the Charles Bridge and walked out to the
middle of it, where he stopped and gazed up at Hradcany
Castle, and then in the direction of Vysehrad, where he had
made his decision. The good weather seemed set for a long
spell, and the brightness of the morning matched his spirits.

He swung his gaze away from the picturesque Hradcany
silhouette and took in the spires of the city. The river itself
was smiling a sort of welcome to him, and with this idea in
mind he headed back towards the first concert hall in the quest
for work.

All he got at first was disappointment. No, there was nothing they could give him to do, a cold man with a brusque
manner said. Bedrich, unused to searching for employment,
took the curt dismissal to heart and left the place with his
feelings bruised.

At the next recital hall too he was unlucky. They might
be able to take him on as a programme-seller on the night of
their next concert, but that wouldn't be for a week. He asked
the manager if he could take his name, but was told it would
be a question of first come first served. This time he didn't feel
quite so crestfallen. If necessary he would be there at five in the
morning to ensure he got one of the programme-sellers jobs.

The streets were becoming hot as the sun climbed the sky

and beat down on the buildings and pavements. As he trudged on through the narrow streets of the old part of the city, past the ancient Gothic buildings, around numerous corners and bends, his spirits dropped again.

It was just before lunch-time when he arrived at the last of the recital halls that he knew of, and he hung back for a moment to mop his face and tidy his hair before presenting himself. He was about to walk in bravely when he noticed some carts drawing up, and groups of men carrying instruments coming towards him along the pavement.

Bedrich made himself as unobtrusive as possible by standing close to the wall, but was examining the men closely, for these were professional musicians, members of the community he had decided to join. True, they were members of an orchestra, whereas he himself had his sights set on being a great solo artist, but even so, these men he was looking at now were already a whole world above him. They lived from music. They played the great compositions of Auber, Mozart, Herold, and Berlioz, and were paid for such a divine chore. He looked at them with curiosity and a little envy.

The musicians who arrived by foot, carrying violins and violas and small reed and brass instruments, went straight into the auditorium. Those whose heavier instruments—the tympani and double basses—were delivered by cart hung about in the sunshine waiting for the pieces to be unloaded so that they could carry them inside.

When Bedrich saw two of the musicians struggling under the weight of the instruments, he moved out from the wall to the group who were stacking them on the pavement. This was his chance, and, taking off his coat as he spoke, he inquired whether they wanted any help. With a warning to "be careful not to drop anything or bang it against the walls", the tallest man handed him two French horns.

When the pavement had been cleared they all went inside and distributed the instruments to their correct chairs.

As the musicians went to collect their jackets afterwards Bedrich picked up his own and slipped it on. He didn't look at the men now. Money hadn't been mentioned, and he hadn't the courage to bring it up. It seemed too indelicate a matter somehow, despite the fact that he needed any coins he could get. He stood apart from the chatting musicians, keeping his eyes averted. He walked to the edge of the area in which the chairs and music-stands were set out, and looked across into the empty and echoing auditorium.

Within seconds he was lost in his own fantasy world. He peopled those empty seats with avid listeners, music-lovers who were facing him with transfixed stares; he placed himself at a piano, playing some composition the tune of which wouldn't come to him. He forced a tune into his mind, and it was a piece by Liszt. He imagined the final notes, the fragment of time in which there was no sound at all, and then the crash of applause and shouts of "Bravo! Bravo!" and the noise of hundreds of feet stamping on the wooden floorboards. The applause increased, and Bedrich took in the auditorium with its imagined audience now standing up and shouting as flowers showered from a hundred bouquets.

"What are you smiling at then?"

The tall musician who had warned him to be careful was looking at him with a half-smile on his own face. The loudness of the voice and the proximity of its owner caught Bedrich off guard, and he mumbled an inanity. He was back in the world of hard reality again.

"Here you are," the man said, handing him some coins.

"Thank you very much."

"I don't think I've seen you around before," the man said.

"Yes, I have been here," Bedrich replied, "at concerts."

"Hear that, Marek?" the man called. "The lad here is a concert-goer."

Marek said, "You were right then, Ota." By the way of explanation he said to Bedrich, "My friend said from the beginning that he felt sure from the way you spoke and the way you dressed you weren't one of the usual idlers who normally hang around scrounging pennies."

"I suppose that I insulted you by giving you a tip," the first man, the one named Ota, said.

"Oh, no, of course not," Bedrich blurted. "You see, I need it, I need money, but I'm willing to work for it."

The two men exchanged glances.

"There's something about this I don't understand," Marek said, putting his hand in his pocket and sorting out some small change which he handed over to Bedrich. "Here you are, boy, that's for helping, but how about explaining to us what you're up to?"

"Well, you see," he began, "I've just left school against my father's wishes, because I want to make my living as a musician. I can't ask him for money, and I must eat. So..." He shrugged.

"Do you play any instrument?" asked Ota.

"Piano and violin."

"Well, all I can say is good luck to you, but whatever else you do, don't let your eyes get filled with stars. Know what I mean, eh?"

"Yes, I think so."

"Good man."

They went off together then, the tall Ota and Marek, his powerfully built friend.

In the days that followed Bedrich became well known around the recital halls. He struck up a firm friendship with the two musicians Marek and Ota, and helped many times with the instruments, always receiving some small payment for his labours. They grew to like the serious boy with his quiet good manners and passionate concern with music. As time went by and they drew him out, they learnt something of his extraordinary knowledge of the subject; on several occasions they came back early from lunch to spend some time with him in the concert hall before their own rehearsal. Sometimes they got him to play the piano for them, and listened with great seriousness to his own compositions. Occasionally they took up their own instruments and joined in. They paid him the honour of giving their attention to his views, and it wasn't long before they treated him as an equal—not just an ambitious boy, but as one of themselves.

He stayed during rehearsals, and they saw him listening, head thrown back as he drank in the sounds. Occasionally he wrote furiously on a little pad of paper. On the morning before the actual concert Ota gave him a ticket. It was a pleasure for the older man to see the gratitude with which the boy accepted the gift.

Bedrich's surges of creative energy kept him up late into those nights on which he wasn't rooted to the cheaper seats at every concert he could afford to go to, or at which he wasn't working as usher or programme-seller. There were so many things he wanted to compose, so many things he wanted to try out—new rhythms, new musical constructions. He lashed himself to frenzies, pouring the notes on to paper as fast as he could write, which was never quickly enough.

During one period he felt as if his being contained a great bottomless pit of fertile ideas which he would never be able to exhaust. But when it came to the execution, and he played back what he had written, and drew on his memories of Liszt, he went to bed convinced he was a presumptuous failure, but hoping he would wake in the morning with the old drive and confidence.

When he awoke he felt worse. He lay on, pretending to be asleep, until Karel and Frantisek went off for the day. Then, in a black mood, he got up and placed the sheets on which he had been working on to the piano's music-stand. He played the music through to the end, and when he was finished snatched the paper and tore it to shreds and threw the pieces into the stove.

Very well, he thought, if I can't be a composer I'll be a virtuoso. For four hours without a break he punished himself at the keyboard, and only gave up when his hands tightened in the agony of cramp.

He was glad of one thing, and it was that he now knew beyond any doubt that he was not just in love with the *idea* of being a musician. He genuinely wanted nothing else in life or from life than music. It was the fact that he still carried on, despite all the disappointments, that taught him this elemental truth. Its knowledge sustained him.

During this time all thoughts of home and family were kept strictly in the background. But Frantisek Smetana, on his farm with his dwindling funds and his large family, had his son Bedrich very much in the forefront of his thoughts. He didn't get up very early these mornings, but he didn't sleep on either. Lying awake listening to the clamour of the dawn chorus, he frequently found himself thinking of Bedrich, and he would stay in bed, chagrin mounting, until eventually he went down to the kitchen in a foul temper.

Albina knew why her father was acting this way. It was wrong of Bedrich to have put up this wall of silence, and she sent him several notes telling him so, but they went unanswered. She grew alarmed and wondered if everything was well with him. Meanwhile she did her utmost to avoid and avert the dramatic explosions which created such tension in the house.

One morning when Barbora came into the kitchen to prepare the breakfast she found Frantisek there before her.

"You're up early, my dear. I didn't expect you down so soon," she said.

He mumbled something which she didn't quite hear, so she asked him to repeat it.

"I said I'll be out all day," he snapped.

"Oh. Where are you going?"

"Prague."

The single word, the set of his lips, sent a chill through her.

"Come on, woman, prepare me something to eat!"

The voice acted like a whiplash, and she hurried about, laying the table and making the food ready. When he was quite ready he sat down, exercising his inalienable right to be waited on. He spoke not at all. Barbora might have been no more than a deaf-mute maid for all the notice he took of her.

Twenty minutes later she went to the door to see him off. He was stepping into the sunlight when she put a restraining hand on his arm.

"Well?"

"If—if you see Bedrich while you're in Prague—you won't —won't hurt him, will you, Frantisek?" It was as much a plea as a question.

Frantisek looked at her for a long moment, then, without replying, left the house.

*　　*　　*

He was shown straight into Josef Jungmann's study, and when the introductions were over and Jungmann had said, "Ah yes, Mr Smetana, then you must be Bedrich's father?" Frantisek came immediately to the point.

"Yes I am," he said, "and I've come here about him."

Jungmann put the points of his fingers together in a pyramid and touched his lips. This man Smetana was about to be hurt. Jungmann was searching his mind to find the least painful way of handing out the wound.

"Well?" Frantisek asked. "Is he making any headway?"

"He may well be," Jungmann said carefully.

"What do you mean? What sort of an answer is that?"

"The only sort of answer I can give you," said Jungmann. He was trying to form a cushion for the shock that would hit this blustering man at any second now.

"You'll pardon my saying so, but I think that a most unsatisfactory reply in view of the fees I pay you to educate my son."

"I can understand—"

"Understand? Understand? Well, tell me how he's getting on at his studies."

Jungmann could see that his efforts at delicacy were failing miserably. This man knew only the bludgeon. "Mr Smetana," he began, "your son doesn't attend this school any more."

Frantisek shuddered under the impact. He clutched at his coat and drew it tight. His voice was a croak when he asked, "Where is he?"

"He left here some weeks ago," Jungmann replied.

"And you allowed him to?" Frantisek was incredulous.

"There was nothing I could do. I tried to reason with him."

Frantisek Smetana felt suddenly old and tired. It was as if all the juices had drained away from him. He sat perfectly still, his head drooping. It was some minutes before he spoke. Then he said, "Why did he leave? Where did he go?"

Jungmann felt genuine compassion for him. He dropped his official, imperious manner. "Your son is in love with music," he said.

Frantisek could feel his gorge rising.

"He's very talented musically," Jungmann continued. "I suppose you know that."

Frantisek said, "Yes, he has some talent."

"He's got a great deal of talent, but, more important, he is passionately involved. He can see nothing else but a future bound up in music."

"And that's why he left?"

"That is why he left my school—to spend all his time in pursuit of the one thing in life that means anything to him."

"But it's such a waste!" Frantisek said, his anger catching alight again. "I had such plans for him. There is so much else he could do, make a good life for himself, insure himself against poverty. Once he qualified in some profession he could take up his music. It has cost me so much."

"Artists don't measure cost in money, Mr Smetana," Jungmann said.

"Don't be an idiot, Jungmann! He's a *boy*, not an *artist*."

"Art recognises no age limits," Jungmann said.

"And where will it get him? Answer me that!"

"It will give him great satisfaction."

"And if he fails?"

"It won't matter. He will have tried, he will have fulfilled himself."

"And broken me," Frantisek added with bitterness.

"We are on different tracks, Mr Smetana. I'm trying to see the whole picture. You can't. You count success by what a man makes in terms of money."

"You've never known poverty, Mr Jungmann, that's clear to me. I have, and I hated it." Frantisek got up to go.

"I'm sorry for you," Jungmann said. "I mean it. I only hope that you're not going to do anything that will ruin the boy's life."

"I shall be the judge of that, and it will be my responsibility," Frantisek said and left the room.

Bedrich was alone in the apartment when his father arrived. He was shocked to see his father, and he could see by Frantisek's face that he was in a rage. But he was not prepared for what happened as soon as his father entered the room. The full-blooded blow on the side of the head knocked the boy across the room. It was the first time since he was a child his father had raised a hand to him.

He stood stunned and afraid, rubbing the place where the sting of the blow felt red-hot. For an instant he wondered if his father was mad. The staring eyes and the drawn-back lips that bared the teeth were alarming.

"You're coming home," Frantisek said. "You're a wastrel."

Then it came to Bedrich what it was all about. "Just listen to me for a moment, Papa," he said.

"Go and get your things."

"*Listen* to me, Papa."

"I'll not have you—"

"Papa, *listen!*" The raised voice took Frantisek by surprise. Bedrich had never yelled at him before. "Now hear my side of it," the boy went on, still nervous, but determined to have his say once and for all. "You want me to be a lawyer, but I don't want to be one. I'd hate it. I'm grateful for everything you've done for me, but, Papa, I can't carry on trying to learn things I'm not interested in—"

"It's for your own g—"

"Let me *finish*, Papa! I don't want to study. And I'm not going back with you. You'll have to drag me out of here, and I'll run away from you. I promise you, Papa, I'm serious. I want to give music a try. I've never been so happy as I've been since I left Jungmann's school."

"You'll come home," said Frantisek. "I'd rather have you working as a labourer on the farm than idling away your time here with your crazy ideas. Great God, what have I reared? Get your things together."

"No!" the boy cried, and, running round his father, he dashed out and down the stairs and away off into the city.

Frantisek waited for him to come back, but when Bedrich didn't return he left the place with a heavy heart and went home to his farm.

Bedrich stayed out until nearly midnight, and when he went up the stairs to the flat he went quietly, on tiptoe. He stood outside the door listening in case his father was still inside.

Havlicek and Buttula found him asleep against the landing wall in the morning.

At times during the week following his father's visit Bedrich was tortured by guilt. Had he really let his parents down? Should he go back? Could the break between himself and his father ever be mended now, or had he cut himself off for all time? His conscience prodded him all the while. He couldn't disregard it. At concerts, during practice, while talking, the questions nagged at him.

In the apartment he became untidy and left his bed unmade, and the room littered with sheets of music. He sought advice from his friends, but didn't listen when they gave it.

The hot months of May and June dragged by, and he became more troubled. Albina's letters told of the unhappiness at home. She said Papa looked a broken man, and that the strain was awful. She said her father seemed to be wallowing in shame, and couldn't bear Bedrich's name to be mentioned.

Later the old man softened and talked frequently of the happiness it would bring them all if only Bedrich would return to the family once more.

Albina came to Prague, and Bedrich wept when he saw his favourite sister. Although she didn't want him to abandon his musical ambitions, she begged him to consider coming home for the summer holidays. As always in the past, he could refuse Albina nothing, and when she told him of the love that awaited him he decided to make the break with Prague, if only temporarily. He needed his family's love, he knew that.

On the morning of July 10th, 1840, he said goodbye to Buttula and Havlicek. He didn't want them to accompany him from the apartment, and he walked out into the streets, looking at the familiar buildings long and lovingly so as to impress them indelibly in his mind. He went to the Charles Bridge and looked at the city. He gazed at the meandering river, at Hradcany Castle and St Vitus's Cathedral, the spires and gables. Then he turned with a thousand pictures in his head, and left Prague for the farm at Ruzkovy Lhotice.

CHAPTER
[7]

IN THE COURSE OF HIS journey home the boy was again assailed by doubts. Was he doing the right thing in going back? What would happen about his music? Was he on the threshold now of abandoning for ever all that he lived for, everything that motivated his existence, filled his mind, gave him the desire to see each new day? Would Ruzkovy Lhotice mean the end of this?

Deep in him he knew he craved the approval of his father and mother and all the family. If he could have this, and their love, of a certainty he would compose better music, be a better musician, attack his musical studies with a freer mind and even more determination. He was convinced that a true artist had to have the comfort of giving and receiving love.

I shall win back my father's love, he told himself, and then I shall go on with my music, and Papa will understand and give me his blessing; so thinking, he put his head back and closed his eyes. Presently he slept, and didn't awake until he was near his home.

His first view of his mother came as a shock. She had aged and looked defeated. She embraced him wordlessly, and clung to him so tightly and for so long that he was brought to the edge of sadness instead of joy. When she finally broke her hold on him she stood back and looked at his face through flooding eyes. "Bedrich, my Bedrich," was all she said.

Frantisek came out then, and walked slowly across the yard towards them. There was a moment of intense awkwardness between the old man and the son who had come home. The unsaid things stood between them like a barrier. The afternoon sun, hanging low in the sky, cast their shadows in elongated black shapes across the ground. Then the old man's arms were held out before him, and Bedrich was running to him to be clasped.

"Welcome," Frantisek whispered, "welcome home, son."

The girls came out, and the youngest ones stood shyly. Bedrich hugged them all in turn, and when he had finished, there was Albina, her eyes shining, racing towards him from the door of the house, Albina whom he loved most of all.

It was his mother who eventually took his hand and said, "Come on inside, Bedrich, you must be tired."

"I slept through most of the journey," he replied.

"That kind of sleep doesn't rest anyone," she said. "Come, I have a lovely meal ready for you."

The children bombarded him with questions about Prague. Some he answered freely, but there were many of which he had to steer clear, for fear of reopening his father's wound.

Frantisek sat without speaking. He felt deeply happy that the boy was home again in the place where he belonged, among the family. Up to now, he realized with a pang, he had never seen his son other than as Bedrich, a worry, a drifter with an unplanned future, a part of himself which always refused to conform. But sitting back and seeing Bedrich now, listening to the children talking to him, and hearing the boy's replies, he saw him for the first time as a young man with a character of his own, someone who would soon be an adult, a person who brought happiness to other human beings. Seeing him in this light, and then aligning it with the fact that this young man was *also* his son, Frantisek glowed with a new pride.

Barbora sensed her husband's happiness, and her anxiety eased so that she was able to bask unreservedly in the joy of having Bedrich home again.

Almost as soon as the celebration meal was over Bedrich felt an overwhelming desire to go to bed. The day, with all its momentous happenings and emotional ups and downs, had taken its toll of him, and he could feel the heaviness in his eyes making the lids droop. Eventually he could no longer stifle the yawns, and asked politely if he could be excused.

Bedrich woke to the sounds of the farm. He lay back, hands joined behind his head, and listened. How quiet it was here, how utterly peaceful! Cattle were lowing somewhere across the fields, and he could hear someone making clucking sounds as the hens were fed. There was a bird on the tree close to the window, singing a duet with another close by, and in the yard one of the workers was watering the pony. There wasn't a solitary sound that was reminiscent of a Prague morning. Prague might be a million miles away, he mused.

"Hello, lazybones," said his mother when he eventually walked sheepishly into the kitchen. "Did you sleep well?"

"I don't think I moved once in the whole night," he said. "What time is it now anyway?"

"Eleven."

"*Eleven!* Why didn't you call me?"

"There was no point in disturbing you. Sit down there now, I have some lovely fresh eggs for you."

Barbora laid a crisp, clean cloth on the table and placed his breakfast before him. When he saw the amount of food he said, "Mama, there's enough there for a regiment!"

"You need building up."

He set about the food, and to his surprise he finished all that was put before him.

"Does that feel better?" asked his mother.

"Marvellous," he said. He wiped his mouth, pushed back his chair, and stood up. He went across to her, kissed her lightly, and asked, "Where's Papa?"

"He went into the village immediately after breakfast. He should be home soon."

He walked out of the kitchen and into the sitting-room. He opened the lid of the piano and ran his fingers along the keyboard.

"Are you going to play something for me?" called his mother from the kitchen.

"No, not just now," he answered. "Maybe later on."

His father's violin-case was there, and he opened it. There

was an overlay of dust on the polished wood, and that made him feel bad. It must have been a long time since Frantisek had taken the violin from its case. Bedrich took it out now, lovingly dusted it with his handkerchief, and put it under his chin. Out of the corner of his eye he saw a movement at the door, and he turned to see his mother moving away, going back to the kitchen. She had been watching.

He put the violin back in its case, his emotions caught in a strange, arrested state. There was a chatter of birds from outside the window, and he moved very slowly so as not to disturb them. On the patch of grass outside—it was still green, though here and there he could see signs of yellowing—two blackbirds with brilliant orange bills were looking for worms. They were strong-looking and alert, almost cheeky, as they made hopping runs and then dug down into the soil. Occasionally they flew on to the fence after cleaning their bills by rubbing them on the edges of stones.

It was lunch-time when Frantisek returned to the farm, and his laughter carried down the country road ahead of him. Even the laughter had a sobering effect on Bedrich. He's happy now, he thought, he's laughing, and he hasn't laughed for far too long. What right did I have to deprive him of happiness? Why did I do it? For music. Music is glorious. Music is love. If I can create, if I can make glory and love, am I not justified in pursuing it, in perhaps hurting someone in the pursuit? But I am only a fledgeling, and there is no guarantee that anything I do shall be fit to be called good or beautiful; therefore, at this stage, can I justify hurting anyone, sacrificing anything of anyone's right to contentment?

"Bedrich! Bedrich! Come here, my son, I want you to meet a good friend of mine." It was his father calling. Bedrich looked at himself in the mirror, and was a little taken aback by the youthful face that frowned at him. He forced a smile to his lips and went to meet his father's friend.

All the afternoon his father walked about humming to himself. Bedrich, trying to find his feet in the house again, once or twice interrupted animated conversations between his father and mother, and was diverted from the kitchen and the sitting-room on various pretexts. At any other time he would have been curious to know what was going on. But he was still in such a state of worried disorientation that, apart from noticing that his mother seemed to be doing a lot of cooking, he didn't bother about much else.

At about three o'clock he strolled along the road towards the village. In places the trees on either side of him grew so close together, and were so thickly covered with leaves, that they met overhead, the sun came through in slanting shafts of light, and he felt as if he were walking down the aisle of a living cathedral. Gradually then the tension in his mind slackened away. He breathed in deeply, put his hands on his hips, and breathed again, standing alone, looking upwards, in the centre of the country road.

With his hands in his pockets, he went on in the direction of the village. He didn't meet anyone he knew. He saw groups of people talking at the doors stopping their conversations as they caught sight of him, then putting their heads together and whispering as they either recognized him or speculated as to who he might be. There wasn't much to talk about in Ruzkovy Lhotice, and the sight of an unfamiliar figure in the streets provided a welcome diversion.

He heard the words "Smetana" and "Prague" a few times, and tried to imagine what it was they might be saying about him. Once again the persistent duality of his thinking took over. On the one hand he could derive innocent satisfaction from regarding these villagers as nice peasant folk who hadn't lived in the great capital, as he had done, simple bodies whose horizons were bounded by the lanes and fields of Ruzkovy Lhotice, and whose conversations were rarely concerned with anything else. He could tell himself: My life has been bigger; I've *seen* more things already than they will imagine in a lifetime, *heard* more than they will ever know existed; and I've also known the country life.

But there was the other side of him which said: These are the people of Bohemia; they are fortunate in that they've seen sunrises on the Blanik, and heard the sounds of animals and birds in every state from birth to death; they are rooted in the soil, and as free as the sun and the wind; they are uncomplicated and emotional and free of the meanness of sophistication;

they love and hate with as much vigour and probably more passion than any city people; they know and appreciate the simple things, and being surrounded by beauty can never be blind to it; for centuries they have had their own music and folklore—and they are my people.

It was Albina who saw Bedrich swinging down the road, and she immediately ran to her father.

"He's coming, Papa, and he's walking fast."

"Good girl, Albina. We're nearly ready, but go out and meet him, and try to delay him for a moment. Hurry, I can hear him."

As Albina ran out to intercept Bedrich the activity in the house increased. Barbora rushed about, Frantisek whispered frantically to the children, the maidservant bore covered dishes hither and thither, and in the room where the piano was the large curtain which had been drawn across from wall to wall, partitioning off one whole area, was tested.

"Is everything ready?" Frantisek asked urgently as his wife came from the bedroom. She was fastening on the jewelled cross she had worn when Machka painted her portrait.

"Yes, dear."

"Good, good." He walked to the door of the music-room, put his head in, and said, "Arnost."

"Yes, Frantisek?" said a man's voice from behind the curtain.

"Are you ready?"

"Yes, yes, quite ready."

Frantisek pulled the door to, but didn't click it shut.

Outside in the yard Albina was saying, "And where did you go?"

"Into the village," Bedrich said.

"Did you see anyone you know?"

"No, but I was looked at and talked about, and I enjoyed myself immensely."

"You're looking happy," Albina said.

"I feel it."

"Are you glad you came home, really glad?"

He looked out over the fields, then turned back to his sister. "Yes," he said. "Really glad, thanks to you." He kissed her cheek.

F

Impulsively, to get over the moment of embarrassment, she took his hand and said, "Come on, let's go in."

The second he walked through the front door, the door of the music-room (which was facing him) opened as if by magic, and the music started. For an instant he stopped in his tracks, and turned behind him to Albina, but she had scurried away to the back door of the house. He turned again, astonishment changing to a feeling not far removed from alarm, as he seriously wondered if he were in some sort of dream.

He stepped into the room. This was no hallucination. This was real music, these were real musicians. He heard them out to the end of their piece without once moving from where he stood, and when they finished there was a tiny hiatus which was shattered by a bursting of handclapping from behind him. The applause triggered off his own reflexes, and his hands had actually come together three or four times before the strangeness of the situation once more broke upon him, and he spun around.

There, arranged in a clapping, smiling group, was the whole family. They had crept into their positions while the music had been playing, and at this moment Frantisek was advancing, still clapping, smiling happily. Then the old man raised his own right hand like a conductor, and brought it down. The children's voices came in together. "Welcome home, Bedrich," they choroused.

Bedrich was at a loss. He looked from face to face and then grinned. This was his father's doing. I don't deserve this, he thought, not after the way I've let him down.

"Well, cheer up, son!" Frantisek was grasping his shoulders.

Bedrich bit his lip.

"This is for you," his father went on, indicating the musicians. "We're going to have a musical evening. Your mother has cooked a feast, some friends will be coming to join us, and you will be the guest of honour and the musical director! Now then, are you pleased?"

"Oh, Papa . . . "

"It's all right, son. You don't have to say anything. I did this just to show you how glad I am, how glad we all are, that you've come home. Now go and enjoy yourself."

The rest of the evening was full of gaiety. The guests came and talked about and to everyone. The children were allowed to stay up late, the musicians played folk-dances; Bedrich danced with all the ladies in turn, and made a fine picture with Albina as they smiled happily at each other and covered the whole floor space with the grace and lightness of youth.

And then he was asked to play the piano. He felt no hesitation about accepting, and he chose a piece by Liszt. There wasn't a whisper of sound as he flexed his fingers and held his hands poised above the keyboard.

He felt particularly good tonight, and he had chosen well, nothing too intricate to begin with, but a piece full of feeling. He closed his eyes and allowed the music to speak to him, passing its message on in turn to those listening to him. He did it by touch and rhythm, by sometimes holding a pause, caressing a note, drawing it limpidly and purely, and letting it hang a moment. He changed the mood by strength and decision. His right hand became firm and decisive, then full of an airiness that weaved a musical filigree. His heart was in communion with Liszt, he himself was lost to those around him. He would not have wanted anything, or anyone, in the whole world to interrupt.

The applause at the end jerked him back to reality, and he felt the pleasure that any man feels at receiving acclaim. They asked for encore after encore. He obliged them with solos, sat in to make a quartet of the trio, and even went to his room and took out some of his own compositions which the quartet at Prague used to play. These pieces brought nostalgic memories back to him.

At the end he persuaded his father to pick up his violin, and got great pleasure when the old man reluctantly agreed. The fingers, though, had hardened; the dexterity had vanished because of lack of practice; the notes were blurred; the exasperation was sad as well as evident. But Bedrich was delighted. He felt that the fact that Frantisek had once again taken the instrument from its case was in itself a great sign. The applause for Frantisek's playing was led by Bedrich, and he was the last one to stop.

This musical evening was the first of a number Frantisek

arranged, and during these initial weeks at home Bedrich was never once asked about school, his future, or his ambitions. And when time passed, and still no reference was made to Prague or Jungmann or the law, Bedrich relaxed and pushed the worries away to recesses of the mind where they were covered over and gradually buried deep.

He walked a lot, across the fields for miles and miles, climbing over hedges, pushing upwards on to the hills, and standing with the wind in his hair as he looked down on the yellow corn rippling in wave motions when the breezes blew over the farmland. He went into woods that were deep-shadowed and cool, and where he was the only human being. He lay down on his stomach and held a blade of grass in the bubbling, clear water of a stream. He did these things on many days, and allowed the impressions to come and go at will, soaking up all the romantic ideas, dreaming his way through the golden July.

There was an afternoon when he lay back and tried to understand the sky. He stared into the blueness and wondered what made it blue. Clouds came across and built up in layers, the white ones fluffy and rounded in cherubic curves, then came the cream ones, and, a little later, those which were a darkening grey. They passed across the face of the sun, and he sat up and saw the countryside alive with changing light. He couldn't have expressed what he felt. He knew only that some time, somehow, he would have to put into music the emotions that were coursing through him from seeing his beloved Bohemia in these, the most wonderful conditions of all.

When the travelling entertainers came to the village he could always be found among the show folk during the day, when they were setting up their equipment. He attended every performance and marvelled at the agility of the tumblers and acrobats. He listened to the singing and memorized the tunes, and on many a musical evening sent his family and their guests into gales of laughter with his uncannily accurate impersonations, embracing everything from accents and pronunciations to notes which were sung appallingly flat. The one aspect of the entertainments he refrained from even gently mocking was the comedy side, for he was always enthralled by the comedians. No matter how many times he saw a routine, he would sit through it with eyes shining and sides aching.

The late September days were shortening before Frantisek brought up the question of the future. After the concert Bedrich gave at the academy at Cetnice when his performance of the concerto by Jan Horalek had brought the audience to a standing ovation, Frantisek, flushed with pride, had nevertheless the twisted hard look of a man who has something worrying on his mind.

Albina, Barbora, Bedrich, and Frantisek were finishing a meal. The father carefully wiped his mouth, and pushed the dishes away from him to make room for his elbows on the table.

"The summer is over," he began, "and now comes the sad time of the year."

"It's been such a happy summer, this year, hasn't it, my dear?" Barbora said.

"Very happy," said Frantisek.

"Bedrich always makes us feel bright and good," Albina said. Bedrich kept his eyes on his fingers.

"Have you enjoyed it, son?" Frantisek asked.

"Yes, Papa, very much."

"It goes without saying that we ... that having you at home has made a great difference to all of us," Frantisek said. "Have you ever thought of staying?"

Bedrich looked at his father. "How do you mean, Papa?"

"Well ..." Frantisek fiddled with a spoon. "I mean I'm getting older, and I am not as capable of seeing to things as I used to be. What I'm saying is that the farm needs a younger man to look after it."

Bedrich experienced an old, familiar, sinking sensation in the pit of his stomach. His father was putting some kind of proposition to him, and in his bones he knew he could not accept.

"Well, Bedrich?"

"I don't know, Papa. I don't know anything about farm work."

"You could learn."

"You really want him to give up his education?" said Barbora.

"No, *I* don't want that. But *he* hasn't exactly shown a burning desire to be educated, has he? I don't mean to be unkind or unpleasant, son, but what I said is true, isn't it?"

Bedrich didn't reply.

"But what about his future?" Barbora demanded.

"Damn it, Barbora, that's what I'm talking about!"

A small, uneasy silence came down on them. After a minute or so Frantisek said, "Bedrich, I want to know your thoughts. I mean, I can't keep on paying for you to go to school if you're not in the least bit interested in it. I only want to do what's best for you, what's best for all of us."

"I know that, Papa." He was suffering all the old feelings of torture and persecution. He sat, pulling at his hair, picking at the scalp, then winding a lock of hair round and round his forefinger.

"What about staying on the farm then?"

"Oh, Papa, I couldn't, honestly, I *couldn't*! I think the life would drive me insane."

"Has it driven me insane? Or your mother? Or Albina, or any of the others?"

"No, of course not. It's just that it's ... it's so humdrum."

Frantisek stood up, and in so doing knocked a footstool over. Instead of picking it up and righting it, he kicked it across the floor. He stood with his palms flat on the table and bent over towards Bedrich. "Why is it," he said, thinly and venomously, "why is it that no matter what is done for you, you always want more? You're never satisfied. You must have it *your* way."

Albina got up, took a step to Bedrich, pressed his arm, and left the room, her face very pale.

Frantisek went to the piano and stood by it, his back to the table. He fingered some sheets of music without noticing what they were, then ran his hand across his eyes, trying to figure out why he and this son of his were so completely different in everything.

He came back across the room and sat down. He looked at

his wife and said, "Leave us alone for a few minutes, please, my dear. I want to thrash this business out."

Barbora went out.

"Close the door behind you!" Frantisek called, and it banged shut. "Now, where do we go from here?" he asked Bedrich.

"I don't know, Papa."

"Don't know, don't know! For Christ's sake, boy, is that all you can say? Now you do some talking," he said. "Justify. Explain. Argue. But for God's sake let me know what's going on inside that head of yours."

Bedrich was stung by his father's tone, and any fears he had had about offending Frantisek's sensitivities fled as he stood up and said, "All right. My thoughts regarding the future are: I *would* like to continue my education. I *still* love music. I *am* grateful, as I've told you before, for the sacrifices you've made for me, but I'll not *beg* to be sent to school. I'd rather leave home and fend for myself."

Frantisek laughed.

"Laughing does nothing to dissuade me, Papa. And remember, I'm not exactly inexperienced at earning money."

"Meaning?"

"Meaning that contrary to any notions you may have had about how I lived when I left Jungmann's school, I earned money by working."

"What did you do for it?"

Bedrich told him about the programme-selling, the jobs as usher, the times he had carried instruments.

When he finished Frantisek said, "I didn't think you had it in you, but I am glad you told me. Now listen, I've been thinking." His voice had lost its edge now, and there was a new look on his face, one of conciliation. "It's as well we had this talk. I'm not saying I agree with those ideas you have about music, but I must say that when you did do some work at Jungmann's the results showed that you had the ability to learn. Your cousin Josef is coming here the day after tomorrow. I'll speak to him. A professor must have some good advice to give on this education business. Meanwhile, let's shake hands. There. No hard feelings?"

"No hard feelings, Papa."

Josef Frantisek Smetana, Frantisek's nephew, was a teacher at the monastery at Pilsen, and when he arrived on one of his periodic visits to his uncle's home Frantisek took him aside and told him about his worries over Bedrich's future. Josef was an understanding man as well as a brilliant intellectual. He felt for his uncle, but he was also aware of his young cousin's dilemma, and the upshot of the conversation was that he undertook to keep an eye on the boy if Frantisek would agree to sending him to school at Pilsen.

On the morning of October 5th, 1840 (Frantisek had celebrated his sixty-third birthday the previous day), Bedrich said goodbye to the rest of the family and set out for Pilsen with his father.

CHAPTER

[8]

PILSEN WAS A THRIVING TOWN with its own musical life, and a culture all its own. It was no Prague, but neither was it a Nemecky Brod. Its very size made it attractive to Bedrich, and he was deeply grateful to his cousin Josef. The town had a sturdy population whose love of the arts found expression in the many festivals that were held throughout the year.

However, Bedrich, under the watchful surveillance of his professor-cousin, immediately turned his attention to his books. He was living with his teacher, a man named Sykora. Sykora was a dried-out individual whose main interest lay in the great tomes in the monastery library.

On the first evening on which Bedrich sat down to practise on Sykora's piano the teacher stormed into the room. "Who told you you could use that instrument?" he demanded.

"Nobody actually told me," Bedrich replied, "but I wasn't told I was forbidden to."

"I'm telling you now. What sort of manners have you been taught?"

"I apologize," Bedrich said. "May I practise?"

"Certainly not," Sykora snapped. "How you imagine decent people can concentrate on anything while you pound out that cacophony defeats me."

"It's not cacophony, sir."

"Don't be insolent. Close the lid at once, and open your books. It would serve you a lot better to concentrate on learning something useful instead of wasting your time."

It was a crestfallen Bedrich who related the incident to his cousin.

"That's just like Sykora," Josef commented. "Anyway, don't let it depress you. I'll try to make some alternative arrangement for you." True to his word, Josef came to Bedrich a couple of days later and said, "I think I've found the answer. I've spoken to Sykora and told him I was taking you away from his house tonight. Have your things packed and ready when I call round for you at seven this evening."

There was a freezing wind blowing when they walked through the Pilsen streets, and Bedrich's hands felt chilled to the bone. He had packed his mittens by mistake, and was still looking for them when his cousin called. Josef was in too much of a hurry to wait.

"Come on," he said, "or this good woman will think we're not coming at all."

The good woman turned out to be Mrs Wildmann, a forester's widow. A mountainous, jolly person, she invited them into a home whose inside was full of the warm sight of polished wood. The stove was roaring and a coffee-pot was already on the boil. Her home spelt welcome from every niche.

"So this is my new lodger, Professor?" she said, holding out her arms.

"Yes, Mrs Wildmann, this is Bedrich."

"Take off your coat, Bedrich," said Mrs Wildmann, "and sit there by the stove. You'll be warm in no time. No, don't bother about your bags. Time enough for them. My son will help you to take them to your room presently. That's it. Now, Professor, will you stay for a nice hot coffee?"

"I'm afraid not, Mrs Wildmann, thank you all the same. I'm late for a lecture already."

When Mrs Wildmann went to the door to see Josef off, Bedrich glanced round the room. His eyes quickly found what he was seeking—the piano. It was standing, draped in an old velvet curtain, in the corner. Covered up—did that mean it was neglected and out of tune?

"Would you like to try it?" the voice said from the door. He hadn't heard Mrs Wildmann returning.

"If I may," said Bedrich, crossing to the instrument, but fearful of what jangle he might hear.

"Let me take this off for you," the widow said, snatching the covering away to reveal a beautifully polished upright. "There you are."

He struck the lowest bass key, and a rich thunder echoed around the room. Absolutely true. He struck the top note, and the sound was hard and clear and true. Encouraged, he played a series of chords, and the piano sounded as good as any household instrument he had played.

"Sit down, Bedrich," Mrs Wildmann said, "you can't play standing up." She pushed the piano-stool in at the backs of his legs, and he began to play some of Cramer's *études*.

When he had finished he turned to see Mrs Wildmann sitting on the side of a chair, elbow on the table, her double chins resting in her palm.

"My word, boy, but you can play," she said. "I've never heard a piano played like that before. Will you—would you do me a great favour, Bedrich? Would you teach my son to play?"

"I'll try," he replied, "but I've never taught anyone before."

"Oh, would you, would you? I should be very grateful. I'll tell you what—you teach my boy, and I'll not charge you anything to stay here. I don't really need the money anyway. Is that a bargain?"

Bedrich agreed, and, strangely enough, from that moment on he felt as if he had known Mrs Wildmann for years.

He worked hard at school and did well in his studies. The letters his father wrote were full of praise and encouragement; in them he said he had been giving considerable thought as to what career Bedrich should aim for. The Civil Service, he pointed out, was safe; it provided security and respectability, and Bedrich could do much worse than think about it as a possible future source of employment.

The boy was determined to please his father. At the end of his first month at school he was delighted with the results he obtained in the examinations. In his room at Mrs Wildmann's house he took out his diary and wrote: *After the first of the monthly examinations I was praised for the marks I received in all subjects. Help me, God, that I may always be able to write such things in this little book.*

On November 8th, he wrote: *I was praised for my papers in Latin and history. My studies are going very well.*

When he had caught up with the rest of the class to the extent that he was able to decrease the number of hours spent poring over books, he began to write small musical compositions. He didn't discuss them with anyone. He wanted to avoid giving the impression that he was relaxing his school efforts, because even a well-intentioned remark or letter to his father could drive the old man into a state of worry again. Instead he committed his thoughts to his diary: *If I wasn't so burdened with study I would compose many more pieces and work them out with greater care and labour.*

Nevertheless, compensations came his way. Accounts of his ability as a pianist spread. Soon came the first tentative approach to him to attend a musical evening at one of the town's grander residences; the discovery that he had indeed a glittering talent to offer; the inevitable further invitations to other and more splendid parties.

He had by now acquired an excellent manner, and was a dancer of quite extraordinary grace and versatility. It was a long way from the village green; the girls he danced with now had none of the rustic abandon he remembered, but he liked their cool beauty. He kept a strict control on the times he spent socializing, however, because he wanted to maintain his success at his studies.

His home and family were for ever in his mind, and among the entries he made in his diary was one which said: *Please, Almighty God, let this year be one of good health, work, and happiness for my parents and sisters, and please enable me to make them happy—that would make me most happy.*

One other thing that made him happy was the memory of a girl he had met at Nove Mesto during the summer holidays. He had gone there to visit his uncle Vaclav Smetana, and at the first sight of his cousin, Luise, he knew that he was in love. So captivated was he by the girl's looks that he had sat down and written a piece of music which he dedicated to her, calling it *Luise's Polka*.

In Pilsen he thought about her a great deal. She walked tantalizingly through his dreams, a beautiful creature without temper, a shining, pure girl who must surely have been placed on earth to love, and be loved by, Bedrich Smetana alone. On nights when Mrs Wildmann was out he sat at the piano and played *Luise's Polka*, and talked as if Luise was there in the room with him. When Mrs Wildmann's son came in and heard him in one of his romantic soliloquy's one such night, he had an embarrassing time trying to explain away his strange behaviour.

At the parties he attended he soon discovered that girls found him attractive enough to seek out his company. It was a flattering discovery which brought with it a sweet exultation.

With scarcely a pang of regret he dismissed Luise from his mind when he met Elisa Goller. He could see clearly that he had been infatuated with Luise, but Elisa Goller was different. She was perfect. She could not be surpassed.

But she was, when Katerina Corvin came along. Katerina combined the very best of both Luise and Elisa Goller. It was amazing, he reflected, how blind one could be. Surely no creature could even compare with Katerina? Katerina was the supreme being, the one to whom his lasting affections would be attached.

At the ball given by the Horovy family he saw a tiny, wasp-waisted picture of a girl who looked as if she had been created by a master of beauty to his own designs. He felt his knees weakening as she was led across the floor by a formidable matron encrusted with jewels. He was standing by himself, in one of the few moments of the entire evening when he wasn't surrounded by chatting admirers, drinking a glass of wine. He glanced about him to see to whom else the girl might be coming. But there was no-one close by, and the girl and the older woman were heading straight towards him.

For some unaccountable reason he started to sweat. His palms became drenched. His forehead became hot, and then the elderly woman was saying, "Bedrich, I wanted my niece to meet you. Klara, this is our musical guest of honour, Mr Smetana." The girl inclined her head half an inch and put out an elegantly gloved hand, as the older woman left them.

There was something about that exquisite little face that took his breath away. "Are you enjoying the ball?" he asked.

"Yes, thank you."

"Yes, so am I," he said. He wanted to pay her a compliment, but was too unsure of himself to try.

"Are you a music-teacher?" she asked, suddenly looking him straight in the face, and causing the redness to rush all over his cheeks and neck once more.

"No, no," he said. "I'm still at school."

"At school?"

"Yes."

Her head went back, showing him the line of her throat, pulling up her breasts to peep, rounded and creamy, over the top of her gown. Her teeth were even and perfectly white. The laugh was like music.

"Does that amuse you—that I should go to school?" he asked.

"It's not that, Bedrich—I can call you Bedrich now?—it's just that I thought you were much older, a man of the world. But we're both only children!"

"You, a child?"

"Well, how old do you think I am?"

"Eighteen," he said. "Nineteen, perhaps."

"*Sixteen*," Klara said, with a sort of triumphant emphasis.

Now Bedrich laughed. With relief. The revelation of her youthfulness demolished the barrier that had made her appear unattainable. There would be no difficulty now in talking to her.

Two minutes later he was dancing with her. On the following evening he called at her house and played some polkas for her. By the end of the week they had been to two concerts together, and Luise, Elisa Goller, and Katerina Corvin were misty figures in his past.

For three months he lived on an emotional see-saw, alternating between peaks of happiness (when Klara responded satisfactorily to his ardour) and dark pits of desolation (when she rebuffed him).

O Klara, Klara! Listen to me, and don't drive me into madness, he wrote. *Let me talk to you, let me influence you, adore you, save you, be your slave! To hope that you would love me in the same way as I love you would be craziness, or impertinence. But I am ready to die for you, my Klara, to die for your name!*

He was never called upon to go to such extremes of love, for, truth to tell, Klara was flighty. She grew tired of the romantic young pianist with his ardent attention, his hyperbole, his passionate recitations. Unfortunately for Bedrich, she was possessed of neither the guile nor the tact to break from him in a gentle way. There was a brutal directness about what she said, and it affected him like a file drawn across an exposed nerve.

He brooded for days. No mortal could ever have suffered as he was suffering. Certainly other people, thousands of them, millions probably, had loved and been disappointed. But with me it is different, he reasoned. It must be. I loved her *so much.* All the others must have kept something back. I didn't. I know I am only just seventeen, but a seventeen-year-old can feel just as much as a thirty-seven-year-old. He took his pen and wrote: *I was not prepared to be so hurt. You degraded my whole self when you rejected me! ... Oh if I could only cry!*

The implied restraint was not long in foundering, and though his grief (that was how he looked upon his disappointment and wounded pride) occupied him fully while it lasted, its duration was short-lived. Indeed, when it was over he was able to think, with a certain degree of wonder, about the amazing resilience of the human spirit. There would be other girls in his life from whose company he could derive pleasure without necessarily making himself upset through total commitment and the threat of rejection.

Karel Kolar and his family had been friends of the Smetanas up to the time Karel, an officer in the Government Finance Department, was transferred from Jindrichuv Hradec, and the Smetanas themselves too had left the place.

During the period when the families were frequent visitors at each other's houses, the Kolars' daughter, Katerina, had been a loud, impulsive little girl known by the adults as "the wild one". She was what, in another place and time, would have been called a tomboy, and Karel at one stage said, "Katy came from a wild egg."

Katerina had been altogether too wild for Bedrich's tastes, but when Karel came to Pilsen on promotion as Finance Inspector it was a very changed Katerina that Bedrich met. Gone was the slightly buck-toothed girl of his childhood. Gone too was the loudness. Instead he saw an attractive young woman who looked at him with calmness and maturity, and had about her an inner quality which touched something in his heart.

He knew the danger signals, and damped down the fires that began to smoulder inside him. Memories of other involvements haunting him, he was as off-hand as he dared to be without offending her. He had always been the one who had jumped in feet first, gushing out declarations of affection, and only half watching the effects. This time, therefore, he kept a rein on his emotions, deciding to hold back to see how things developed. Perhaps in a week, three weeks, a month, he would find that his feelings for Katerina Kolar had been born of impulse and nostalgia, and nothing else.

His studies had gone well in the past year, and he had achieved a fine balance between school-books and music. Scholarship and music were, for him at any rate, at variance with each other at all times. Basically he just wasn't interested in academic subjects. He was persevering with school for only one reason—to satisfy his father.

When it came to studying, the effort to exclude the other half of his existence—music—was great. It took massive will-power not to get up, "just for half an hour", to play some tune that was running through his mind, or to practise, "just once", an exercise that had almost beaten him earlier on.

His cousin Josef listened to him frequently, and privately was very moved by Bedrich's wonderful talent. But Josef had made a promise to his uncle, and though he never discouraged Bedrich he saw to it that the youth kept up his progress at school. He listened to Bedrich's talk, to all the dreams of the future, the explanations of the genius of Liszt, the admiration for what Mozart had done. He heard all of it, and, bursting to speak, kept silent. Of course, in his wisdom he knew that by listening, even though not commenting, he was helping, acting as an invaluable safety-valve for his young cousin. Bedrich realized this too, and he expressed his gratitude more than once.

Josef was there that day in May 1842 when Bedrich met Katerina Kolar on her return to Pilsen from Horelice, where she had been staying with her great-uncle. He saw the look on Bedrich's face, the expressions that came and went on it revealing his thoughts.

It was a windy Sunday afternoon, and there had already been showers at lunch-time. It was no day for walking. The Kolars and their visitors remained indoors, and the talk for most of the time centred on how Katerina had been getting on at her great-uncle's house.

"We move around quite a lot, you know, Josef," Karel said. "It seemed unfair to have Katerina's education disrupted so much, so when her uncle suggested we send her to him it seemed a good idea. Not that we liked not having her with us."

Bedrich was sitting well back in a deep chair, gazing at Katerina. He'd been letting the general conversation pass him by, interested only when Katerina was talking. When he heard Mrs Kolar says, "The last we heard of you, Bedrich, you were in Prague," he reddened and said, "Oh, Prague, yes. But ..." How could he put it? "I wasn't much of a scholastic success, I'm afraid."

"Too many distractions?"

"Yes, you could say that."

"I won't ask you if you've kept up your music, because we've been hearing great things about you here already."

He was at a loss again.

"You're as keen as ever, I take it?"

"Yes," he said.

"And as modest, I'm glad to see," said Mrs Kolar warmly.

"It's not that—though thank you very much for saying it. It's just that ... well, there's such an enormous void between what you'd like to be able to do and what you can actually do. I sometimes fret about whether I'm musically too ambitious."

"A young fellow without ambition is only a shell," Karel interjected. "Am I right, Professor?"

G

"Yes, it's the driving force to greatness, true enough," said Josef guardedly. "But of course it's got to be controlled."

"How can you control it?" Mrs Kolar wanted to know "I mean, if you control it, aren't you in danger of stifling it altogether?"

"I wouldn't say that," Josef said. "Of course, the danger does exist, naturally. It would be stupid to say otherwise. But there is equally a danger in being governed absolutely by ambition. It could get hold of a person to such an extent that he could become just as much of what Karel called a shell. Can you see that, Bedrich?"

Bedrich had been following his cousin closely. "Yes," he said, "what worries me is that I might not recognize my limitations once I had reached them. It must be a terrible situation to be in, where you are blind to your own limitations and still press onward, seeking a goal which you can never reach."

"This is becoming far too serious," Karel said. "Katerina, what about playing something for us?"

"Yes, that's a good idea," her mother said. "Katerina has been studying music at Horelice. Indeed, her uncle Josef says she shows a good deal of promise. Perhaps we could get an opinion from Bedrich."

"Oh, Mama!"

"I'd love to hear you play, Katerina," Bedrich said.

"So that you can criticize all my faults?"

"Of course not. Who am I to criticize anyone's faults? You should hear me!"

"Perhaps we'll have that pleasure too," Karel said. "Come along, Katy, don't keep our guests waiting."

Josef Smetana was watching his cousin, saw Bedrich's eyes unblinkingly follow Katerina as she went to the piano. Josef glanced at Mrs Kolar, who was also watching her daughter and Bedrich. He could tell there was something happening between these two young people, right there in front of them. Mrs Kolar's eyes met Josef's, and she hunched her shoulders in a tiny but definite sign of satisfaction.

While Katerina played, Bedrich looked with all his eyes, listened with all his ears. He couldn't be sure, but it seemed to him that this slim, lovely creature (impossible to believe she had ever been the noisy little girl he had so utterly disliked) invested piano-playing with more tenderness than he could remember ever having heard. He sat with uncritical ears, and saw the girl as though in a dream.

Afterwards he praised her lavishly and persuaded her to play some more. While she played he stood by her side, one hand on the piano-top, the other covering his eyes. It was astounding that so few years could have brought about such a huge transformation, and it was like a work of fiction that a girl so young and so divine in appearance could make such heavenly music.

He himself yielded graciously to persuasion and played some of his favourite Liszt, but with little heart in what he was doing. He allowed his fingers to go mechanically on, while his mind was crowded with images of a future linked with Katerina.

Going back to Mrs Wildmann's he was unusually quiet.

"Katerina had quite an effect on you, Bedrich," Josef said. "You are attracted to her?"

"Very much."

"The old process all over again, eh?"

"You mean Smetana falling head-over-heels, blind, intoxicated in love, walking about in a trance, swearing this is the real thing for life, being disappointed, disillusioned, distraught, and then some time later starting all over again—that's what you mean, isn't it?"

"There is a ring of familiarity about it," Josef said.

"Did you go through this kind of agony?"

"Maybe not exactly the same, but on similar lines, yes."

"How does one know when one has got over it?"

"It's difficult to say. You grow out of it. It's harder for a romantic, though."

"Thank you very much," Bedrich said tartly.

"You're very sensitive, Bedrich, too sensitive."

"I don't happen to like sarcasm," Bedrich said.

"I wasn't being sarcastic. But whether you like the description or not, you're still a romantic, and romantics find it hard to shrug off romantic ideas."

"All right, cousin, thank you for the lesson."

Josef laughed. "Bedrich, Bedrich, Katerina Kolar *has* knocked you over, hasn't she?"

"No, she hasn't! I just think she's ... "

"Beautiful? A goddess? A rare jewel?"

"Oh, shut up!"

"Very well, I'll keep quiet about her after this. But do remember, Bedrich, we *are* cousins, I *like* you, I hate seeing you making a fool of yourself. That's all. Katerina is a nice girl, and frankly I'd like to see you both becoming regular companions. But for the Lord's sake, boy, don't keep carrying on in the grand manner. Give it a chance. Don't expect others always to have the same hundred-per-cent attitude to you as you have to them. And, Bedrich...." He put his hand to the back of Bedrich's neck. "Don't snap back at me, because what I've said I said sincerely."

Bedrich put his own hand up and covered his cousin's. "Thanks," he said. "I do appreciate it."

Six months earlier he would have dismissed Josef's advice. Not now. He pondered on it and saw the logic, and as a result withheld many of the things he would normally have said to Katerina. However, as the weeks passed the strength of his feelings for the girl, instead of diminishing, grew. Very slowly he trickled the signs of his affection in her direction. She responded favourably. He paid an increasing amount of attention to her. She accepted it with warmth and apparent delight. He paid her compliments. She returned them. He implied he was fond of her. She told him he made her happy.

This degree of success liberated his old urges, but even still he forced himself to proceed with caution. Fearful that Josef would pour well-intentioned scorn on the affair, he didn't discuss it with his cousin. He had to get some of it out of his system, however, and the diary would accept it mutely and pass no comments.

Oh adored one, how wonderful it is to get love for love, one heart in return for one's own! he wrote. *How wonderful to know that one is loved! Never before have I experienced Heaven—until now! ...I devote to you my heart ... my whole life.*

The diary was the only recipient of these thoughts, and he looked upon it as on an understanding friend.

Are you curious, my dear little book, he wrote, *about the identity of she who lives in my heart? I shall tell you, because I know I can always rely on your silence. It is Katerina, my Katy....*

Since Josef didn't talk about the matter, and Bedrich guarded himself against disappointment by remaining silent about it, nobody at the Smetana home at Ruzkovy Lhotice suspected anything. But when Bedrich went to the farm for his summer holiday in 1842 he was carrying with him, and treasuring, the knowledge that the Kolars would soon be coming on a visit. So it was an extraordinarily light-hearted brother that Albina greeted.

There was a dramatic and disturbing change in him only a few days later when a letter arrived at the house with the news that Karel and his wife and daughter would not, after all, be able to come for the promised visit. Without explaining why, he was bad-tempered and moody. He had no time for the children. He was unapproachable, and his presence in any of the rooms meant an atmosphere of tension that was most unpleasant.

The holidays stretched out bleakly ahead of him, not so much weeks in which he would be with his family as weeks in which he would be separated from Katerina. It was only when there was but a week left that he brightened up again, and then only after an exchange of letters between his own and Katerina's parents in which the suggestion was made that during the next school year he should live in the Kolars' house. Suddenly the Smetana family saw the Bedrich they knew and loved once more—gay and tender and co-operative.

But there was a shock awaiting the love-sick Bedrich when he returned to Pilsen. Katerina, instead of greeting him rapturously, as he had hoped, was rather cool and aloof. He couldn't understand why she had changed towards him. Something must have happened during the holidays.

His unhappiness was very obvious to Mrs Kolar, and, though she didn't talk to him about it, she too noticed her daughter's coolness, and was disappointed. "You're not being very nice to Bedrich," she said to Katerina.

"Just because I don't fall in with every suggestion of his?"

"It's not only that—you are so curt with him."

"Well, at times he gets on my nerves, he's so *serious*."

"I think that's to his credit."

"But, Mama, there's plenty of time to be serious. I'm young. I want to *enjoy* life."

"He is very, very fond of you."

"I know, and I'm fond of him. He's a very nice friend, but I want some freedom of my own."

"Well, don't hurt him too much. He's very sensitive."

Katerina made an effort, and Bedrich climbed the ecstatic peaks again. But once his demands became intolerable, Katerina flirted outrageously in his presence. The young bucks of Pilsen paid her many compliments, and she enjoyed their cheeky charm. All Bedrich's glowering and pouting gained him nothing. The more he exhibited his distress, the more she paraded her flirtatiousness. He was right back at the stage he had vowed never to reach again—ill with depression and bitterness.

One morning, after a (to him) particularly loathsome scene during which she told him she had her own life to lead, she flounced out of the house leaving her diary and a pair of gloves on a chair behind her. For several minutes he remained slumped on the settee with his eyes closed. When he sat up he saw the diary. Its presence there challenged him. He stood up and walked towards it, then halted. Remembering the things he wrote in his own confidential little book, the thought of what he had been about to do nauseated him. He went to the window and looked out. He just caught sight of Katerina's retreating figure. There was nobody else in the house. He went back and stood looking down at the diary. It contained all Katerina's secrets. The idea of looking through it, uninvited, was obnoxious. And yet . . . and yet . . .

He picked it up, then put it down immediately. To pry was to cheat.

He went back hurriedly to the window. There was no sign of anyone.

The book lay on the chair, teasing him.

He reached it in three running strides, and, shouldering aside his guilt, opened it. The page that stared at him was the last one on which she had written. The words burned into his eyes, and farther.

I must—even if I don't want to—I must realize that Bedrich loves me. I must be kind to him, but I cannot give him my love, because I don't feel any for him.

He snapped the book shut, and with a little cry ran to his bedroom.

I cannot give him my love, because I don't feel any for him.

He could think of nothing else.

When he woke up and looked in the mirror and saw his swollen face he recalled what his mother used to do when he was a child. He took a clean handkerchief, soaked it in cold water, and pressed the pad over his eyes.

The summer of 1843 would see the end of his schooling in Pilsen, and facing him then would be the tussle of wills with his father. Bedrich's mind was already made up—he was going to risk final alienation by refusing to become a civil servant. He was almost nineteen and a life in an office was anathema to him.

He had survived the trauma of learning Katerina's thoughts about him, but, unlike previous occasions, his affections had strengthened. There were now two primary objectives in his life—to be a musician and to win Katerina.

Under the date of January 23rd, 1843, his diary bore the entry: *With God's help and love I will one day acquire Liszt's piano technique and compose as beautifully as Mozart.*

And on May 31st: *I am living for Katerina. Katerina will be my goal, and her picture will spur me on to achieve what my heart desires.*

At a point where many musicians would have had their musical studies behind them Bedrich was still in what he termed his "time of darkness in musical education".

Invitations to give recitals and attend parties still poured in on him, and he accepted most. The thrill of being listened to and applauded gave him confidence. He turned his attentions to composing dances and salon pieces, and readily admitted that he was influenced by what others wrote. He made the admission without excuse, because he knew that, never having been taught composition, he had to feel his own way through the various phases.

Although still sticking meticulously to his school study timetable, he nevertheless managed to turn out composition after composition. Polkas, waltzes, nocturnes, impromptus, fantasies, quadrilles, and overtures were torn from his packed brain. And all the time he courted Katerina Kolar.

Professor Josef Smetana, that kindly guardian angel, watched his young cousin with mounting concern. He was more convinced than ever that the Civil Service would never see Bedrich Smetana, and little by little he relaxed his emphasis on academic studies.

At Ruzkovy Lhotice, Frantisek exulted in the correctness of his forcing tactics as far as Bedrich's education was concerned. The boy had done him proud. The school examination results had been uniformly good, and it would be only a matter of months before Bedrich would go into Government Service with a good salary, security, an enviable position in the community, and the wherewithal to ensure the family's wellbeing.

Josef couldn't bring himself to write to his uncle. He put the task off week by week, and felt uneasy about his own weakness of character. If Bedrich were forced (assuming that anyone could force him) to give up music, then, Josef knew, the youth would undoubtedly suffer a mental breakdown.

As the last school term neared its end Josef made up his mind to visit his uncle Frantisek with the intention of trying to talk sense into the old man.

It was a stormy meeting. Frantisek roared and swore, and called Josef a scoundrel and a cheat and a traitor. Josef held his temper. He had prepared himself for vituperation and accusations. He let his uncle talk himself out, and knew the end had come when Frantisek deflated before him and said softly, "And after all I've done, to think my son will wallow in poverty and low life, and that he was helped there by the son of my own brother!"

"Have you finished now, Uncle Frantisek?"

A shrug and a wave of despair were his answers.

"I've listened to everything you've said," Josef began, "now kindly listen to me. First, I'm not a cheat or a traitor, or any of the things you called me. I'm not angry that you said what you did. You're upset, quite naturally so. You wanted something from Bedrich, and you're not going to get it. I promised to keep an eye on him for you, and I did. He worked well. You've got the school reports to prove that. But in the same way that you never wanted to stay a brewery worker, your son doesn't want to be a lawyer, or a civil servant. He wants to be a musician, and nothing you say or do will change that. And with all respect I suggest that it's about time you faced that fact, and put out of your head the silly notion that he's going to end up as a wandering player. He's got too much talent and—thanks to you—education for that to happen. But mainly talent. Talent is a precious thing, Uncle. Some people acquire it; Bedrich is one of those lucky beings who was born with it. Don't try to frustrate it. Cherish it. Thank God for it. Accept it with the gratitude such a gift deserves."

They talked for many hours, and finally Frantisek gave in, grudgingly, and agreed that his son should go his own way. That meant to Prague, in October, for musical studies.

Josef of course passed the good news on to Bedrich. The look of sheer disbelief, and then delight, was a sight Josef would always remember. Then, as though catapulted, Bedrich ran to him and clasped him in wordless thanks.

Katerina was given the story by Bedrich himself, and in the telling he let his speech pour out the wildest of his thoughts for the future. He didn't notice her silence, the occasional tightening of the eyes as she winced, the signs of impatience. He was riding high on a wave of relief and joy, and he criss-crossed the room, gesticulating, occasionally stopping to look upwards and into the future. And, as he went on spilling out his thanks for the understanding of Josef, the kindness of his family, and of his father in particular, Katerina couldn't help but share something of what Josef's victory meant to Bedrich.

She was smiling at him and with him as he ended his torrent and came and knelt by her.

"Isn't it wonderful?" he said.

"I'm very pleased for you, Bedrich."

"It means all the world to me," he said. "I've been trying to think of all the ways we can celebrate during the coming weeks."

"Then you haven't heard?" she asked.

"Heard what, Katerina?"

She drew a deep breath. "I thought Mama would have told you, but of course she hasn't seen you since the letter came." There was that vulnerable, pathetic look on his face again, but she had to press on and break the news to him. "We've got to leave Pilsen. Papa has received notification of transfer to Mlada Boleslav. We've got to leave within a few weeks."

Bedrich sat back on the carpet, utterly deflated.

In his diary he wrote: *I feel as if I have been struck by lightning.*

On the Sunday morning, July 23rd, after a night of restlessness, he watched the Kolar's belongings being loaded on to the carts. Nobody took any notice of him. The removal men were busy, and probably thought he was one of the family.

Presently Katerina came out, dressed in her going-away clothes. She saw Bedrich and came towards him. For a moment she stood in front of him, and when she saw him crying the tears came to her own eyes. She put out her hand, and he took it; the salt drops splashed on the backs of her fingers.

"Goodbye, Bedrich," she whispered.

He couldn't answer.

Mr and Mrs Kolar came, and Katerina stood back to allow them to talk to Bedrich. The other children said goodbye, and the family, Katerina excepted, trooped out to the waiting carriage.

Katerina stepped up to Bedrich once again. Again neither of them could speak, and then Karel's voice from outside called, "Come along, Katy." She left Bedrich alone in the hall and went to join her family.

The only consolation he had was the invitation Karel had

extended to him to come and visit them at Mlada Boleslav. But that was weeks ahead.

That night he went to Mrs Wildmann's house and asked her if he could play her piano.

On August 6th he was presented with his matriculation document by the school authorities, and he walked away from the buildings with only one backward glance. It was devoid of regret that he was leaving. He had formed no attachments there, didn't feel he was leaving anything of himself behind. He had come out honourably, but now all that school represented was a closed chapter.

On the way through Prague he posted a letter to Katerina telling her he would arrive at her home in seventeen days' time.

The vacation dragged by far too slowly for him. He counted off the days to the 23rd, and when the date drew close he became cheerful, because the separation from Katerina was now reckonable in hours. However, complete happiness returned only at the moment he walked into the Kolars' home at Mlada Boleslav.

His stay there was, in his own words, "like a wonderful fairy-tale". Katerina's welcome was warm and sincere, and for fourteen days the two of them were rarely out of each other's sight.

At the end of October 1843 he left his home at Ruzkovy Lhotice for Prague, and this time there would be no charade, no double life split between school and music, no pretences to be kept up. Now he would be on his own, faced with the stern reality of trying to carve out a living from the profession, the art, which had almost rent him asunder.

BOOK

[*2*]

CHAPTER
[9]

THE PRAGUE HE SAW through the eyes of a nineteen-year-old took Bedrich by surprise. The buildings were the same—and yet not as he had remembered them. The river was as beautiful as ever—but there was an uncompromising harshness in its impersonality. The friendliness of the streets was gone. He was disconcerted and afraid.

The hopes he'd built up when he learnt that the Kolars would be sending Katerina there for advanced piano tuition were dashed when he met her, for she seemed in a hurry to get away from him. While Bedrich was left to his own devices (and the twenty sovereigns his father had handed him now seemed terrifyingly inadequate) Katerina was under the roof and tutelage of Maestro Proksch.

She was ambitious, both musically and socially. If a barrier were required to cut her off from elements that ran counter to her ambitions, then she would have no hesitation about erecting one. Besides, Bedrich had to learn to stand on his own feet and keep his worries to himself.

He tried, and was bruised by the screaming loneliness.

The money he had was needed to cover lodgings, food, a piano, and all other necessities, so he searched out his cousin, a comely woman named Pepi Gilicek, and struck a bargain with her for bed-and-breakfast lodgings.

Two lawyers and myself lived in one room, he wrote later. I had my food at an inn—when I could afford to pay. In those first two months I often went to bed hungry, and there was a period of three days when, apart from the morning cup of coffee and a roll, no bite of food crossed my lips.... There was no piano, I couldn't afford to buy one, and was too ashamed to borrow one.

Several times he met Katerina in the streets, but these accidental meetings only caused him sorrow.

Staying with Proksch, he confided to his diary, *she is as distant from me as if she were in America. I don't know Proksch, and Proksch doesn't know me, so I cannot go to his place. And even if I did go, I believe Katerina would ignore me. When we meet in the streets she rushes away. I do not know what I shall do.*

A cloud of lassitude descended on him. He had no means of practising the piano, and his money was running out. He was hungry, in need of companionship, in need of solace, and he was gripped by a pervading sense of hopelessness which grew steadily more pernicious.

One day he took stock of himself, and what he discovered made him so angry that he swallowed his pride and borrowed a copy of *Musiklehre*, by A. B. Marx, to study the theory of music. He realized that he had slipped very close to the point of no return, and by the beginning of December had taken such a hold of himself that he made another decision, and begged a music-dealer to allow him the use of a piano on which to restart practising. And when the pleadings were successful he played all day long, "because I want to become a virtuoso, better than anyone else."

There was no money to be earned from composition—at least not by an 'unknown'. He found this out the hard way, by submitting pieces he had written to all the music houses in the city. The manuscripts came back with curt rejections. He visited the houses personally, persuaded impatient men to listen to his compositions, and heard gloomily the oft-repeated phrase, "Yes, very promising, young man, but come back to us when you've had something published."

How could he get something published if they all said the same thing? But, of course, fretting about the system got him nowhere. So, though he detested giving in, he stopped composing in order to concentrate on playing.

He was eating less and less, making do with whatever small bits of food he could buy with the coins he received from doing menial jobs. His health deteriorated rapidly.

After fainting one morning before lunch-time he gave serious thought to abandoning the whole dream, and trying for the Civil Service. In his state the prospect offered him the chance to eat well, to be free from worry, to be a joy to his father. What was the point of starving? Another week, he decided, I'll give it one more week.

Almost exactly a week later Mrs Kolar was walking in one of Prague's main streets with Katerina when she stopped in her tracks and tugged at her daughter's sleeve.

"Look, across there, isn't that Bedrich Smetana, the one looking into the cake-shop?" she asked.

Katerina followed her mother's pointing finger. "Yes," she said, "it's him all right. Come along, Mama, don't let him see us."

The emaciated figure turned away from the window and walked along, staring at the ground.

"Come on, Mama."

"My God, Katerina, what has happened to the boy? He looks as if he's dying." Even from where they were standing Mrs Kolar could see the scrawny neck, the untidy hair, the wasted, shrivelled body inside clothes that seemed too large. "He looks terrible," she said. "What's wrong with him?"

"Oh, I don't know, Mama. He's probably feeling sorry for himself."

"Haven't you any feelings, Katerina? Are you so hard you can't see what I see?"

"Mama, where are you going?"

Mrs Kolar didn't answer. She was already half-way across the road, waving, trying to catch Bedrich's attention.

"Bedrich!" she called. "Bedrich!"

But a delivery-cart was clattering by, and her voice was lost in the din. The traffic was heavy at this time of day, and by the time she managed to dodge her way across, Bedrich was thirty yards away. She broke into a run, and the passers-by stood aside and looked after her. She was blind to their curiosity.

H

Breathless by the time she caught him up, she managed a gasped "Bedrich!" and he turned around, surprised, and ashamed at the figure he cut before her.

It looked to her as if he was about to turn and hurry away, and she grasped his arm. He was like a frightened animal.

"Bedrich, my poor Bedrich, how—are you all right?"

"Hello, Mrs Kolar. Yes, thank you, I'm fine. Just surprised at seeing you."

She could feel a lump rising in her throat. "You're so thin," she said. "Your arm is like a child's. Have you been eating?"

He was horribly self-conscious now that she had announced her concern over his appearance.

"I'm all right," he replied, and, in an endeavour to shift the talk from himself, asked, "How is Mr Kolar, and the rest of the family?"

"They're all very well, Bedrich, bless you for inquiring, but I can't get over the sight of *you*." She was looking at him in horror. She turned to see if Katerina was coming, raised her hand to indicate to her daughter where they were, and again looked at Bedrich. "Come on," she said, "I'm going to give you a good square meal, and then I want you to tell me how you got into this condition."

She picked out the nearest good restaurant, and after his first embarrassment he ate ravenously, wolfing down everything ordered for him. When he finished he was profuse in his thanks.

"Now, Bedrich, tell me everything," said Mrs Kolar, and by astute questioning she drew him out. She was unable to control her reactions, and on innumerable occasions expressions of exasperation and sympathy escaped her. Long before the end, however, she had made up her mind what to do.

"I want you to go back to your cousin's," she said, "polish your boots, get out your cleanest clothes, and have a good wash. Then meet me by the Church of Our Lady in Carmelite Street in an hour from now. And hurry, there's no time to be lost."

He excused himself and walked hurriedly out of the restaurant.

"I just don't understand you, Katerina," Mrs Kolar said

when they were alone. "I can't understand your lack of feeling."

"But how was I to know, Mama?"

"You've got a tongue in your head, you've got eyes!"

"I've been busy, Mama, studying very hard."

"So busy you couldn't spare a thought for a friend of the family who was obviously on the verge of collapsing? Katerina, if I thought all the love we've lavished on you had no better effect on you than that, I'd be a very disillusioned mother."

"You make me feel dreadful, Mama."

"I should think so! There'll come a time when *you* are old, or lonely, or sick, and all I hope is that no-one will be as blind to your condition as you've been to that boy's. Honestly, you'd imagine he was a hateful person instead of someone who adores the ground you walk on. I hope you *are* ashamed."

Katerina's expression gave ample evidence that she was.

"You're very young, Katerina, but you've got to learn that human beings are important, to each other as well as to themselves. If there is ever an opportunitity to help someone you should accept it. You're not much of a person if you close your eyes to it."

Katerina learnt then what it was that made her mother the woman she was.

Bedrich was baffled about what Mrs Kolar was up to, but he rushed around the little room sorting out what to wear.

Pepi Gilicek, surprised to see him back and in such a hurry to get warm water for a wash, wanted to know what was going on. He was very vague.

"I don't know," he said, "Mrs Kolar sent me back."

"Mrs Kolar—that's your Katerina's mother, isn't it?"

"Yes," he said. "Pepi, have you got any black polish?"

"I know where there there is some."

"Get it for me, please, would you?"

"Yes, sir, of course, sir! Washing yourself, cleaning your boots—you want to be careful, young man, she may be taking you to a priest to get you married!"

For an instant, stupidly, his heart raced. Then he laughed and carried on.

Pepi saw him to the front door when he was leaving, and her well-intentioned banter rang in his ears as he broke into a half-trot to meet Mrs Kolar in Carmelite Street.

He saw Katerina and her mother before they saw him, and again he wondered where Mrs Kolar was going to take him.

She looked him up and down, taking in the change in his appearance in one swift look. "That's better," she said, "a lot better. You look presentable now, more like the Bedrich I remember."

He kept his eyes off Katerina. He couldn't bear to look at her.

"Come along," said Mrs Kolar, and went to the kerb to hail a cab.

When they were seated inside, Bedrich summoned up enough courage to ask where they were going.

"I'm taking you to Proksch," Mrs Kolar replied.

"Proksch?"

"Yes, you've surely heard of him. Katerina is—"

"Oh, yes, yes, of course I know of him," Bedrich cut in. "Every musician in Prague knows of Proksch. The finest teacher of piano, of music, in the city, if not in the country— but I could never afford even to *think* of having him as a teacher."

"You just leave that aspect of it to me, Bedrich," Mrs Kolar said. "You concentrate on playing well when we get there."

Bedrich was dumbfounded. What could the woman be thinking of? Proksch was famous all over the land as one of the great masters of teaching, a considerable composer in his own right, an eminent man who, rumour had it, ruled his students like a martinet, but gained fantastic results, charged huge fees, and was looked up to and feared by most of the *cognoscenti*. He took only the cream of young pianists, and there was always a waiting-list of people wanting to join his academy. It was said that Proksch gave a better musical education than that provided by the great Prague Conservatoire.

Fear was gnawing at Bedrich as they drew up outside Proksch's residence.

"Now remember, when the time comes for you to play, give it your very best. Put all your heart and soul into it, and leave the rest to me."

Bedrich nodded nervously and fell in behind Katerina and her mother.

Something he didn't know about Proksch was that the great teacher was blind, and so when they were ushered into his presence Bedrich was nonplussed to see the maestro fumbling for Mrs Kolar's hand. It was only when he saw the eyes suddenly opening and closing, and the head inclined unnaturally to pick out the direction of sounds, that Bedrich realized that the eyes were sightless.

The voice was loud and rasping and authoritative.

"Mrs Kolar? Good. How are you? I'm glad to see you. You've come to ask me about Katerina, I suppose. Well, she's making progress. Is there anything specific you want to discuss with me?"

Mrs Kolar seemed to gather herself before answering. "Yes," she said. "I'm glad, naturally, to hear that Katerina is making some progress. But that's not what I came here to talk about."

"Oh?"

"I've come to see you about a young man. He's here with us in the room."

"What's his name?" Proksch's eyes were closed tight in concentration.

"Bedrich Smetana," Mrs Kolar answered.

"Never heard of him." It was said as though it were a total dismissal. "What is he? Another prodigy?" The word was used with biting disdain.

"He's a pianist," Mrs Kolar said.

"All the people who come here call themselves pianists," Proksch rasped. "Most of them shouldn't be allowed to polish pianos."

Irritation began to prickle Bedrich.

"He's a very good pianist," Mrs Kolar was saying in her most determined manner.

"That's something else they all say at the beginning," Proksch said. "But I'm the only judge whose opinions I value. Anyway, if you're going to ask me to take him on, the answer is no. I have too many pupils. Is that all?"

Bedrich opened his mouth to say something, but Mrs Kolar waved him to silence.

"I want you to hear him," she said.

"I'm a busy man, Mrs Kolar. If I were to listen to every—"

"I'm a very determined woman, Mr Proksch. You won't put me off that easily."

Proksch laughed suddenly. "I admire your spirit, lady," he said. "All right. Where are you, Smetana? There's the piano. Play your party piece."

Asked in this manner, Bedrich had a good mind to refuse, but Mrs Kolar was beckoning to him to go to the instrument and start.

"Hurry, young man, I haven't got all day," Proksch said.

Again Bedrich wanted to say something, to lash back at this unmannerly individual with his overbearing impatience. He bit back the words, and instead went to the piano. He adjusted the stool carefully, taking his time over it so as to compose himself and still the anger that was gripping him. When the seat was exactly as he liked it he sat down, arranged himself, emptied his mind of everything but the Liszt piece he had decided on. He would give this Proksch something to listen to.

Proksch was sitting down now, making no effort to hide his impatience, visibly fretting with annoyance at the time it was taking this Smetana person to begin playing in whatever dreadful way he, or Mrs Kolar, or anyone else thought passed for musicianship.

But as soon as Bedrich started, Proksch straightened up in his chair, looked to where he knew the piano was, and cupped a hand behind an ear the better to catch every note. With his head he made little bird-like movements as he twisted this way and that, and kept time on certain passages with the free hand.

Mrs Kolar watched him with a hawk's alertness. Proksch was impressed; no matter what he might or might not say, all his attitudes and expressions showed that Bedrich's playing was surprising him.

At the end he dropped his hands to his lap and said loudly, "Mmm-mm."

Before he had a chance to say anything else Mrs Kolar said, "Thank you, Bedrich. Now, would you and Katerina please excuse us for a moment? Just wait outside." When the door closed behind them she turned to Proksch, who was prowling around the room, feeling his way from one familiar piece of furniture to another. "A little better than one of your piano-polishers, don't you think?" she said.

"He has a certain aptitude, that I will admit," Proksch replied.

"You're a grudging man with your praise. Why don't you say what you think—what I *know* you think?"

"How do you know what I think?" he shot at her.

"I've only got to watch you."

A small look of pain showed fleetingly on his face. "You've got an unfair advantage over me." he said.

"I'm still waiting for you to admit that you think Bedrich Smetana is—"

"Yes, he's good in some ways, but in others ... "

"He's better than most people who come here, isn't he?"

"If I say he didn't sound like a blacksmith hammering on an anvil it doesn't mean that I think he's good." Proksch said.

"But he interests you, doesn't he?" Mrs Kolar persisted.

"Yes, I must say he interests me. There are certain things, though, that disturb me a little. There's some showiness about his playing—a kind of *bravura* I'm not altogether in favour of. It probably comes from some idiotic teacher. Who taught him?"

"That's just the point," she said, "the boy is virtu-ally self-taught."

Proksch stopped prowling and turned towards her. "Self-taught?" he asked incredulously. "Impossible."

"Yes, he is. He's had *some* lessons, of course, but not for a long time."

"You mean he's a young man with a talent that is running wild?"

"Yes, that's exactly what I mean."

"Incredible," Proksch commented, and then remained silent for several minutes. Then he said, "I'm even more interested. Let us discuss it further."

The upshot of the discussion was that Josef Jan Proksch, because of Mrs Kolar's persistent persuasion, and his own instincts, agreed to accept Bedrich as a pupil. But not before he called him back into the room to play for him once more. And this time the crusty old perfectionist listened with even more attention.

When Bedrich had finished, Proksch asked, "Is it true what Mrs Kolar says, that you are virtually self-taught?"

"It's true," Bedrich said defiantly.

"Well, you've done quite well, considering," Proksch said.

"I've always done my best," said Bedrich. Proksch's laugh angered him, and his sharp intake of breath was heard by the maestro.

"Self-teaching leaves gaps," Proksch explained. "Particularly when it comes to interpretation. You see, young man, to me your playing has the imprint of someone who is short on theory, and theory has to be learnt. Not from books, but from someone who knows it and who can impart the knowledge. Someone like—and I make no bones about it—myself. Shall we concentrate on perfecting your musicianship?"

This was Bedrich's first inkling that Proksch was going to take him on, and his delight was made bleak by the realization that he could never afford the fees.

Mrs Kolar, keenly aware of Bedrich's discomfort, said, "Bedrich, would you please leave us again for a moment? There is something else I wish to discuss with Mr Proksch."

Thankful for the understanding Katerina's mother was displaying, Bedrich excused himself and went out.

Mrs Kolar then spoke to Proksch, explaining Bedrich's penurious state. She persuaded the maestro to take Bedrich for one crown per lesson. Not only that, she also arranged that Bedrich should pay as and when he had the money.

Recording the events of the day in his diary, Bedrich wrote: *I would have been forced by my lamentable financial circumstances to abandon all my plans to become a virtuoso, and to slide down into the position of a civil servant or clerk, had not help from Heaven come to me in my hour of greatest need and distress.... Though I was well aware that I was not in a position to pay Proksch his fees, I was very happy that I would be receiving lessons in the theory of music. I did not worry how I would pay. I put myself completely into God's care.*

It was in March 1844 that he had his first lessons from Proksch, and over and over again the teacher dinned into him that "mere talent", as he called it, of itself was useless for a musician who hoped to become great. "Without education, without a knowledge of theory and the background of composing, you will always be just another pianist," Proksch said.

The longer Bedrich stayed, the more he came to see how right Proksch was. And as the teacher's manner mellowed Bedrich warmed to him and found him a good friend. Proksch asked him to bring his own compositions and play them, got him to talk about all sorts of things. During these early sessions the maestro made few comments. But in his mind the blind teacher was building up his own dossier on the character of Smetana.

Then one day he began making observations out loud, explained that each man has different talents, and differing facets to his talents. He illustrated what he meant by going to the piano and playing snatches of music in various styles. He spoke of a person's natural inclinations and said that these inclinations should be smothered if they were based on shaky principles, in other cases the inclinations should be catered for so as to make strengths out of natural ability. He had closely examined all Bedrich's possibilities, searched out the weaknesses, devised special exercises to eradicate them. He developed other exercises to explore the youth's areas of strength, but, more than anything else, he reawakened the craving to compose. He brought into him a closer, more perceptive relationship with the music of Beethoven, Chopin, and Bach, and inspired him to more ambitious work.

For a time Bedrich was utterly captivated by what Proksch told him, and what he learnt for himself, of Chopin's compositions. The beauty and intensity of expression to be found in the Pole's piano-pieces, the melancholy that came through the music, the knowledge of Chopin's sickness, all added up to a romantic figure with which young Smetana wanted to, and did, identify.

He talked to Proksch about it, felt twinges of disappointment when the teacher failed to bubble over in reciprocatory enthusiasm, but, instead, launched out into a lecture on the riches to be found in Beethoven and Berlioz. Because he respected the blind maestro, Bedrich swallowed his disappointment, listened carefully, studied more.

His horizon was expanding, pushed outwards by a man whose thinking was modern as well as classical. "Contemporary music *is* important," Proksch would say. "Don't listen to oafs who seek to dismiss it. They do that in all ages, and they prove nothing other than that they are fools or small-minded, narrow-thinking bigots. Modern music has its place, an important place, and we are now in the age of musical heroism."

So now Bedrich became a Beethovenist. A friend from Pilsen, Arnost Nesvadba, fed his hunger for more talk of the German, and introduced him to the artistic society, Konkordia. There he met fellow enthusiasts, among whom he was able to exchange ideas and opinions.

Josef Proksch was well pleased with the new pupil. Early in their relationship he had suspected, and then found out for certain, that Smetana was an emotional young man, one who expressed himself, whether verbally or musically, in extremes. Intuitively he had led Bedrich to Berlioz, had demonstrated how that immensely talented Frenchman with the gift for grandiloquence had made music of a quality that was uniquely high. Probing for a responsive chord, Proksch found it.

Bedrich was doubly happy, of course, because studying under Proksch meant that he saw Katerina frequently. She, it appeared, saw him now in a different light. Her attitude towards him softened again.

Love, Bedrich discovered, now meant something different to him. It was altogether quieter, less feverish. It was the difference between a genuine affection for and pleasure in a person's company and the wild, tempestuous infatuation which used to whip him.

But there were still complications in his life, and the one which cast the largest shadow was money, for he had none.

Was he always to be scourged by the miseries that lack of money brought? He felt helpless. Money had always meant rows, hunger, bickering, depression. Money meant his father complaining about expense; it meant poor and rich people; it meant embarrassment; it meant relations turning against each other.

For him now it meant the agony of going to his unpaid-for room in his cousin's house, and her unspoken request that he either find the rent somewhere, or vacate his bed so that she could let it to someone who would pay. For she too was in need of money.

He took to sneaking into the house, and slipping out early in the mornings before anyone was awake. But Pepi Gilicek wasn't deaf, and often at night, warned by a squeaking stair, she would come out of her room and stand silently looking up after him as he tip-toed to his bedroom. He felt small, diminished as a human being, whenever he resorted to these furtive movements. But what else could he do?

Arnost Nesvadba asked himself the same question. What could his friend do? Arnost hadn't much money but what he had shared gladly, and with a degree of tact that eased the way for Bedrich to accept.

He often paid for my meals, Bedrich wrote. *Sometimes he went to a certain inn and paid for a month's meals for me in advance. He paid for my piano, and he was altogether a source of tremendous assistance.*

There was a pact between them that they wouldn't talk of these things, but Nesvadba's money couldn't last for ever, and the day came when it ran out. That day the two friends went hungry, and life took on a threatening greyness.

Once again relief came from a surprising direction. When the news got around that Count Leopold von Thun, a wealthy aristocrat, was seeking a resident music-teacher for his children, many musicians in Prague applied for the post, for it was a good one that offered all-important security, an enviable home, and good pay. The one applicant who wrote with no hope of being considered was Bedrich Smetana, and his surprise therefore knew no bounds when he was later called for an interview.

The Count and his wife, Countess Alzbeta Felicia von Thun, were waiting for him when he arrived at their palace in the heart of Prague. Used to meeting and mixing with the aristocracy, Bedrich was not at all nervous about meeting these people, but the surprise at even being called there made him rather wide-eyed. The Count's first glimpse of the young man prompted him to wonder if there hadn't been some mistake, and, glancing at a piece of paper in his hand, the Count asked, "Are you Bedrich Smetana?"

"Yes, sir, I am."

The Count exchanged looks with the Countess. "You're much younger than I expected," he said. "To be frank, I am a little surprised."

"So was I, sir. I still am," Bedrich said.

"Why is that?"

"I didn't think I had a chance of my application being noticed."

"Oh, I see. I can easily explain that—you were specially recommended to me."

Then it dawned on Bedrich, and he said aloud what he was thinking. "So he even did that? What a man!"

"Yes," the Count said. "Jan Kittl is a very considerate man."

"Kittl!"

"Yes, isn't it him we are speaking about? But I can see from your expression you meant someone else."

Bedrich was looking open-mouthed at his prospective employer. "But Jan Kittl is—" he began.

"Acting Director of the Prague Conservatoire," the Count supplied.

Bedrich shook his head in amazement. "*He* recommended *me?*" he said.

"Gave you a very strong recommendation," the Count said.

"But I'm not even a student of the Conservatoire," Bedrich said.

"Yes, I know that. You're studying under Proksch."

"And Kittl actually recommended me?" He laughed.

"He's heard you on a number of occasions, and had very high praise for your abilities. That's why I singled you out, but, as I said, I am rather taken aback by your youthfulness. Look, would you mind playing something for us?"

Bedrich was still smiling with disbelief. "Not at all," he said. "Is there something special you'd like me to try?"

"There's some music on the piano," the Count replied.

A glance at the first sheet showed that it was an intricate and difficult composition by Richter, and Bedrich hadn't played it before. But the confidence he had won since joining Proksch did not desert him, and he played the piece through at sight.

Any doubts the Count may have had were dispelled immediately. When Bedrich finished the Count said, "The job is yours if you want it."

"Thank you very much, sir; I should be delighted to accept."

"When can you start?"

"Immediately, if you wish."

"Splendid. You can move in as soon as you are ready. Your room is prepared. By the way, I see you are familiar with that Richter piece."

With appealing ingenuousness Bedrich said, "No, I've never seen it before."

"Truly?"

"On my honour."

The Count turned to his wife. "I'm beginning to see what Kittl meant, aren't you?"

A charming woman, the Countess stood up and, smiling warmly, approached Bedrich with a hand held out to be taken. "Welcome, Bedrich," she said. "I'm delighted you'll be joining us."

"Oh, incidentally, I trust the ... remuneration will be satisfactory," her husband said to their beaming new music-teacher.

"I'm sure it will be, sir."

"You know the amount?"

"No, sir."

"*Really?* Here you are accepting a position and not knowing how much you are to be paid! Well, it's three hundred crowns a year, and, of course, your accommodation and food will be provided free. Is that all right?"

All right? It was riches beyond his wildest dreams, and Bedrich could scarcely believe his good fortune.

Pepi was overjoyed, not to say relieved, when Bedrich broke the news to her. She clasped him and did a little dance with him around the kitchen, then insisted that he bring her all his clothes so that she might wash and iron the washable ones, and darn and press those which were in need of attention.

"You must look your best now that you are going to live in a Count's palace," she told him. "And for goodness sake, when you get your first money, buy yourself some new boots and jackets and trousers."

"When I get my first money, Pepi," he said, "the first thing I shall do is pay back some of what I owe you, and Arnost, and Jan Proksch."

On the day he was to meet his pupils he prepared a speech with which to greet them. Ten minutes before the lesson was due to start he went into the music-room of the palace and silently rehearsed the phrases. He had been thinking a great deal about the things he would have to do. Words like "discipline" and "authority" had been going through his mind. These were things he would have to pay attention to.

There was a knock on the door, and he turned around to face it. "Come in," he called, trying to make his voice sound like a combination of Jungmann's and Proksch's.

The door opened and a tiny girl with blonde ringlets came in, followed by another, slightly older. Then another child entered, and another, and another. Five! Then a tall, thin woman with a severe hair-style and tubular, black clothes followed them in, and, at a word from her, all five children, standing in a row, curtsied.

Taken aback by the sight, Bedrich stood there, unsure of what to say.

The woman came across to him and said, "I am the childrens' governess. I understand you are Mr Smetana."

"I am," he said. "I am pleased to meet you."

The woman turned stiffly to the children. "This is Mr Smetana, children, and don't forget your manners."

She introduced them separately, the names going in and

out of Bedrich's head as each child came to him and shyly shook hands. There was something very appealing about them, and, as he watched their faces, he had a distinct memory of the day he was taken to his first teacher, Jan Chmelik, when he was only five years old. So when the governess took her leave Bedrich pushed aside all notions of saying anything from his prepared speech. Having natural sympathy for these mites, and a love of all children, he decided to be himself. He laughed and told them small jokes, and gradually broke down their shyness and apprehension, and had anyone been listening outside the door he would perhaps have been surprised at the sound of gaiety coming from within.

Bedrich soon elicited that he was their first music-teacher. He would be starting from scratch. While the discovery at first frightened him a little, it slowly gave him a sense of relief on two counts—first, that it freed him from comparison with anyone else, and, second, that he would not have to eradicate any wrong habits which could have become ingrained during the tenancy of another (and maybe careless) teacher.

The children loved him from the start. They worked hard and willingly for him, and, as they were all talented and pleasant, he derived great satisfaction from bringing them through the various stages of learning.

The Count and Countess were more than pleased. This young man was a jewel of a find, they frequently told each other, and it was wonderful to see how happily and rapidly the children were progressing. Instead of finding music a chore, the youngsters quite obviously adored it, and they looked forward to their lessons. The household seemed much sunnier from the day Bedrich Smetana took up his duties.

Bedrich of course wrote to Kittl and thanked the Director for his kindness in recommending him for the post. Kittl wrote a charming reply saying he had been delighted to do it, that he had only done it out of conviction, and that he was very pleased to hear from Count Leopold von Thun that Bedrich was doing famously.

Although the Count was an eminent man, he was not one who clung too rigidly to unnecessary formality. Certainly he was wealthy and well bred, but he was also equipped with a perspicacity that allowed him to see that much of the trappings of aristocracy were based on outdated conventions which separated class from class. He was also quick to recognize that his new employee was someone out of the ordinary. Here was a young man of unquestionable talent, dedication, professionalism, enthusiasm, and likeability, and yet basic ordinariness of personality.

So instead of remaining merely a paid member of the staff, Bedrich became almost a member of the von Thun family. He was encouraged to talk about his desires and ambitions. He told them of his love for Katerina Kolar; of his family, his problems, his hopes for the future; of his admiration of Beethoven, Liszt, Berlioz, Bach, Chopin; and of his belief that one day he would write great national music which would show to the whole world the beauty of Bohemia, Bohemia's people, and Bohemian thought. They listened intently as he spoke and gestured.

"My children fell in love with him," Countess von Thun was to recall. "When he played for us we were entranced. He played Chopin very often, and we lived, as it were, through the deep melancholy of that musical poet.... But above all, Beethoven was, for Bedrich, a giant. Indeed, Bedrich introduced me to Beethoven's musical soul, and helped me to drink in the beauty of his creations."

In the evenings, when the children were in bed and dinner over, Bedrich (who now dined with the Count, Countess, and whatever guests happened to be visiting) would go to the piano, and, explaining in words as he went along what was in the artist's mind, play pieces by his favourite composers.

He still went to Proksch to continue with his own studies, and he paid back the maestro the fees he owed. At Proksch's own musical evenings, which had been a feature of the Prague musical scene for the past ten years, he frequently played in public. On March 9th, 1845, he and Katerina played four-handed the Rondo from Herz's Fourth Quartet, and the sheer happiness of thus sharing a performance with his beloved left him in a state of euphoria for days afterwards. But he didn't press himself or his love on her as he had done in the past. He took things much more quietly. His inner contentment made him calmer, and Katerina found the new Bedrich more to her liking.

Each summer the von Thun family left Prague for one or other of their castles—Mon Repos and Ronsperk—and Bedrich was invited to accompany them. These were times such as he had never known. With no teaching duties, he concentrated on his own music, and became drunk with the magnificence of the surrounding countryside. Older now, he could look at a landscape, see it, marvel at it, and analyse its richness. And having done so, he went back inspired to his blank music sheets and wrote at speed the notes that cascaded through his brain.

Every day except Saturday and Sunday.

"He travelled every Saturday to Prague or Mlada Boleslav to see Katerina Kolar," Countess von Thun recalled. "Already his heart was bursting with love for her.... He returned on the Monday morning, and then he always talked to me about her with shining eyes."

From his pen came his *Bagatelles et Impromptus*—a work that expressed his feelings about love, its sweetness and its sadness. Predictably, the dedication was to Katerina.

A Page for the Diary was written in triumph at the peacemaking between him and Katerina. And there were many more: *Remembrances of Pilsen,* a polka dedicated to Katerina; five waltzes; six preludes for organ (dedicated to Count Leopold von Thun); two études; a polka and allegro; the song *Sorrow* written to Wieland's German text, and the song *Invitation* written to Jacobi's text; and *Czech Melodies.*

The talent for composition was bursting into full bloom. A thrilling thing was happening in Bohemia, and Bohemia knew little about it.

[10]

BEDRICH FINISHED HIS STUDIES with Josef Jan Proksch in May 1847. On June 1st he gave up his job as music-teacher to Count Leopold von Thun's family. He was twenty-three.

The three years he had spent with Proksch were the most artistically rewarding he had known, and the two and a half years with the Thuns as happy as any in his life, but now he wanted to cut free, to go out into the world and try to set it ablaze with his knowledge and ability.

The Thuns were sorry to see him go. There were tears from the children, and tender farewells from all the family.

"You know you can come back any time you like, Bedrich," the Countess told him.

"Any time," her husband added. "Come and visit us. You can look upon our home as your home. There will always be a place here for you. And thank you for all you have done for our children, and for all you have given to us."

Bedrich recommended Katerina for the post he was vacating, said his own thanks, and bade goodbye to the kind people under whose roof he had lived since the age of twenty.

Uppermost in his mind was the desire to become a success as a virtuoso, to make enough money to become independent, and then marry Katerina.

I wanted to travel all over the world, he wrote, *to be acclaimed as a great soloist, to save what I earned, and then seek a position either as musical director of a large orchestra or as an independent teacher.*

His first excursion took him back to Pilsen, the home-town of his cousin, Professor Josef Smetana. He went with great hopes and a raging thirst for acclaim.

Josef had in fact reacted with gusto at the suggestion that Bedrich's concert tour begin in Pilsen. "But bill yourself as a *Czech* artist, play *Czech* music," Josef had advised.

Bedrich would have none of it. "I must play *great* music, Josef," he said. "That will be my only criterion. Music that is international and glorious."

"I fear you may be making a mistake, Bedrich. Our concert-goers are provincials, you know. They are conservative. They don't take kindly to things they're not familiar with."

"But I'll *make* them familiar," Bedrich answered. "They're not stupid. They're music-lovers, and they'll learn, and they'll love what the great composers have written."

He had bought new clothes, and a long time before his recital was due to start was ready and waiting. But the music-lovers of Pilsen stayed away. Bedrich Smetana's name meant nothing.

Finally, when he could delay no longer—the few people who had trickled in out of curiosity were growing increasingly restive—Bedrich walked out to the piano, his heart heavy, an anti-climatic gloom enveloping him. He looked at the rows of empty seats staring vacantly back at him, bowed to the thin hand-claps. There was no triumph in this return. The new clothes had been bought in vain.

But the spark of headstrong independence in him suddenly ignited, and he went to the piano determined to show Pilsen what fools its so-called music-lovers had been to stay away. He would force these cynics down there in their cheap seats to applaud in a way they had never done before. He failed. They didn't applaud. They actually talked among themselves; some even voiced their dissension as he went from Schumann to Bach to Beethoven to Liszt, and two people got up noisily and walked out, talking loudly about pianists "with the nerve to come here and force rubbish by unpalatable foreigners down our throats." At the end of the recital Bedrich barely bowed and hurried off.

There was little Josef could do but offer sympathy, and this

Bedrich fiercely resented. "You'll have to concentrate on the Czech angle," Josef said.

"And be dictated to by people who wouldn't recognize greatness if it were spelt out for them, Josef? Never. But you'll see, the remainder of my tour will prove my point that it is only here that the professed lovers of music are deaf dolts."

His optimism, however, proved groundless. The other concerts were financial disasters. Few came, and those who did grumbled. Northern Bohemia had no love of "unpalatable foreigners", and in any case summer was a time to be out of doors.

His disappointment was honed by bitterness. But if he became temporarily bitter he did not become soured. There was more of the stuff of manhood in him now, and from his reading he knew that disappointment was the lot of most artists at some time or other in their lives, and that, indeed, with some it was a companion for life.

A new germ of an idea was already growing in his mind. Why not set up his own teaching academy? There were a number already in existence, and music was enjoying such a vogue in Prague that the waiting-lists were monthly becoming longer. He had proved that he could teach; his name was familiar in music circles in the city. After appearances in the subscription concerts of December 17th, 1847, and January 7th, 1848, he had been mentioned in glowing terms in the music columns of the newspaper *Bohemia*. The references had dealt with "his superb technique" and "his absolute mastery".

Spurred on by such encouragement, he filed an application to the relevant Government office for a licence to open a music institute. The date was January 29th, 1848. He still hadn't figured out how to obtain the necessary capital, but every morning he watched the post, waiting for a reply to his application. February dragged by, and there was no letter. He had almost given up hope when, in the first week of March, he received a terse notification that his application had been received, and "passed for consideration". He threw the letter from him in anger. Government departments were all the same. Couldn't they give him a direct answer without all this time-wasting? He was impatient with all the political tension in the country which gave rise to such pointless prevarication. How much longer would they keep him waiting?

The day he was granted permission to open an academy there came to his mind a fresh confusion. He had no premises, no equipment, no money, and had done nothing to obtain financial backing. Monetarily he was an innocent, and, like most innocents when confronted with problems, he was helpless. Musicians knew him, but in such an uneasy economic climate money sources were scarce. People were unwilling to gamble on a young man of twenty-four who couldn't show even one published composition with his name on it. He begged and implored. Sometimes he resorted to bluff, and even tried ranting. But it was all to no avail.

He lost sleep and became physically and emotionally rundown. There was no chink of light at the end of the dark corridor down which he was sliding. Defeat and humiliation faced him every way he turned. He had got to that stage when oblivion (which in this case meant death) beckoned invitingly, and for four ferocious days he drifted ever closer to accepting the invitation. It promised an end to suffering, a blessed relief from injustice, a cessation of the weariness of being thrust into trough after trough of despair. Even God, it seemed, had forgotten him.

On the night on which he had decided to commit the act of self-destruction he sat at the piano for what he believed would be the last time, and in a fever of desolation he played through the pieces he had always loved most. His soul found expression through his fingers, and a storm of feeling eddied through the lonely place. It was his farewell.

And then in the mind's eye he saw a picture of a great occasion—a concert platform, a pianist of unbelievable ability, a boy crouched forward, alone in a vast throng of people, waves of applause rolling through the auditorium, and the boy shining-eyed with wonder at the genius of a man named Franz Liszt. An idea he had had once before came to him again.

He stopped playing abruptly, took out pen and paper, and began to write a letter.

*   *   *

Franz Liszt had a lot on his mind. He was getting ready to leave Weimar, and there were scores of things to be attended to.

He was sitting at a desk sorting out papers when Princess Sayn-Wittgenstein, his mistress, came in from the hall bringing some letters which had just been delivered. She observed him quietly for a few moments, and, not wishing to disturb him, silently placed the envelopes in front of him. As she was taking her hand back he took it and placed it to his lips.

"Still busy, my dear?" she asked.

"I'm tired," he replied. He looked at her and smiled. "You're so considerate and kind," he said, "so good for me." He turned from her and glanced at the little bundle of letters she had put down. "More?" he said. "Always letters, letters, letters. I wonder how many of them are begging letters this time."

She left him alone.

Presently, when he had finished what he was doing, he looked again at the mound of envelopes in front of him. For a while he thought about ignoring them, leaving them until later, but, idly, he took the top one, looked at the neat hand-writing, felt the bulk of the package, and then took up the ivory letter-knife and neatly slit the envelope open.

The first few lines of the letter revealed it for what it was—another plea for help. Every post brought them, and he frequently burst out in exasperation that people thought "because you're a well-known musician you must have money to throw away." He turned impatiently to the signature, *Bedrich Smetana*. So who was Bedrich Smetana? The address on the opening page was a Prague one, but the name meant nothing to him.

There was something untidy about the pages, as if the writer had spilled water which smudged the ink. He was about to throw the letter into the wastepaper-basket when he glanced at the pages of music. There was something fresh about the first few lines which arrested his attention, and on an impulse he went to the piano, smoothed out the sheets, and propped them on the music-rest. Then he began to play.

Princess Wittgenstein, in another part of the house, heard the music and stopped what she was doing, surprised to hear

Franz playing. Not recognizing the piece, she approached the room quietly and entered. As the last chords died away she crossed the room and put her arms about Liszt's shoulders and said, "That was beautiful, Franz. I didn't know you had been working on a new composition."

"I haven't," he said without looking at her.

"Ah, the letters," she said. "Chopin has sent you something new."

"No," he replied. "Somebody neither you nor I have ever heard of—Bedrich Smetana. And it is beautiful, isn't it?"

She was puzzled. "An unknown who writes like that?" she asked. "And you've never even heard his name?"

"Never. He lives in Prague, he has sent me six pieces of music, and beyond that I know nothing." He turned within the circle of her arms until he was looking up into her face. There was a small frown of concern knitting his eyebrows together.

"What is it, my love? What are you thinking?" she asked.

He fought for a moment, trying to crystallize his thoughts, but, as always when confronted by this marvellous woman, gave up the effort, and spoke aloud in an uninterrupted stream. "I was just thinking about this Bedrich Smetana," he began. "There's something . . . disturbing about this situation. I mean, we live our lives so narrowly, wrapped up in the confines of that part of society in which we happen to be at any given time, and even though we think we know a lot, we know nothing. Look, take us—we think we understand the world, people. We mix, we travel, we entertain, we read. As a musician I imagine I am aware of most great music. And yet a letter arrives from some poor wretch in Prague, a letter I almost throw away, and within minutes what happens? I realize there exists a whole world of talented people I'd never ever thought about!" He relapsed into silence, then got up and walked about the room.

She went over to him and took his hand and said, "Come, sit down." When he was sitting alongside her she said, "There is no reason for you to feel upset."

"But there is," he insisted. "I should be more *aware*. It's unfair that I should have so much, and this poor devil so little."

"Franz."

"Yes?"

"What does he say in his letter?"

"I've barely glanced at it."

"Well, let us see, shall we?"

"You read it to me."

She got the letter from the desk and started to read, at first to herself. She looked up after she had been reading for a little while and remarked, "He seems more closely acquainted with hunger than with the means of satisfying it."

Liszt was fiddling with the stem of a flower he had lifted from a vase. "To think I don't even know what it means to be in need," he said. "Nor do you." The vehemence with which he said it made it sound like an accusation.

She read the remainder of the letter aloud, and several times her voice broke so that she had to stop and gather herself.

" ...*I am enclosing my cycle 'Six Characteristic Compositions', Opus One, which I beg you to accept as a token of my burning admiration for you, Great Maestro,*" she read, and looked towards Franz, who had placed the flower on the ground in front of his shoes, and was gazing unblinkingly at it, his mouth working silently.

The afternoon sun was slanting in through the windows, and it caught and highlighted the deep red velvets and rich brocades of this civilized and opulent room. For a moment, as she glanced around, the Princess saw it as though from a distance, saw herself sitting there, elegantly dressed, at home amid the valuable furniture, the paintings; saw the man at her side, head bowed, famous, and now troubled; and she thought about the room in Prague where a young man with the ability to create gentle beauty was starving and in despair. Four hundred sovereigns was all he wanted; a loan of four hundred sovereigns for two pianos to open a music-school.

She felt the letter being taken out of her hands. Franz was reading on. " ...*I guarantee with my life that I will repay the loan. I have no guarantor. I have only myself and my word, but my word is sacred to me.*"

Once more their eyes met.

" ...*You are the only person to whom I have confided my*

despair and my distress. But the only thing I would beg of you is that you do not delay too long over replying—regardless of whether you can help me or not. All I want is to know one way or the other as soon as possible. As it is, my state of mind is such that I could not say with any certainty that Bedrich Smetana will still be alive in even two weeks from today's date."

The quietness that hung over the room was oppressive, and it was broken only when Lizst went back to the piano and played again the music that had come in the envelope from Prague.

He was still playing when the sunlight at last deserted the room, and the greyness of the onrushing evening forced him to lean closer to the pages to read the music.

Light rain had been falling all day, and Bedrich, out since early morning, had been wandering through the narrow, twisting byways of the Old Town, occasionally stepping into a covered gateway to lean against a damp wall before going on. He found his steps leading him into the Jewish cemetery, a high-walled, private, sacred place, thick with age-old, black tombstones and elder-trees around whose branches and trunks the mists swirled. In here there was a quietness that was not of the night kind. He wondered what it was about the silence that made it different. And then it came to him. Of course, it was the silence of the dead.

He felt no fear or uneasiness. He walked slowly among the tombstones, many of them slanted, keeling over as though they themselves wanted to lie down to rest eternally. He peered at the writing on the stones, but could make no sense of the strange characters. He wondered what the stones said. He wondered what, if he himself were to die today, or tomorrow, someone would write on his stone. "Bedrich Smetana, died aged 24 . . . " What else would there be to say?

He touched the stones as he walked among them, rubbing his fingers over the soft moss, and he experienced a sort of affection for the monuments and those whose bones lay beneath. It felt right that he and the long dead should be on intimate terms, because in a way he felt dead already.

After a little while he went and sat beneath one of the trees, and though the wetness seeped through his coat and trousers, he didn't mind. There was no sound in the place, and he was grateful for that. He remembered how, at one period of his childhood, he had been afraid of the darkness, because he thought it was peopled with the ghosts of the restless dead. Yet here he was, sitting alone in a graveyard with the short, wet day greying into night, and he was untouched by anything save melancholy.

Nobody came all the time he sat there, and when he left nobody in the streets turned to look at him. He walked down to the river, then along its banks and on to Mayor's Island. He stood a long time, gazing at the Hradcany, its harsh lines blurred and round-edged in the murk. The Vltava, which danced and glittered so attractively in the summer sun and which froze with hard, clean, white ice in the cold season, slid past him, now grey-black, oily-looking, unfriendly. And somewhere inside him there played the thought that the river would provide a private way out of his misery. No-one need know. There was nobody about. It would be easy just to go down into those dark waters, and not fight.

An iciness gripped him until he shivered violently, and then he hurried away from the place, going he knew not where.

Hardly knowing how he got there, he found himself in the gloom of St Nicholas's Church in the Old Town, standing before the altar, and his soul was pouring out in supplication.

A long time later he left the church, feeling easier in his mind. When he let himself into his room he found the letter from Liszt. It was lying on the pillow of his bed, and bore an address in Krzyzanowice.

Quite calmly he read the words in it over and over again. One paragraph he read until he knew the sentences off by heart. It said: *The compositions you sent me are of the highest standard. They are beautifully emotional, and composed with a great gentleness. I honestly believe them to be far above anything I have come across recently.*

Then, suddenly, his emotion swelled again, and he sat crying on the edge of his bed.

Later, before he slept, he read the end of the letter once

more. *Should my way lead me to Prague this summer, as it is likely to, it will be a great pleasure for me to visit you and thank you personally for dedicating your "Opus One" to me. Meanwhile, my dear friend, permit me to assure you of my perfect respect, and sincere affection. Franz Liszt.*

A new light had come to illumine the frightful darkness of Bedrich Smetana's life.

CHAPTER

[11]

THE FOUR HUNDRED SOVEREIGNS Princess Wittgenstein had enclosed with Liszt's letter allowed Bedrich to secure the premises and equipment for his music-school, and early in July 1848 he sent out notices that he was opening the new institute, "for the teaching of pianoforte", in a house on the corner of Old Town Square and Zelezna Street.

Now that fate was at last looking benignly upon him, he became absolutely clear-headed in the pursuit of his ambition. No longer was he blundering blindly. Indeed, he surprised himself by the certainty with which he attacked the new project. This business-like Bedrich was a far cry from the drifter he knew himself to have been only a few weeks before. He sat down and drew up his plans, mapped out the course he wanted to take.

He asked for, and obtained, permission to quote Count Leopold von Thun as patron of the new institute, and in the programme of studies he prepared and sent out he emphasized that it was his intention to teach, not only the technique of pianoforte, "but also the appreciation of music, and the theory of composition and artistic presentation". In this he was sticking close to Proksch's programme.

The announcements repaid their careful preparation, and among the earliest list of registered students appeared the names of Countesses Nostitz-Rhinecke, Lobkowitz, Sporkov, Bellgarde, and Wolkenstein. But there were also the children of ordinary non-aristocratic folk—children like Marie Palacka,

Matilda Bellotova, Ludevit Prochazka, and Augusta Kolar (daughter of actor-dramatist Josef Jiri Kolar). They all received the same attention.

Proksch himself soon heard about Bedrich's plans, and, indeed, in a letter to his brother said: *It is interesting that Mr Bedrich Smetana, until lately my private pupil, has announced the opening of his private institute based on my system.*

Proksch, far from being annoyed, was secretly flattered. But Proksch's own position in Prague was undergoing certain tremors brought about by the continual upheavals of political pressures.

Many in Bohemia were discovering nationalism, were being made aware that they were an ancient people, that their ancestors, the Slavonic people, had first appeared in Central Europe as far back as A.D. 800. A burning pride was beginning to sweep through the land, gathering into its flames hordes of men and women eager to suffer gladly the birth-pangs of a nation. Already a revulsion against the German language had begun, as well as a deep-rooted desire to spread their own language into the schools and homes, the salons, the shops, and, ultimately, the printing houses and Government offices. And amid all this Bedrich's earlier nationalistic tendencies were being whipped up into an ever-strengthening love of people and homeland.

Ardent Czechs were casting their eyes beyond the boundaries of their land, and avidly perused every report of the struggles of the Irish, who were still, and with increasing success, trying to shrug off the yoke of centuries of English oppression. Czech balls were organized in Prague. Fiery young intellectuals held rallies and preached nationalism. Fervour grew, the movement consolidated, and Bedrich was caught up in it. But where his contemporaries (like Karel Havlicek, who was now in the forefront of the nationalistic-writers' bloc) were motivated primarily by political motives, Bedrich was prompted by love and pride. Music was his *métier,* and music would have to be his voice, his method of expression. At the same time he felt unable to remain a mere onlooker, so in an effort to salve his conscience he became a member of Svornost, the National Guard.

It wasn't always easy to divorce his nationalist self from the musician that he was, and in time he gave up the struggle. He would pour his nationalism into his music. After all, wasn't that basically what he had wanted to do for years, since the first time he had determined to write great and beautiful music which would sing to the world of his beloved Bohemia?

He was now a young man of substance, albeit one who had the sad, mysterious eyes of the aesthete. The reputation of his school was spreading, and he had to begin to search for teachers. It was a mature, financially secure musician who vetted the applicants, rejected (with care and sympathy—his own days of struggle were too close to allow him to forget) the unsuitable ones, and finally chose those who fulfilled all his requirements.

And this was the same professional young man who continued to court Katerina Kolar, in between teaching at his academy and composing. She shared his love of country, and when the opportunity arose was instrumental in persuading him to compose his very first patriotic song, *Song of Liberty*, with words by her uncle, J. J. Kolar. Afterwards came two marches, strongly smacking of the stuff of revolution, and on a visit to his parents he reached a new milestone—his first composition for a large orchestra, the "Festive Overture" in D.

He was no longer apologetic about his career in front of his father. He carried himself with an air of confidence, and with his newly grown beard, city clothes, thick hair brushed straight back from his forehead, and wide knowledge, he was a man to be listened to.

But there were occasions, when he was out in the fields or pushing upwards to the hills for the views that set his head leaping with exultation, on which he resented the conventions which laid down that he couldn't run or jump about, or do any of a hundred things that every boy does without thought.

He went yelping down a slanting field, jumping in the air in imitation of a spring lamb. At the bottom there was a wood which he entered on tip-toe, playing a fantasy game of hide-and-seek, reliving days of his childhood, enjoying himself in a way that should have nothing to do exclusively with childhood. When it was over he walked happily among the trees through the changing green light, kicking and scuffing the brown-leaf carpet, occasionally stooping to pick up a bit of dead branch and hurl it upwards across a clearing to see if it would remain aloft. In the open spaces of the woods he lay down and just gazed upwards, watching the leaves shivering in the wind that hit the trees high up, but left him snug on the ground.

One afternoon he came unexpectedly on a group of children playing a private game involving dances, songs, and chases, and he stood hidden on the edge of the glade as their silvery sounds bounced back and forth in delicious echoes. It was an experience he stored away. When the children suddenly ran off the glade was left empty of their sounds and the colours of their clothes. Their going filled him with sadness because his own childhood was over, gone for ever. Nothing he could do would ever again enable him to play with the same innocence and enjoyment as these children had just shown him.

He walked back across the fields as the sun slid down and the evening star gleamed brightly, anxious, it seemed, to dominate even if only for a while before its glitter would be lost in the competition.

That was the night he sat down and started on his "Festive Overture".

The family could see he was preoccupied, and, since he didn't want to talk or go visiting and mumbled about "getting down to do some work", they took the hint and retired early for the night.

For some time now he had had the tunes for the "Festive Overture" in his head, but had put off setting them down on paper until he could decide on a form. He had flirted with the idea of scoring the piece for full orchestra, but had dismissed it more out of fright than anything else. When he thought about the number of notes he would have to write down, the harmonies and rhythms and melodies and instruments he would have to visualize and then keep fixed in his mind, he had bypassed the whole idea as too big and complex for him. But tonight, somehow, after his walk in the fields and woods, he felt he could do it. His stomach was quivering with excitement, and his fingers felt weak as he gripped the pen. He crossed himself quickly, made a quick mental prayer, and wrote the first line without hesitation.

The day's experiences had unlocked his hesitancy, and right through the night he worked on the first draft. It didn't come easily. He had to tear away the layers of memory to remember some of the things Proksch had taught him. He sat at the piano and tried various passages and found the effect was bad enough on the piano; it would undoubtedly be five times worse on violins, violas, and cellos, not to mention brass and wood-wind. He walked away from the table once and out into the night, his mind made up to discard the whole business. But he came back and tried again, and again, and again.

He looked at what he'd written, couldn't discern anything, saw the notes swimming at him in a watery whirlpool, and decided to go to bed. Next morning his eyes felt gritty. They had caked up during the night, and the rims looked red and angry. Making a note to see a doctor about glasses, he went downstairs and ran to the papers he'd been working on. His mind clear and rested, he rushed over the pages, and, yes! the thing *was* taking shape, and looked as if it were working out as he had hoped.

The lovely image of childhood he had seen that day in the woods remained constantly with him for months. It came into his mind at frequent intervals, and with the knowledge that his own childhood could never come back, he longed for the next best thing—to have children of his own.

In Prague he was becoming well known both as a teacher and recitalist. In the streets people sometimes pointed at him and spoke his name. The regular concerts he arranged for his students (again copying Proksch) were well attended and received good notices. Life was good, and sometimes as he crossed Old Town Square he whistled as he walked, buoyant with success and the joy of being alive.

His pupils worked hard and well, all of them intent on pleasing a teacher who was kind and patient and so willing to give them all the help they needed. His self-absorption dis-appeared. He became an outgoing personality, always ready to laugh, always ready to listen, always ready to entertain in his inimitable fashion.

He took Katerina to balls and concerts, lavished her with carefully chosen gifts, and won from her, with little conscious effort, a deep, lasting love. As a couple they were welcomed to functions of all kinds, he the brilliant young musician-personality, she his coolly beautiful companion, articulate, amusing, and talented.

On the night of the Artists' Ball he called for her in a cab, and caught his breath at her beauty when she appeared in a simple white gown. He was wearing the mask of Gluck, the composer, and in the ballroom they danced with the abandon of a young couple who know there is something special about the occasion. There was laughter and gaiety on all sides, and the orchestra played with a verve that transmitted itself to everyone on the packed floor.

At midnight he guided Katerina towards the open balcony windows, and when they reached them he said, "Shall we go outside and take a breath of fresh air?"

She didn't say anything, but nodded smilingly as she took his arm and stepped into the warm night. They both stopped and looked for a moment at the dancers gliding by. It was like looking into a moving picture.

"They're all so happy," she said.

"Are you?" he asked.

"Yes."

"How happy?"

"Very happy."

She squeezed his arm, and he felt tall. They walked along to a dark spot away from the windows where the music sounded muted. He leant on the rail, she snuggling close to him. The sound of horse's hooves on the cobble-stones came up to them, and presently a cab came around the corner off to their right and down past the trees until it stopped just below them. For a second or so the horse pawed the ground, and then a man came out of the building, said something to the driver, and then called back over his shoulder, "Marie! Marie, are you there?"

There was an answering call, and the man crossed the pave-

K

ment, to reappear almost immediately with a laughing girl in a silver wrap. Gallantly handing her up, the man climbed in behind her, stumbled, laughed out loud, and then the cab drove off.

When the cab had gone the city relapsed into silence, warm lights showing in some far-off windows, the spires standing straight and black in the night sky.

Bedrich removed his mask and turned to Katerina.

"Katerina."

"Yes, Bedrich."

"Will you marry me?"

"Yes," she said, and he kissed her.

On the morning of August 29th, 1849, at St Stephen's Church in Prague, they were married.

CHAPTER
[12]

ALL THROUGH HIS WIFE'S pregnancy Bedrich had been
the epitome of consideration. In the hot months of the
summer, when Katerina was irritable and awkward and sick,
he found immense reserves of patience, danced attendance
on her, brought her delicacies and gifts, and saw to it her work
was made as light as he could make it. He gave in to her
whims, indulged her fads, and during the period when she
expressed the opinion that he probably now no longer loved
her because of her unattractive physical condition, he spoke
softly to her and assured her he loved her even more because
she was carrying his, their, child.

On January 7th, 1851, their daughter was born. Katerina
chose the name.

"I'd like her to be called Bedriska," she said, "after her
father."

The baby was strong and bawled lustily, and in a short
time was following movements close to her with alert eyes.
Friends of the Smetanas came to the house and joined in the
admiration. Students came with gifts of small knitwear and
sleeping garments. Musicians came with their congratulations,
and drank to the health of the child; and one evening Proksch
arrived, insisted on the small bundle being placed in his arms,
and held it with excessive caution. Then he handed the baby
back to Katerina. He stood for a while after the baby had
been taken, then put out a hand and said, "Bedrich!"

Bedrich went to him, saying, "Here I am."

Proksch felt for him, and then put an arm round Bedrich's shoulder and hugged him without speaking.

Parenthood meant increased happiness for the Smetanas. Sometimes, when he was alone, Bedrich wondered whether he possessed enough seriousness to carry out his responsibilities fully. He didn't know the answer, but he compared himself with his own father and found many differences. His father, it seemed to him, had had very definite ideas of what a father should and should not be.

"In a way I don't feel any different," Bedrich said to Katerina.

"Different from what?" she asked.

"Different from the way I felt before we had Bedriska."

"You mean you don't find any change at all?"

"Oh, I find some changes, naturally. But I don't feel any *older*."

"Well, you're not much older, after all," she said laughingly.

"No, but I always thought fathers were sort of stiff, serious people. Fiercely responsible about their children's wellbeing and future—as my own father was, and still is. But I don't feel that way, and I worry about it a little, sometimes."

"Well, I don't feel like a mother, either. So if you're wrong I'm wrong too, and we can console each other!"

There was a completeness about Bedrich's life that astonished him whenever he thought about it. There was the joy of being a musician, composing, teaching, being praised, earning money, being married to a girl he loved and who loved him, and having a baby of his own he could go and play with, cuddle, rock, tickle, or murmur to any time he wanted.

Four months after the birth of Bedriska, Katerina became pregnant again, and on February 26th, 1852, another daughter was born. This one was christened Gabriela, though at home they called her Jelcinka. She had a new sister in May 1853, and this one's name was Zofie.

Bedrich lived in a state of idyllic happiness, and his life revolved around Katerina and the three little girls he adored. Instead of remaining at the academy he was for ever rushing home to see them, kneeling down on the floor to play with them, never showing the faintest signs of irritation when they soiled his clothing, or woke him in the middle of the night.

When one of them developed whooping-cough he stayed beside her cot for three nights, sweating with fear, his face stretched and pale with distress every time the little body was torn by the terrible sound in the throat. When the child recovered he relaxed and went out alone in the streets, breathing in the clean air in huge gulps.

The following day he composed a very gay and colourful polka, and, when it was finished, he wrote *For Our Girls* on the top of the first sheet.

Though he loved all three of his daughters, Bedriska held a very special place in his heart. She was his first-born. It was she who had brought him that first feeling of incredulity as he had gazed at her and tried to grasp the fact that she was his own flesh and blood, born from part of his substance, a proof of his manhood, a baby of his making, and his for as long as he lived. These things would always mark her out as different from the others.

She had been born imbued with her parents' love for music, and when Bedrich saw her sitting behind him listening to his piano-playing, he remembered the times when he himself had sat listening to his own father playing the violin. By the time she was three she was allowed to come and listen to rehearsals of chamber music, and never once did she interrupt, though some of the sessions went on for as long as two and a half hours at a time.

More than anything else she loved dance rhythms, and without much persuasion would venture on to the floor, holding her embroidered dress daintily between tiny fingers, and tossing her dark-ringleted head as she kept time with improvised steps of her own. She used to beg Katerina to dance the quadrille, and her father the merrier folk dances.

In the same way that Frantisek and Barbora had sat in the evenings discussing Bedrich as a child, so Bedrich and Katerina talked of Bedriska and Gabriela and Zofie. But July 1854 brought illness to the family again, and after a week of sleepless nights in Lupnik in Moravia, where they were on holiday, Bedrich and Katerina, sitting up in chairs alongside Gabriela's cot, heard the child struggling for breath. At twenty-past eleven on the night of July 9th the child made a last unavailing effort to stay alive; then its face went purple, the eyes rolled back in their sockets, and with a pathetic, convulsive shudder Gabriela died.

Numbed, Katerina remained motionless. Bedrich leant into the cot, and, sobbing, picked up the lifeless body of his daughter and called her name over and over again. "Gabriela! Gabriela! Jelcinka, oh, my Jelcinka, Jelcinka!" But no calling could bring the life back, and he was still holding the body, stiffening now, against him when Katerina, crying desperately to herself, took it away from him and laid it back in the cot. She took his hand then and led him out of the room. He threw himself face down on their bed and cried inconsolably until sleep overtook him.

He was dry-eyed all the next day, but in the afternoon he took Bedriska and Zofie out of the house and into a field of meadow-grass, where he sat and stared at them in the sunlight. And when a bird sang he wondered angrily by what right it did so on a day such as this.

He grieved over Gabriela's death for many long months. At the school, though he remained gentle and patient as ever, he no longer joked. He was seen walking in the streets with a look of permanent pain on his face; the bounce went out of his steps, and his shoulders drooped.

At home he did his best to conceal his grief from Katerina and the children. Indeed, it was only with Bedriska and Zofie that he managed to return to something like his normal self. He immersed himself in their games in an effort to bury the spectre of death. He spent hours with Bedriska at the piano, teaching her (at her own repeated request) to play. It was always he who brought the lessons to a close, even when she wanted to go on. But in him there was a strong resolution never to push her, never to force her.

In his diary he wrote: *A the age of three she is singing songs, with a good ear for pitch, and she gives an impression of understanding the text remarkably well for a child of her years. Already she plays the piano with a lot of promise. I feel she has a natural musical talent.*

Katerina, pregnant for the fourth time, and busy looking

after the home and caring for her two daughters and her husband, regained an even emotional keel more quickly than Bedrich, and by doing so she was able to sustain him with her love and comfort. By the time the summer of 1855 came he was almost back to his normal self again, though by now an infinitely more serious man than he'd been a year before. But his blazing musical zeal and ambition were starting to surface once again. Disconsolate tinkerings on the piano became serious experiments with musical forms. Occasional scribblings of notes on music-paper became concentrated efforts at composition.

By the time summer was in Katerina felt Bedrich was all right to be left on his own for a while, and she said that she was thinking of taking Bedriska and Zofie with her to her mother's for a short holiday. Bedrich immediately agreed with the plan. Katerina could do with the break, and it would be good for the girls to see Grandmother Kolar.

Accordingly, he kissed them all goodbye, and to Bedriska he said, "Don't forget to sing and play the piano for Grandma and Grandad."

"No, Papa, I shan't." The child put her arms around his neck and kissed him. As always when a child showed him affection he felt very humble.

Katerina lifted the children into the waiting carriage, and came back to Bedrich.

"You won't be too depressed, will you, Bedrich?"

"No, my dear, I'll be fine. I have lots of work to do."

"If you do feel upset, pack a bag and come and join us." They kissed, and he helped her up into the carriage. She mouthed the words "I love you" to him and then they were gone.

He went into the house and threw himself into the work that had piled up. He worked late every night for a week, and wrote little letters to Katerina telling her how, in the mornings, he missed the little children's presence, but that he was not feeling morose because his work was heavy and going well.

Then one morning he received a letter from Katerina with the word URGENT printed on the envelope. His heart dropping inside him, he ripped open the envelope and read the hastily written note asking him to come quickly as Bedriska had been taken ill with scarlet fever.

The doctor was in the child's room when he arrived, and Bedrich instantly saw the concern on the man's face. He pushed past and went to the child, who was tossing and turning fitfully on her pillow. As he bent down to the red, sweating face, he felt the heat coming off it in waves. He turned in alarm to the doctor, to Katerina, to Anna Kolar, but their expressions gave him no consolation.

To the child he whispered, "Bedriska. Bedriska, my pet, can you hear me?"

She turned her head, and for a second her eyes flickered open, but there was no sign of recognition.

"Bedriska! It's papa. Can you see me?"

A hoarse voice poured a flood of incoherencies at him, and he strained to make sense of the disconnected words and phrases. They were meaningless.

"What's she saying?" he asked the doctor. "I don't understand."

"It's the fever," the doctor said. "Her mind is wandering. She's raving."

"Can't you *do* anything except stand there? Help her! Make her better!"

He was on his knees on the floor, the child's clammy hand pressed hard against his mouth, his tears drenching it.

She died the following morning, September 6th.

The inscription on Bedriska's gravestone said: "Here lies our child, gifted by God in spirit and heart; in her were embodied all her grieving father's most beautiful hopes, and her mother's greatest happiness. Her departure to the world of the angels has taken away everything from us, for ever."

It said only a little of what they felt. No words could describe what they went through. Barely seven weeks before her new baby was due Katerina collapsed and was confined to bed, where she lay sorrowing through the interminable hours.

She was in no condition to give consolation. She was in desperate need of it herself. From her husband she got none at all in the first three weeks, for the brutal truth was that Bedrich went out of his mind.

Sanity fled from him and left him gripped by a silent madness. He locked himself for hours in his room, an empty husk of a man who sat and stared ahead unblinkingly. The movements he did make were in sudden bursts of energy, when he beat his face with his fists in a terrible frenzy, crazed with a desire to inflict pain on himself.

When knockings were heard in his room they went in and found him standing by a wall, hitting it with his head until the blood ran down his face. When they tried to restrain him he flung them off. His strength was uncontrollable.

He walked through the house hollow-eyed, the blackness above his cheeks making the orbs appear enormous; he had the appearance of one of the walking dead.

It was the lamenting of his wife that finally brought him to his senses. He heard the sound as though from afar, and it grew quickly until his ears felt they would burst; his first words since Bedriska died were: "Where is she? Where is Katerina? Take me to her, quickly! *Now*."

Katerina's mother, Anna Kolar, guided him to the room.

The madness left him.

He went to the bed and said her name: "Katerina."

Her eyes closed tightly, she shook her head.

"Katerina," he said again, this time urgently.

She turned towards him in a little while, but her eyes were brimming.

He fell on his knees, groping for her fingers.

"Katerina, Katerina ..."

Anna Kolar left the room and quietly pulled the door shut behind her. This was a private moment for two people whose hearts were breaking, and though she loved them both and wanted to try to comfort them, she knew she had no place in the room at that moment.

There were nights after that when Bedrich woke up to hear his wife softly crying in agony, and he went to try to comfort her. His own need was enormous, but he recognized Katerina's as greater. He sat with her, patting her hand gently, leaning over her, murmuring sounds of consolation and comfort.

When she became hysterical and screamed all through the eerie pre-dawn hours of a wind-lashed morning, he pressed a cold flannel on her forehead and held her to him until she calmed down. He answered her fearful stridency with soft depth to his voice. And all the time his heart was sobbing out in pain.

When the new baby was born on October 25th she arrived to less rejoicing than had greeted any of the others. For Katerina the event was no more than an end to her hugeness; she took little interest in the baby. Bedrich tried, but he could not switch off grief and turn on joy at command. The best effort he could make (and it was for his wife's sake) was to lift the new-born child, and say, "Isn't she beautiful?" with as much conviction as he could muster.

After her confinement Katerina grew stronger in mind as well as in body, and as she progressed, so Bedrich's task of bringing consolation to her eased somewhat, and he was left again to the torture of loneliness and grief.

There were nights without end when he sat in his study, his mind and heart sick with memories that would not leave him, memories of his dead babies and of his wife's weeping. They stayed painfully fresh, undimmed by the passing of time, and he wondered what he could do. He turned to composition, and found his concentration could not be maintained. Certainly he could still write music, but it came out as fragments, mere snatches of melody he could not develop. Always the memories flooded back and arrested his progress. Sheet after sheet of music was screwed into balls and thrown into his waste-paper basket.

He gave up the struggle in the end, and sat down to let his mood dictate the style and content of his composition. He began to write in musical form something of the memories and the sorrow and the despair. It came easily to his pen, because his whole being was suffused with emotions. The instruments told the whole terrible story. The opening was full of weeping. Hearing in his head the sounds of Katerina's crying for the dead Bedriska, he wrote it down for the violin. Remembering his own efforts to still his wife's tears, he chose the soft mellowness of the cello for his own voice. And, torn by the memory, he gave the piano the passages that depicted the outbursts of despair that were incapable of being assuaged.

The love that he and Katerina had felt for the child, a love that was swamped by the realization that she was gone from them for ever, was torn from his being and expressed on those pages. And then, gradually, as the work on the trio progressed, he started to feel freer, liberated from the darkness by telling the world of the things that were closest to his soul. And by the time he had finished his Piano Trio in G minor he was already nearly purged by the confession he had made. He had come to realize too that his sanity would depend on his being able to immerse himself in more and more work.

The trio was the most personal thing he had ever written, and it was many weeks before he showed it to anyone. But once it was completed he was able to tackle other things. He began to study again, and examined more closely the works of Schumann and Chopin. Schumann held him under a spell for a long time, and his own compositions showed distinct traces of the German's influence; however, he noticed it in time, saw what he thought could endanger his own natural tendencies, and veered away from copying.

Trying to form his own orchestral style, he went through periods of acute frustration when the best he could do was turn out experimental works whose artistic incompleteness drove him frantic with disappointment.

Little Katerina, the new baby, was a weak and sickly child. Bedrich's wife, Katerina, was almost perpetually ill. Other musical institutes were opening and attracting those students who lived close to them away from Bedrich's school. The music critics were not taking him seriously as a composer, made vicious attacks on his compositions, and rudely and publicly advised him to stick to piano-playing. Where was fate's benignity now? Was there nothing to sustain his hopes and ambitions? Was Katerina ever going to be well again? And what about the baby? He didn't know which way to turn. Hopelessness was always at his shoulder, a fearful shadow waiting to pounce and drag him into its fetid abyss.

The baby died on June 10th, 1856, and Bedrich gave up completely. Two children dead in quick succession, a wife fading away before his eyes, financial difficulty confronting him, mockery from powerful critics being heaped on him daily, and now the third of his little daughters stretched in the stillness of death. He felt he could take no more.

He shed no tears. He was beyond that. He was thirty-two years old, and he was an old man whose will and sap had all gone from him.

[13]

ALEXANDER DREYSCHOCK was a contented man on whom success, when it came, rested lightly. As a pianist he was famous, not only in Bohemia and Moravia, but in all the countries of Europe in which he had given recitals, and in many other countries to which accounts of his brilliance had been reported back.

But of late much of his happiness had been dissipated by knowledge of the misery in which his friend Bedrich Smetana was sunk. He admired Smetana both as a man and as a musician. Smetana, he felt, was one of the few men of great musical talent to have appeared for some years, a composer of truly phenomenal ability who would do for his country what Bach and Schumann had done for Germany.

He knew him as a kind and extremely vulnerable human being, a person whose sensitivities had been receiving an unbelievable lacerating at the hands of hardship and personal tragedy. And yet out of these experiences had been born works of gentleness and deep human perception. Smetana, Dreyschock believed, was one of those people on whom nothing that delighted or saddened was lost. Until, that is, the death of his third child.

Since then poor Smetana had disintegrated. His appearance reflected the snuffing out of the last sparks of ambition and self-respect. The beard had become unkempt and straggly, the hair wild and uncombed, the clothes wrinkled, the conversation stilted and disconnected. It made Alexander Dreyschock a very worried man.

"You must believe in yourself again, Bedrich," he implored.

"I did, once," Bedrich said in a flat voice.

"But *now*, I mean," Dreyschock insisted. "You must, you've got to."

"Can you tell me how?"

"Man, you're an artist, a great artist. Isn't it enough to know that?"

"I don't know it. I thought once I had the makings of . . . of something."

"Oh, nonsense!"

"Is it?" Again the lack of life in the voice.

"Of course it is, and you know it."

"I know nothing, Alexander, nothing, any more."

"You're feeling sorry for yourself, aren't you?"

"No, not even that now."

"What did Liszt tell you?"

A small smile. "Oh, that! It didn't cost him anything."

Dreyschock, uncharacteristically violent, grabbed Smetana's shoulders and shook him. "Don't talk like that!" he roared. He let go of Bedrich's shoulders and turned his back on him. When he spoke again it was more quietly. "I know you've had frightful things to bear, and truly, Bedrich, my heart bled for you. It still does, but good Lord, man, you've still got to live your life, and you owe it to Katerina, to your Zofie; and yes, even to the . . . to the others, to do what you're destined to do."

"You're like Liszt, you're kind," Bedrich said.

"I'm not being kind—and Liszt wasn't being kind!"

"And the critics?"

"Damn the critics!"

"They create opinion, Alexander. They *know*."

"They know nothing."

"They've helped you."

"It suited them. They know nothing. I don't give a curse for any of them. I do what pleases me, and if they don't like it they can—" he used an oath. "Now, forget them."

"And keep on, is that what you want me to do? To keep on and enjoy being publicly crucified? And take everything that comes my way, and smile as if it doesn't affect me? I'm not made of stone."

"No-one knows that better than I do," Dreyschock said, and left, more worried and discontented than ever.

He was half-way down the street when he turned and went back to the Smetana house, in through the front door which he had left open when he walked out, into the room where he had left Bedrich. His arrival back caused no comment.

"You might tell me to mind my own business," he announced, "but I can't, man, I can't. I have too much regard for you. I feel for you too much."

Bedrich looked at him with those great, haunted eyes.

"Do you even know what I'm trying to do?" asked Dreyschock. "I'm trying to salvage something. I'm—" But the eyes just held their uncomprehending stare, and he walked out of the room, this time banging the front door loudly.

Katerina came shuffling into the room to Bedrich, and was about to talk when she was seized by a paroxysm of coughing. When she recovered herself she said, "I heard Alexander's voice raised, and he banged the front door when he left. Was he angry?"

"I don't know," he said dully.

There was no communication between them any more. She had no strength to make the effort needed to re-establish their relationship. Weariness had made her captive, and illness was sapping all her energies.

Bedrich never left the house other than to go to the institute, and he didn't teach any more. His concentration was gone; the student numbers were dropping; debts were mounting. At the school he sat in his own room moping the hours away; he took no interest in what was going on in the city, knew nothing of the impending arrival on September 6th of a great musical figure.

Late in the afternoon of September 6th Alexander Dreyschock came to the house and asked to see him.

"He's in the music-room," Katerina said. "Alexander, can you do nothing for him? He's like a dead man."

He patted her hand. "Leave me alone with him for a while. But in the meantime I want you to go and get ready. We're going out, all three of us."

She drew away, and put a hand to her mouth almost as if in

fear. "Oh, no," she said. "I couldn't go out. I haven't been outside the door since Katerina was taken from us. I don't feel
well enough."

He leant forward and took hold of both her hands, so thin
and frail that he felt he could crush them to pulp by squeez-
ing hard. "Please, Katerina. It's for Bedrich."

She was still very hesitant. "But I look terrible, my hair—"

"You have beautiful hair—you are a beautiful woman, and
I want you to look good tonight."

"Oh, you lie so charmingly, Alexander."

"I'm not lying. But hurry, my dear, it's very important."
Then he went to the music-room and knocked before going in.

Bedrich was sitting at his desk, his head on his arms in
dejection.

"Come along, Bedrich, we're going out for the evening,"
Dreyschock announced in a tone of voice he hoped would not
be resisted.

"Ah, it's you, Alexander. I heard your voice in the hall and
wondered who it could be. It's not often we have visitors at
this time."

"We're going out," Dreyschock repeated. "Katerina is getting
ready."

"Katerina?" Bedrich couldn't understand. He sighed and
smiled again, and said, "Well, it will, perhaps, do her good.
But you can forget about me."

Dreyschock began to propel him towards the door. "Be a
good fellow and don't argue," he said. "There is somebody
I want you to meet."

"No, Alexander, I don't want to meet anyone. Thank you,
but I . . . I can't face people."

"You will want to meet this person. Now, come on, *hurry*,"
and he walked Bedrich to his bedroom, where he waited until
a clean shirt and his best suit were lying on the bed ready to
be worn. Then Dreyschock, seemingly deaf now to all protesta-
tions, stood over him while he washed, trimmed his beard,
and changed his clothes. Finally he led Bedrich downstairs
again, out across the pavement, and sat him in the farthest
corner of the waiting cab. This done, Dreyschock went back
into the house, called for Katerina to hurry up, and went into

the music-room. Rummaging about among the folios, he eventually found what he was seeking, and then sat down to wait.

When he heard Katerina giving last-minute instructions to the maid about looking after Zofie, he went out to the hall and stood there until she came down the stairs. There was a pathetic shyness about her as she stood before him. "You look wonderful," he told her, and took her arm.

"Where are we going?" Bedrich wanted to know as soon as the cab started to move.

"To my house," Dreyschock said.

"And who are we going to meet?"

"You'll see soon enough."

At Dreyschock's house the main room was all set out ready for a reception, but Katerina and Bedrich were taken to Dreyschock's bedroom, where they took off their coats and hats.

"The person I want you to meet will be here presently," Dreyschock told them. "But I want you to sit here till I come for you."

He left them sitting nervously on the edge of their chairs. They barely talked as they listened to the noises of cabs arriving, voices raised in greeting, the buzz of conversation, the shuffle of feet in other rooms. Then there was a small hiatus as a last cab drew up to the front of the house, and when its occupant, or occupants, entered the main room there was a sudden burst of hand-claps. Katerina and Bedrich looked at each other. Within seconds Alexander came into the room and said, "You can come with me now."

Bedrich helped Katerina to her feet, and followed Alexander. When they entered the big room all Bedrich could see was a ring of faces, most of them familiar. The noise of excited conversation was deafening, but Alexander was saying, "Stay close behind me," and shouldering his way through the throng, which fell back and formed a passageway as he said, "Excuse me, please." Bedrich kept his eyes downcast with embarrassment. Eventually, bumping into the halted Dreyschock, he heard Alexander saying, "May I present Bedrich Smetana!" Bedrich looked up, and in that instant, as their eyes met, Franz Liszt embraced him.

He could never remember afterwards what Liszt said to him,

L

or what he said to Liszt. All he knew was that the man he had idolized was standing there, face to face, holding his hand, actually speaking to him.

Franz Liszt himself had to fight down the feelings that welled up on meeting this humble, tragic-looking man who was old beyond his years, from whose eyes sadness poured out, and from whose pen such glories had already issued. Dreyschock had said nothing about Smetana being at the reception. The confrontation was a total surprise.

And then Dreyschock was coming in between them, handing something to Liszt, and saying, "It is Bedrich's newest work. Would you play it for us?"

Liszt took the folio, looked at the title, Piano Trio in G minor, and, with a little bow, said in a quiet voice. "It would be an honour."

The guests found seats. Softly protesting, Bedrich allowed himself and Katerina to be ushered to chairs in the front of the semicircle. He didn't look at Liszt, this great man on whom Dreyschock had perpetrated such a trick.

Liszt settled the sheets of music, paused for composure, and began to play. Bedrich closed his eyes. Katerina bowed her head, and music such as that room had never heard flowed from the piano.

When he was finished Liszt dabbed his eyes with an immaculate handkerchief. Most people in the room were crying. And then the applause shook the foundations. But Liszt didn't move. He sat with his chin low down against his chest. He was overcome.

Then he got up and came over to Bedrich, but couldn't speak. He bent over Katerina, embraced her, and said in a broken voice, "He is a genius. Your husband is a genius."

Liszt was in Prague to prepare the performance of his *Estergon Mass*, which was to take place in St Vitus's Cathedral on St Wencelas' Day, but though he knew he would be extremely busy with his rehearsal schedule and all the social obligations he would be expected to fulfil, he made his mind up on the instant he finished playing the piano trio that he would have to do something for its composer. The man looked desperately in need of something. It could be encouragement, Liszt thought, though why a person with this sort of talent should still need encouragement, he could not fathom.

He drew Dreyschock aside. "Thank you, Alexander, for giving me that Smetana composition to play," he said.

Dreyschock searched Liszt's face. "I know you were affected by playing it—I could see that—but you just said: 'Thank you.' Your reaction to this piece of music seems very like my own."

"And yours was—what?" Liszt asked.

"I felt as though I was eavesdropping."

"That's precisely what I felt. In fact, Alexander, I couldn't even *say* my thanks to Bedrich, I felt that much of an intruder into his world of grief."

He looked over his shoulder to where the crowd was standing in knots, drinks in hands, heads together, talking. Only two people were talking to the Smetanas, and Bedrich was taking no part in the conversation. He was standing with his head inclined meekly, a lost expression on his face.

"Look at him," Liszt went on. "He's so . . . what is the word? Humble? Or sad? Or vulnerable?"

"I think of him as vulnerable."

"I couldn't even talk to him," Liszt said. "But that music, my God. . . ." He shook his head, then looked into Dreyschock's eyes. "Whatever it was that made him write it must have been appalling. Do you know?"

"Yes, I do."

Dreyschock told him about the children, the illnesses, the deaths. Liszt repeatedly interrupted with "God in Heaven!" as the story came out, and when Dreyschock finished, Liszt's expression was one of agonized disbelief.

"But at least this trio is a masterpiece," he said. "There must be some consolation for him in knowing that his suffering wasn't all completely wasted."

"They derided it," Dreyschock replied bitterly.

"Who?" More disbelief on Liszt's face.

"The critics."

"I don't believe it."

"They tore it to shreds."

"Then all I can say is that you Czechs are fools!" Liszt said.

"Our critics are."

"All critics are, but yours more than any. Is it any wonder that man looks as he does? They're destroying him."

"Franz, he has taken more than he can bear. He doesn't believe in himself any more. That's why I handed you that score to play without warning. I knew it was an unfair thing to do, but I had to gamble on it. That man needs help, and because he idolizes you I had to take the chance. From now on ... well, what more can I say?"

"If I can do anything to convince him to carry on," Liszt said, "then, Alexander Dreyschock, you'll have done posterity a great kindness."

Late the following afternoon Bedrich was alone in his music-room when he heard someone at the hall door. Was this Dreyschock? He stood up, ready to chide and thank simultaneously, but it was not Dreyschock he saw when the door opened. Franz Liszt was coming towards him with outstretched hands. Bedrich swallowed hard. This was almost too much.

Solicitous for the comfort of his distinguished visitor, Bedrich pulled up the most comfortable chair in the room, plumped up the cushions, and said, "Here, maestro, sit here."

"My name is Franz," Liszt said, "as yours is Bedrich. I hope I may be allowed to call you Bedrich, and you must call me Franz."

Almost every day until he left Prague at the end of September, Liszt came to Smetana's house. He drew Bedrich out of his shell in long, easy conversations, played Beethoven, Chopin, Schumann for him; got him to play his own compositions; discussed the modernists; argued, and gradually but firmly brought back to life the fires that had gone out. With consummate skill and an avoidance of patronage, he reawakened Bedrich Smetana; and towards the end of his visit he had the thrill of knowing he had been successful.

"It's astounding," Dreyschock said. "You've worked a miracle. The man is alive again. He glows. He's restless to start composing."

"But there is one thing left to be done," Liszt said. "He

must get out of Prague. The indifference or the ridicule will kill him if he stays here."

"There we think alike," Dreyschock said. "I'm going to suggest to him that he goes to Göteborg. He'd be happy there. They'd appreciate him."

"That's good," Liszt agreed. "You can give him some letters of introduction, perhaps?"

"Yes, I'll provide him with several," Dreyschock said. "And, Franz, I don't have to tell you how much your help has meant to me."

Within a few days Franz Liszt was saying goodbye to Bedrich, the two men holding tightly to each other, Liszt saying, "And when you are free, come and visit us at Weimar, won't you?"

"I'll try," Bedrich said.

"I've learnt a great deal from you in these past few weeks; I'd like to learn more."

"Learnt? From me?" Bedrich couldn't believe his ears.

"Yes, a great deal. About beauty and about emotion and about humanity. As I said, I want the opportunity to learn more. So remember, we shall be waiting for you in Weimar. And, Bedrich, you should give some thought to the possibility of getting away from Prague for a time. Go and work elsewhere. It would do you good. And now, my dear friend, I must be away. Until we see each other again, may God bless you and help you to create more musical riches."

Dreyschock came around to Smetana's home two days after Liszt left. It was a smiling, neatly dressed Bedrich who took his hand firmly. They talked music for about an hour, and to Dreyschock's delight his friend was brimful of new ideas and plans.

In a rare lull in the conversation Bedrich said, "You know, you have no idea what Franz Liszt has done for me."

"I think I have," Dreyschock said quietly. "You've got back your self-confidence and your interest. What do you intend to do?"

"Compose."

"But you're not making much money now, are you?"

"True."

"Do you mind if I suggest something?"

"Of course not."

"Leave Bohemia."

Dreyschock was pleased to note there was no outburst. He mentally thanked Lizst for having prepared the ground.

"Why do you say that?" Bedrich asked.

"I think you need a change of environment."

"Any other reason?"

"I think the clowns who influence musical taste in Prague are rather too anti-Smetana at the moment. Get out of the place, disappear for a while, forget them, and you'll have no pressures bearing down on you. You'll be free to do good work."

Bedrich thought about it for a while, then said, "Where shall I go?"

"Göteborg. It's a good city. They are good people there, and they love their music."

More deep thought before Bedrich asked, "You've been there?"

"Yes."

"But Sweden is a long way, Alexander—supposing Katerina didn't like it when we get there?"

"Perhaps you should go on ahead and see the place, see if you would like it. You could look for a home and send for Katerina. Think it over, Bedrich."

He thought very deeply about it. He began to take solitary walks in order to be able to work out his future.

Conditions in Prague had changed. The nationalism which, so short a time ago, had seemed on the verge of overpowering everything in its path had withered and died. Time had passed by Bedrich, events had occurred without his knowledge. The ardour was snuffed out, and to retain an enthusiasm for what had dramatically become unfashionable ideas was dangerous.

The wisdom of the advice given by Dreyschock and Liszt was apparent to him, but what caused him to hesitate was his reluctance over forcing a long land and sea journey on Katerina.

He would have to go, she said. It would be the best thing he could do. She would wait behind until he had found an apartment and then join him later. "It will give me a chance to rest and get strong for the journey, my dear. You must do it. And the sooner the better."

So on October 11th, 1856, he left Prague, and travelled via Hamburg, Kiel, and Copenhagen to a new life in Göteborg.

His first glimpse of the sea as the ship sailed out into the Baltic so fascinated him that he stayed on deck most of the night, shivering with excitement and cold, and then went to bed with his head swimming in a ferment of anticipation. Pray God, he thought, that I am leaving behind for ever the misfortune that has stalked me.

CHAPTER

THE TRIP INTO THE HARBOUR of Göteborg (Bedrich had
been up early, standing alone on deck in the darkness) had
been full of trepidation and barely suppressed excitement as
the riding-lights of anchored ships slipped by them, and the
voices of the sailors at their stations came downwind to him.
And then there were the waterfront lights, casting their long
beams in rippling parallels across the tide.

The dawn had come, grey and pearly and mysterious, creeping up the eastern horizon until it caught the city of Göteborg
and held it, a series of black outlines, as though painted with
exquisite precision on a gigantic canvas. The moment was short
but unforgettable, and he shivered. And then the sky
brightened, the black greyed, the greyness lightened, and the
buildings took on colours and depth; and he wondered what
this new place held in store for him.

He was trying to understand (and make himself understood
by) the reporter of the *Göteborg Gazette for Trade and
Shipping* when a man joined them, excused himself, and said
in German, "Would you be Bedrich Smetana?"

"Yes," Bedrich answered.

The man put out his hands, his face beaming with relief,
and said, "Ah, welcome to Göteborg." And then in Czech,
"But let me introduce myself. My name is Josef Capek." They
embraced, and the reporter, perplexed and tired, and puzzled
by the gushes of foreign language that burst from the two men,
left them.

Josef Capek had come to Göteborg in 1847, and already had made a home for himself in the city, as well as a reputation as a violinist, organist, and composer. Dreyschock had written to him about Smetana and asked him to meet and look after him.

In the nine years that he'd been settled in Sweden, Capek had often pined for his native land, but had fought all inclinations to return. Memories of disappointments and penury were still very close to the surface, and though he missed his country and its people, he cherished the security Sweden had given him.

Standing now on the deck with his fellow-countryman, Capek felt lonely no longer. Here was someone who spoke his language, who could be shown around, who was a musician, who could give him at first hand the news and flavours that no letters could ever give. And if Dreyschock was right the man was a fount of ability.

Capck asked Bedrich how many cases he had and what cabin he'd travelled in, then told him to stand by the rail and not to move. Then the busy little violinist hurried off. When he returned ten minutes later he said, "Now, my friend, all is taken care of. I've paid a porter to collect your luggage and have it delivered to my place. So let us go and have some coffee, and you can tell me all about Prague."

Arm in arm they went down the gangway, Bedrich continuing to thank his voluble companion, Capek dismissing the gratitude and emphasizing that it was a pleasure to be of help.

When Capek hailed a cab Bedrich put a halting hand on his arm and said, "No, my friend, if you don't mind. I'd rather walk."

"But it's a long way."

"I'd still rather walk," Bedrich said. He was remembering the first time he'd seen Prague, and wanted his first impressions of Göteborg to remain just as clear in his mind.

When they at last reached Capek's home and were both seated sipping hot coffee, Capek said, "And now, friend, tell me about Prague."

Bedrich sat back, closed his eyes, and took Josef Capek back to the villages outside Prague, along the valley of the river, through the dells and glades, round the curves of the river's course, and finally brought Prague with all its loveliness and majesty into the room. And when he had finished there was a great quietness in the room, and Capek sat as though in a dream. After some time he leant forward, put a hand on Bedrich's, patted it, and whispered, "Thank you."

On the day after the *Göteborg Gazette for Trade and Shipping* announced his arrival Bedrich held his first concert. There hadn't been much time to publicize it, and it was held in a small hall which was two-thirds filled. He was extremely nervous, anxious about the reception the Göteborg citizens would give to him, an unknown and unheralded pianist.

When he came on to the platform his legs felt so weak that he was fearful he might fall down and make a foolish spectacle of himself. Just before walking to the piano he caught sight of Capek sitting there smiling his encouragement up to him. Always, it seemed, there was a memory for the occasion. This time it was Albina who came to mind. "Play for me," she had said, and it had worked. Very well, this time I'll play for Josef Capek, he thought, and he went to the piano with the smiling, encouraging face of Capek before him.

At the end of the recital the audience got to its feet and bellowed "Bravo! Bravo! Bravo!" until he sat down again, exultant though shy, and played his encores. And it was with the utmost reluctance that they let him go at the end.

As he walked off, the cheers and handclaps ringing out, he said aloud, "Yes, I like it here."

And then Capek was hugging him and saying, "Dreyschock was right. Oh, he was so right!" He accompanied Smetana to to the room where his street clothes were, and while Bedrich was changing, Capek kept up a stream of complimentary remarks.

"Thank you, Josef," Bedrich said. "The audience seemed pleased."

"Pleased? They were delirious. Surely you have no doubts about staying here now?"

"I should love to stay," Bedrich replied.

"Then you must—"

He was interrupted by a knock on the door. When he opened

it Bedrich heard a man's voice saying, "Ah, it's you, Mr Capek. Is Mr Smetana there?"

Capek, standing back from the door, said, "Yes, Mr Magnus, will you come in?"

Magnus, a wealthy merchant, a distinguished-looking man with iron-grey hair and wearing clothes of quality and great cost, strode into the room, followed by two women and two men. He went straight to Bedrich, who was standing bashfully by the wall, stuck his hand out, and said, "Mr Smetana, forgive me bringing my party to burst in on you unannounced like this, but I felt I just had to shake your hand and congratulate you on a memorable evening's entertainment."

"Thank you very much," said Bedrich.

"Mr Magnus is one of our city's greatest patrons of music," Capek offered by way of explanation. "And a most generous one."

Magnus dismissed it with easy grace.

"You enjoyed it then?" Bedrich asked, more as a conversational bridge than as a real question.

"Enjoyment would be an understatement," Magnus said. "Am I right?" he said, turning to his companions.

"It was a sheer delight."

"Glorious evening."

"Magnificent, Mr Smetana." This latter from a strikingly handsome woman with piercing, bright eyes and a head of rich, black hair which was parted in the centre to reveal an immaculately straight line of milky-white scalp. She smiled as she spoke, and her voice was rich and warm.

Bedrich, suddenly aware that he was staring straight into her eyes, blushed and turned back to Magnus, who was saying, "Tell me, Mr Smetana, have you decided to grace us with your presence for long? I did read that you were hoping to remain here for some time."

"Yes, sir, I—"

"Don't call me 'sir', Mr Smetana. I made up my mind as a very young man never to call anyone 'sir'. And any man who is as gifted as you should never dream of subservience. I seem to be lecturing to you, Mr Smetana, but I believe in speaking my mind."

Bedrich was taken aback by the directness, and tugged nervously at his beard and laughed.

"Mr Magnus is right, you know, Mr Smetana," the dark-haired woman said.

The small room had become suddenly warm, crowded as it was by the seven people in it. Magnus saw the look of strain on Bedrich's face, and he ushered his party towards the door. "Come," he said, "this poor man is tired, and it's unfair of us to have descended on him like this. But, Mr Smetana, *do* decide to stay. And I hope we shall have the pleasure of another concert soon. Good night, and once again, thank you."

There was a chorus of "thank you's", and the last face Bedrich saw was that of the dark-haired woman whose eyes held his for a moment before she turned away quickly and was gone.

His second recital was held on November 12th, and this time every seat in the hall was occupied, the overflow standing round the walls and sitting on the dusty floor of the centre aisles. The reception was rapturous, and the Stockholm weekly paper *Ny Tidning för Musik*, which came out on the following day, gave the event a glowing review. At the end of the piece appeared this paragraph:

> Mr Smetana intends to remain in Göteborg and to establish there a music institute. He has already been offered, and has accepted, the post of Musical Director of the Society for Classical Vocal Music.

The offer of the post came as a complete surprise, and when Capek told him that the Society had been born out of the wild enthusiasm created by Bedrich's first recital he felt a quiet pride growing in him, a stiffening sense of purpose such as he had not known since the early days of his academy in Prague. It was heartening to find his belief in himself taking solid root again. Liszt's unstinted praise had begun it. Now his acceptance in Göteborg was adding strength to it. Revitalized, he started to make new plans.

Magnus came to see him after the second concert, a buoyant Magnus who was alone this time.

"You know, Mr Smetana, I suppose by material standards

I'm a wealthy man," he said, "but compared with you, I'm a pauper, a cultural pauper."

"Oh, come now," Bedrich said.

"No, I mean it. It is the rare ones like you who are rich beyond description. What have I ever created of any real worth?"

"Your business empire."

"That's only money—goods and chattels."

"It requires talent. I have none of that kind of talent."

"You'll never need it. And it's not talent, not in the real sense of the word. Anyone could acquire it. Application, that's all it is. A little flair, possibly, a lot of luck. But luck has no part in what you've got. I'd exchange all I have for a vestige of your great gift."

"I'm very flattered," said Bedrich.

"My life has been one of tedium, coercion, I suppose, a certain amount of tyranny; but what have I done that's of lasting value? What have I done of which any person can say, 'He has made beauty where none existed'?"

"You must have made people happy—your employees."

"Not happy, my friend. Grateful, perhaps. And for what? For ensuring they get what is theirs by divine and natural right—enough to buy the necessities of life."

"Not every wealthy man can claim as much," Bedrich remarked.

"But it pales to insignificance alongside what you can do. You *create* beauty, memories, magnificence. You bring me the taste of serenity. . . . But enough of this. I am holding a ball in a couple of weeks from now, and should deem it an honour if you would come."

Bedrich went and, when he was announced, felt peculiarly alone without Katerina at his side. But as soon as Magnus came forward to meet him and ushered him towards a circle of people the feeling vanished. Besides, there was a tingling sensation in his stomach when he noticed the woman with the black hair and piercing eyes standing smiling at the end of the line. Her presence he found pleasantly exciting. He barely heard the list of names as the men and women were introduced, and he shook hands and murmured his appreciation of the congratulatory things they said.

Then the woman was in front of him, smiling enigmatically, and he was fumbling so much for something to say that he completely missed her name.

She was at ease, gracious. "I'm delighted to be able to shake your hand, Mr Smetana," she said. "It was all rather chaotic the last time we met, wasn't it?"

"Indeed," he said. My God, he thought, is that the best I can do?

Later, when he was standing with Josef Capek, he caught her looking at him across the ballroom floor. He turned so that his back was facing her and said to Capek, "Josef, don't look now or it will be too obvious, but there is a woman over there under the portrait, directly across the room behind me. Who is she?"

Capek made an elaborate business of looking around the room, eventually sweeping his glance past the place Bedrich had mentioned. "There are three ladies there," he said. "Which one do you mean?"

"She has dark hair, and is wearing a red-velvet dress."

"Oh! You've met her before. She came with Magnus—"

"Yes, I know, but what is her name?"

"That's Fröjda Benecke. *Mrs* Fröjda Benecke."

Bedrich turned around again so that he could see her. "She's a very attractive woman, don't you think?" he said.

"She is. But she *is* married."

Fröjda Benecke was still looking in their direction, with a firm, unashamed, level look.

"Don't become involved," Josef said.

"Just because I ask a woman's name, that doesn't mean—"

"That you're interested in her?"

"Of course I'm not! I just think she's an attractive woman, that's all."

He couldn't get to sleep for a long time that night. Fröjda Benecke's face wouldn't leave him. He tried to banish it by thinking of Katerina, but Katerina was a long way away in Prague, and he couldn't conjure up a picture of her strong enough to displace Fröjda Benecke's for long.

Prague did not want to accept me, so I left, he wrote to his parents on December 23rd. *It is nearly always true that a country will never accept its own artists. They have to leave home to make a name for themselves. They have to go away to earn a living. I was struck by such a fate. I am homesick for my own country. I miss you all, and I am lonely for my wife and child.*

Lonely he was, but he was powerless to rid himself of thoughts of Fröjda Benecke. The memory of her was both disturbing and enchanting, and the first composition he wrote in Göteborg was called *Ball Visions*. He dedicated it to this woman whose vision tormented him. She came to him one day and asked him if he would accept her as a pupil, and though he was sure he was about to walk across hot coals in thin shoes, he said yes.

From that day on he knew he was in love with her. They didn't speak of their love, but every action, every word, every gesture, was of such a tenderness that they both knew. It was secret and holy and illicit and incontrovertible. They were both caught in a flow of feelings which it was impossible to struggle against.

He was tortured because of what he felt. His emotions were in a tangle. *And yet I love Katerina still,* he wrote. *But if I truly love her, how could I love Fröjda Benecke? Katerina gave me my children, suffered for me, made me happy, meant the world to me, loved me, loves me, means the world to me. Perhaps I don't love Fröjda Benecke. Do I? How can I know? If she were to disappear from my world tomorrow—but no, I can't bear to think of such a thing. Surely that means I do love her? If I do I am being unfair to Katerina. If Katerina were to leave me—no, I can't bear that thought either. I should die if she left me. What manner of man am I? A cheat? I don't know. I love them both. And that is wrong. Fröjda Benecke is married too. She loves her husband and her children. She loves me. How can it be? What are the answers? Are there any?*

Mrs Benecke was only the first of many who came to him to be taught. True, teaching music was in itself only a means to an end, but, like Josef Capek, he found that in this northern city it brought him ample security and, what was more, freed his mind again from the strain of monetary worries. The few months immediately after his arrival were a time of discovery and enjoyment.

The people were ripe for experiments, and, given the reins, he was able to indulge to his heart's content all his inclinations to broaden their appreciation of composers of whose works they were well-nigh ignorant. He was a propagandist for contemporary musical romanticism, and if there was a reluctance to accept it in existence in Göteborg he never knew about it. The people took him to their hearts. He opened their hearts and their ears, and in turn they gave him affection and acclaim. He did not have to pander to inbred tastes, nor was any form of condescension required. He was in a position to enlighten and educate, and Capek was alongside him to encourage the re-emergence of his ambitions. Capek and Fröjda Benecke, who, in the absence of Katerina, became the staff on which he leant.

On April 18th, 1857, he performed Beethoven's Piano Concerto in C. Part of the review on the following morning said:

> Mr Smetana's playing, full of feeling and life, cannot but create fresh interest in everything he tackles; but towering above all was his performance of the Beethoven concerto.

In his diary that night he wrote words that mirrored his elation. *Today the newspaper contained a kind review of my concert. Among the sentences of praise was the statement that no pianist has performed Beethoven's concerto as perfectly in this city. I am delighted, but not deluded, because as far as I am aware only one pianist of reputation has ever played here.* As a boy he had often said, "I love true things", and his concern for truth had now peeled the newspaper's praise down to its basic worth.

By the beginning of May he had made the decision to bring Katerina to Göteborg, and on the 16th of the month he bade adieu to Capek and Magnus at the dockside as he set off on the journey to Prague to assist in packing up the family belongings.

All the way to the house, on the morning of the 24th, he was running over in his mind the things he should say to Katerina.

It was a bright summer's day, the sun high in the clear heavens, Prague looking its most beautiful. Slivers of surprise shot through him that the place had not changed. It was just as it had been. He didn't know why it should have changed, nor in what way he expected it to differ—and yet he was surprised.

He paid the cab-driver and put down his bag. Then he lifted the brass knocker and let it drop against the door. The bang echoed through the house. He held his hands ready to shoot out and embrace his wife, but no sound of footsteps came to him. He grasped the knocker again and crashed it against the stud. Almost immediately he heard the sound of running feet within. As hands fumbled with the locks on the inside, and he stood laughing on the outside, a loud admonitory whisper hissed at him: "Quiet! *Please!*" And then the door opened, and it was not Katerina at all who stood there, but her sister, Alzbeta. His hands dropped involuntarily as Alzbeta's mouth fell open with shock, and he knew instantly that something was wrong.

"Come in, come in," Alzbeta said.

He bent and picked up his bag, and went into the hall. "Katerina, is she all right?" he asked.

For answer Alzbeta held on to him, and when she broke away from him he saw that she was crying.

"What—" he began.

"Ssh! Don't talk loudly," she said. "Zofie is very ill."

Terror gripped him. He was already past her in the hall when he asked, "What is it?"

She whispered the two dreaded words, "Scarlet fever."

He ran on and saw Katerina, small and worn-out, ill-looking, letting herself backwards out of Zofie's bedroom. When she saw him she uttered a small cry and ran to him and collapsed in his arms. He carried her, pathetically light, downstairs, and when she recovered he knelt down beside her where she lay on the couch and said, "How is she?"

"She's sleeping," Katerina answered. She put her hand up and ran her fingers through the hair on the back of his head, and then pulled his face forward until it was resting on her breast.

M

He wept silently, and Katerina's arm tried to still the heaving of his shoulders.

Zofie pulled through the illness, but the fever left her very weak and recuperation was painfully slow. Bedrich tried to brighten Katerina by telling her of Göteborg, of his triumphs there, the kindness of the people, the good life that awaited them as a family. Katerina listened, but didn't enthuse, and Bedrich knew once again the despair that hollowness carries with it.

The news that his father had died on June 12th hurt but didn't shock him, and he left, quiet but composed, to attend the funeral.

It was raining when they lowered Frantisek's coffin into the grave, and Bedrich thought that it was a bleak day on which to be put down among the worms. He couldn't find the right words to comfort his mother, and walked, supporting her arm, back to the cab for a silent ride back to his brother's home. In time he said his goodbyes, and as he drove away he was overpowered by the conviction that the magic of the Smetana family life had been crushed out of existence with the going of his father.

He wanted to leave Bohemia now as soon as possible.

[15]

KATERINA TRIED HARD TO APPEAR cheerful about leaving
Prague, but the truth was that the prospect frightened her.
She woke every day feeling sickly, and her strength seemed
to be slipping inexorably from her. Sweden was so far north,
and people told such awful stories of the hardship of the
winters there. And then, too, leaving Prague meant surrender-
ing her last ties with her family who were so good when it
came to the provision of help and consolation.

She tried to put a brave face on things, but the efforts were
transparent and didn't fool Bedrich. Why is it, he wondered,
that every time my life has some form of structure, something
else causes it to founder? Always, always there is opposition
of some kind or another to fight, to try to knock down, to try
to sweep aside.

He sat alongside Katerina one day and painted for her the
good life they would have in Göteborg. He told her of the
money to be made (and spent) from teaching, the fulfilment he
himself could obtain from doing work he loved doing and
which was appreciated, the warmth of friendships, what a
splendid fellow Capek was. But he stopped half-way through
when he saw the lack of interest on her face, the insipid look
that passed for a smile, and he stamped out of the room. He
went straight to his own room and paced up and down the
floor. When he heard the knocking on his door he didn't
bother to open it, but said, brusquely, "What is it?"

"Bedrich, can I speak to you? It's Alzbeta."

He let her in and said, "Well?"

"I've been watching you and Katerina," she said. "I'd like to try and help. Would you allow me to?"

He shrugged. "What could you do? Work a miracle?"

"I'd like to come with you," she replied quietly.

"To Göteborg?"

"Oh, I know it would be an extra expense for you, but I'm worried about Katerina, and worried for you, Bedrich. I think that if you'd permit me to come along I could help. I'd look after Katerina—she needs a good deal of looking after. You wouldn't have to worry so much." She dropped her eyes, and almost apologetically added, "I know I've never talked a lot about your music, but I admire it tremendously, and I know you should have a free mind to concentrate on it."

He gazed into that shy face whose mouth had surprised him with the unexpected things just spoken. "I don't know how to put it, other than to say thank you, thank you very much indeed, Alzbeta."

They left Prague on September 3rd.

"We'll take the journey quietly, my dear," he said to Katerina. "We'll stop at Dresden for a day or two so that you can rest. And perhaps I'll go and see Franz Liszt at Weimar." But even the trip between Prague and Dresden took a lot out of Katerina, and when he saw her tense, exhausted condition he decided that they would put up at the town's most luxurious hotel. Katerina needed petting, and he gave it to her.

At the end of the first day she said, "Are you not going to see Franz?"

"Well, I would like to go, but it wouldn't be fair to leave you feeling unwell."

"Come here," she said. "Bend down. Now, listen, you know how much Franz means to you—"

"Not as much as you, my love."

"In a different way."

"You know I love you."

"I know you do. But you can prove it by doing what I ask."

"I'll do anything you ask me."

"Very well, go and see Franz."

"Are you sure?"

"Yes, quite sure."

He stood up after kissing her cheek lightly.

"I shan't be away more than a day or two, and you'll be in my thoughts all the time."

Katerina did indeed remain in his thoughts during the journey to Weimar, but on the outskirts of the town he began to think of other things, and all of them had to do with music and the man he was on his way to meet. He was let into Liszt's house by a servant, and as they walked through the hall he heard the unmistakable sound of Liszt himself at the piano. Cascades of notes bounced off the walls, and he motioned the servant away as soon as they reached the open door to the music-room. He leant against it and drank the sounds in, watching the profile of the great maestro, flowing hair flying as the head tossed, nose bent almost to the keyboard during the softer passages, steely fingers racing with blurring speed as they stabbed out the notes on the showier parts.

When it was all over, Bedrich coughed lightly and said, "Franz."

There was one moment of uncertainty with the profiled head arrested in frozen movement like a frightened animal, and then Liszt had turned and in one movement was bounding across the room shouting, "Bedrich! My dear friend, how good to see you!" The embrace was long and warm. Then Liszt stood back and said, "Come over here and sit down and let me look at you." His eyes darted all over Bedrich before he said, "Now, tell me, how are you? How is your music?" He plied Bedrich with questions covering everything that had happened since their last meeting. He wanted all explained, wanted all the details, went back over happenings he hadn't understood.

Finally it was Bedrich's turn, and in that elegant room he made the great man tell of the developments at Weimar, the comings and goings of composers, the espousal of new causes, the fights, the controversies and triumphs over the works of Goethe and Schiller, the tempests of opinions over the works of Wagner, Liszt's own experiments with the symphonic poem. As he warmed to the subject Liszt moved over to the piano and gave examples of what he was talking about, and by brilliant talk and illustrations captured Bedrich's imagination.

It was four days before he arrived back in Dresden, and when he did turn up Alzbeta and Katerina saw a man revitalized and impatient to begin work again.

He couldn't get to Göteborg soon enough. "I've got to get back quickly," he told his wife. "I must make a start. I feel at the moment I could conquer the whole world—that's what that visit to Weimar has done for me. But first I must conquer Göteborg."

But he had forgotten that he possessed a formidable shyness which would need conquering. Consequently it was April 1858 before he presented his first big surprise to the Göteborg musical public; on the night of the 15th an astonished, bewildered audience heard the great overture to Wagner's *Tannhäuser*. They were still in a state of numbness when two pianos were pushed on to the stage, and two pairs of students from Bedrich's new academy came and sat at them to play Liszt's Scherzo.

This was puzzling, new, not easily assimilable music, undershot with an excitement difficult to define; the morning paper expressed something of the general reaction when it said:

> The new Germany of music was represented strongly, and, without daring at this stage to try to analyse it, we feel that it could well be that this kind of music will secure some strong supporters from among us. . . . If the aim of musical art is to write something of the utmost difficulty to perform and of great complication when it comes to understanding, then we are forced to admit the truth of the statements made by the supporters of the new trend—that such music as we heard last night has never before been written.

Göteborg was captivated by Smetana's gentleness, but was now also slightly perplexed by the singleminded way he drove on with the new experimental music. Even Josef Capek, who followed Bedrich with the docility of a house pet, had to be convinced that the new direction was a good and right one.

Bedrich was living on an emotional tightrope, pushing on with ideas that were treated with some suspicion, devoured by love of Fröjda Benecke, worn out with worry over Katerina's health, guilt-ridden at the unfaithfulness of his thoughts.

One night, after a late rehearsal for a concert, he sat at the piano long after everyone else had left. It was a still, May night and he was in nostalgic mood, letting his fingers roam over the keyboard, softly playing. Presently he became aware of footsteps approaching him. The hall was in darkness apart from the pool of light around the piano. The footsteps, hardly a man's—a child's, perhaps?—seemed to be coming from a long way off.

He continued playing, caressing sentimental lines of melody from the piano, and wondered who could be approaching him. Leaning his head away from the piano, he asked. "Who is it? Who's there?"

There was no answer.

He asked again, but still no reply came to him. The music was bringing a calmness to him, and he was unconcerned about the unseen person in the hall with him.

At the same moment as his name was spoken he smelt the perfume, and there, on the edge of the pool of light, stood Fröjda Benecke.

Forgetting himself for once, he ran to her, and before he knew what he was doing he was crushing her lips hard against her teeth. She didn't resist. Indeed, she folded into the curves of his body and stayed passively that way until he came to his senses and released her.

Eyes wide with alarm, he stood back from her and said, or rather blurted, "I'm sorry."

"There's no need to be," she said.

"But what I did was wrong. I had no right to."

"And I had no right to come here."

"Why did you come?"

What was she to answer? The whole truth? Or only part of it? The word Katerina came to her. Then the word Zofie. Only part of the truth then.

"I came to try to offer you some comfort," she said. "I came on a blind impulse. I came here to tell you that I know you are suffering, and that I love you, and that I'm sure that as long as I live I shall love you."

He moved towards her, but she made a tiny, definite gesture of restraint which halted him. "No, don't come to me again, because I don't know if I could stop myself if you touched me."

"Then why do you tell me such things?"

"Because they are true."

"And yet you won't—"

"Bedrich, listen, try to understand what I'm going to say to you. I was wrong to have come here, but in some strange way I felt that if I could tell you that I loved you, even though we can never—no, *must* never—dream of ... I don't have to say it, you know what I mean. Don't you?"

The heat was gone from him, and he felt ashamed. "I know," he said.

"What I am trying to say is that I felt the need to tell you, so that you should know that two women love you for yourself. In your moments of despair the knowledge may help you. That's all I wanted to do. I know the torture you've been through—I've been through it too. I love my husband and my children, and I'm no stranger to guilt. But I've come to terms with the fact that though I love you, I love my husband no less."

He was standing by the piano, and he tinkered idly with the top C note. Without looking at Fröjda Benecke he said, "What you've told me has made me both sad and happy. It must have taken courage to come here."

"Of a sort, I suppose."

"It's not been wasted. Will you accept my thanks?"

"I have one other thing to say."

"Yes?"

"I'd like to meet your wife."

He glanced at her to make sure she was serious. "Why?" he asked.

"I don't know why. I would just like to."

"You won't say anything to her that might hurt her?"

The look of incredulity on Fröjda's face pierced him, and he apologized instantly.

Over the following weeks Fröjda became a frequent visitor to the Smetana home, and never, by word or action, did she betray her real feelings for Bedrich. What she did do was to reawaken in the sick Katerina the awareness of what a unique man she had married, and the relationship between herself and Katerina became one of deep friendship and mutual concern about the happiness of the man who had drawn them together.

The confrontation in the deserted concert hall helped Bedrich too, because from that point on he was able to control his passion for Fröjda. He still loved her, but the yearning was now stilled. She could never be his, but part of her affections would be his alone for always. His guilt too left him. It was assuaged by Fröjda's friendship with Katerina, leavened by her frequent presence in his home, made innocent by something akin to an understanding on the part of Katerina. He would never fully understand the working of the female mind.

After several months of strenuous work Bedrich took the family away from Göteborg for a summer holiday at the resort of Särö. At first he spent much of his time with Zofie, taking her round the sights and going on trips with her. He played games with her, bought her sweets, joined in her fun, told her stories that captivated her.

Katerina had no energy to do anything or go anywhere. The pains in her chest were worsening, and her skin had taken on a pallor. Her lips were thin and blue, and the skin on her nose shrunk until the bone showed through it.

Bedrich couldn't look at her without becoming upset, and when he became upset she became deeply distressed. So for her sake as well as his own he bottled up his feelings, immersed himself in looking after Zofie, and in the late hours of night committed some of his anguish to papers in letters which he rarely sent. Only Proksch, still alive in Prague, always highly esteemed as musician and friend by Bedrich, heard of Bedrich's thoughts about returning home.

Bedrich had opened up his heart in a letter to his old teacher, telling him that the climate in Sweden was adversely affecting Katerina's hopes of recovery, and that he thought he should return home. He felt better once he had communicated the things that were troubling him. No doubt Proksch would send an answer, perhaps even a confirmation that to return to Prague would be the wisest decision.

With the punishing schedule of academy work lifted from him, he let his thoughts stray again to his ambition to compose a symphonic poem based on *Richard III*. Before writing anything down on paper he spent several nights just recalling everything he knew and felt about Shakespeare's king. Once he had it crystallized in his mind it would be easier to tackle.

He decided to try the composition in a style that would owe nothing to any of the romantic composers, to experiment, to let his imagination run wild. He would try to express the king's character in music. And he would make something of the ferocious dream Richard had had before the battle. He would try to show too that Richard was a human being who longed for love, but was destined not to have it. As the shape of this strange being emerged, a man beset by wickedness and haunted by the ghosts of the people he'd murdered, Smetana himself became a man yet again caught in a fever of excitement and ambition, restless to get on with the task that lay ahead. When he finally felt the moment was ripe to start he flung himself at the work at a pace and with a willingness that cut him off from all contact with the people around him.

The night hours paled into morning, and he kept at it. He snatched sleep as though angry at having to waste the time doing nothing creative. He barely replied to questions, ignored Zofie, paid scant heed to Katerina, whipped his flagging body and spirits until the early morning of July 17th, when he dropped his pen, pushed the last page from him, and slumped in exhaustion on the table.

I wrote it with happiness and love and with all my strength, he told Liszt in a letter, *and more than what I've done with it I could not at present accomplish.*

But if the effort had temporarily exhausted him it had but whetted his appetite for more work of a similar nature. He was no sooner over his tiredness than he was mentally sketching out the shape of his next composition, which would be based on Schiller's *Wallenstein's Camp*.

He had never been inside a military camp in his life, but had read every line of Schiller's work and was familiar with the descriptions. And the dream he'd had had been of such start-ling clarity that the details remained in his head for days.

As soon as they returned from Särö he began work on the new composition, writing down ideas which he wanted to in-corporate in it. He had decided to use *Wallenstein's Camp* only as a general background. There was much of his own imagination he wished to utilize. And the fact that he was far from Bohemia, and filled with an exile's yearnings, heightened his sense of atmosphere.

So from the distillation of his thoughts came the picture of soldiers gathered together, noisy, irreverent, tired from long hours on the march. The Capuchin priest was the clearest single character he saw, and he identified with this man of God who was trying so hard to get the unruly soldiers to raise their thoughts to finer things.

He painted in the distractions, the laughter, the dancing flute that tempted them to dance rather than listen to words of the deity and things spiritual. He felt for the priest who had to combat the earthly pleasures of drink and talk of women. He knew what mockery meant, and what it could do to a man.

He remembered nights full of loneliness when far-off foot-steps had sounded in the dark—and these footsteps he trans-lated into the tramp of sentries. He made his music become soft and quiet to represent the growing silence of the sleeping camp, built it up again as the soldiers of his dream stirred with the clangour of a new day, more marches, a new expedition. But above all they were Czech soldiers, his own people.

He finished the score on January 4th, 1859. Years later he would say of the work, "I endeavoured to create a national character in my music. I tried that with all my being."

But in that January Katerina's health had deteriorated to such a degree that he feared she was about to die, and in his panic to let her see Bohemia once more before her life ended he made hurried preparations to leave.

He still had Proksch's reply to his letter in his bureau, and had read it through many times. *I would strongly advise you against returning to Prague,* the old man had written. *I feel for you in your concern over your dear Katerina's health, but there must be some place where the climate would be kinder than it is in Sweden. Here in Prague you would lose all the freedom that has enabled you to do such good work. Everything is as it was when you left. A few powerful, talentless men are holding sway, and anyone who wants anything has to humiliate himself and beg for small favours. It has become a privilege to beg. The alternative is to starve. Please consider carefully before deciding to come back.*

But that had been written in August, and since then the winter had taken its toll. He wrote to Katerina's mother, and with a heavy heart told her: *Our earlier fears for Katerina's health have, unfortunately, been confirmed. Not only has her condition not improved, but it has seriously worsened.... The greatest guilt is mine, because it was I who moved her here to a foreign country. I came here in the first place in search of financial security, and now it looks as if I have lost everything. It is my wish to leave Göteborg for ever, and I am clinging to the hope that a return to Prague will have a favourable effect on Katerina's health.*

He dreaded what he would find in Prague, but Katerina's condition overrode every other consideration.

Mrs Kolar came to Sweden to help, and on March 17th Bedrich gave his farewell performance. On the day before the concert the Göteborg paper noted:

> Tomorrow night will see the farewell concert of Mr Bedrich Smetana, and it will be with deep regret that the people of our city, who have benefited so much from his talent as a teacher and as a composer, will see him go.

A performance of Handel's *Messiah* was cheered to the echo, and, to a storm of hand-clapping, Bedrich was called to take several bows and be the recipient of adulatory speeches as well as a silver conductor's baton presented by his students.

On the 9th of the next month he began the journey home.
Several times Katerina lapsed into unconsciousness, and the small group stood grim-faced around her, her mother distraught and at the same time fighting determinedly for her

daughter's life, Bedrich praying silently, Alzbeta apparently paralysed with shock.

Whenever Katerina's eyes flickered open, they all knelt by her and tried to talk her into holding on. But Katerina was already too far gone, and words meant little to her. She had no will to live. The pain in her chest was excruciating, and she waited for the next bout of unconsciousness to take her beyond the barriers of pain.

They were a day's journey from Dresden when she whispered Bedrich's name. He bent down to her, holding her thin, small hand tenderly. "Where am I?" she asked hoarsely.

"Nearly home," he said.

"Are we in Bohemia?"

He looked at Katerina's mother, who shook her head. "No," he said, "not yet. But it won't be long now. Tomorrow we shall be in Dresden."

She sighed deeply. "Dresden. That's good. I like Dresden. I was happy there when we stopped on our way to Göteborg. Do you remember?"

He couldn't trust himself to talk.

"You do remember, don't you, Bedrich?" she asked again.

"Yes, I remember, Katerina."

Her eyes closed, and she winced as a spasm of pain shot through her. Presently she opened her eyes again and spoke. "It was when you went to see Franz Liszt, and you were happy when you came back, and seeing you so happy made me feel fine."

The effort of talking was making her weak, and Bedrich pressed lightly on her hand and said, "Try to rest."

She smiled. "I would like to see Dresden just once more," she said.

"Of course you'll see Dresden," he said. "You'll see it many times."

He felt rather than saw the movement behind him, and he glanced round in time to see Katerina's mother going to a corner where she pressed a handkerchief to her mouth to smother the sounds of crying.

"Bedrich." It was Katerina. "Bedrich, if I"—she took a grip

on herself before saying the word—"if I die, there is one thing I want you to promise me you'll do—"

"Sss-ssh! my love, you mustn't talk of dying. You're not going to die."

Talking was becoming more of an effort every second, and Katerina's face showed a look of impatience. "I want you to promise one thing."

"I'll promise you anything in the world."

"If I die I want to be buried in Bohemia, next to my darling little Bedriska. Do you promise?"

She never heard his reply. The waves of blackness overcame her, and she drifted off into oblivion. He let go of her hand and tucked the blanket up close to her chin to keep her warm.

He stayed with her all through the night. She recovered consciousness three times, but didn't speak. Just before dawn she spoke to him again. Her face was contorted with pain, and she opened her eyes and said, "Hold me to you, Bedrich, hold me, hold me!"

He cradled her in his arms, felt her body stiffening spasmodically. He had taken out his pocket-watch, afraid that it would stick into her side where she lay against him. The watch, a solid-gold one presented to him before he left Göteborg, was lying face upwards. He looked out of the window of the compartment and saw some of the outlines of the approaching town. Katerina sensed him looking away from her, and she asked, "Where are we now?"

"Coming into Dresden," he whispered.

Her eyes opened wide and she said, in a stronger voice than she had been able to use since they left Sweden, "You do remember how very happy we both were here? I feel happy now again...I think...I think I'd like to stay here."

She closed her eyes then, and in a few seconds her head dropped sideways and she remained very still.

He called for Alzbeta and her mother, and they took Katerina's body from his arms and laid it down and pulled the sheet up over the face.

He put the watch back into his pocket slowly and very deliberately. The time it showed was seven minutes past five. The date was April 19th, 1859.

He opened his attaché-case and took out his diary.

It is all over, he wrote. *Katerina, my beloved wife, died this morning at five o'clock, quiet and happy. Be with the angels, my darling, be with God.*

After the last shovelful of soil had been placed on the grave at Olsany, on the outskirts of Prague, he stood by himself, untouchable. He was deaf to the words of sympathy that were spoken to him by friends, by Proksch, old and ailing, by the students who had come to share his grief, by the families of both sides. An arm was placed about his shoulders, and almost angrily he shrugged it off. His sisters came and tried to lead him away. He was immovable.

In the end he spoke. In a dead voice he said, "Leave me alone."

Reluctantly they drifted from him, but stayed in little clusters by the gate of the graveyard. They waited, looking anxiously in his direction, but he never moved, never once gave any sign that he was aware of their presence.

Albina, the sister he adored, walked slowly across the grass to him, stood a few feet off, and then approached him and said, "Bedrich."

He gave no sign of having heard her.

"Come," she said gently.

He shook his head, and his hand moved in a small gesture to her to go away. She went back to the people by the gate, and they whispered together and then moved out into the road, where they climbed into the carriages and drove off, leaving one carriage behind for Bedrich.

He stood there until it began to get dark and a little rain fell. It beaded on his bared head, and he fell to his knees and hugged the wet mound of brown earth, the earth that covered Katerina and his children.

Muddied, he finally got to his feet, went out to the road-way, looked back once, and then, ignoring the waiting carriage, walked into the murk of the coming night.

CHAPTER

[16]

JUNE WAS ONLY TWO DAYS OLD when Franz Liszt himself came to the door of his home in Weimar to welcome his friend whom tragedy seemed to be stalking. He led Bedrich inside, and was the first person who managed to get him to talk of the events that had precipitated him into his present state.

Liszt was a good and sympathetic listener, full of patience and understanding. It was a calm and consoled Bedrich who slept soundly that night for the first time in nearly two months.

The following morning Liszt didn't refer at all to yesterday's sorrow, but took Bedrich to the music-room immediately after breakfast and asked him if he had brought the score of *Richard III* with him as requested. When Bedrich produced the piano transcription of the symphonic poem Liszt asked if, as a special favour, he would play it. Bedrich was hesitant, but Liszt insisted. Unable to refuse his friend, Bedrich played.

At the last note Liszt broke into clapping and came across the room to Bedrich and patted him on the back.

"Powerful and moving—simply magnificent," he said. "The work of a genius. I said it of you before. I repeat it—you *are* a genius. And in case you think I am saying it to boost your spirits, I am *not*. Go over and sit where I was sitting. I want to play something for you."

When Bedrich was settled in the chair Liszt placed some music sheets on the piano. "This is something an unknown young musician from Prague sent me nine years ago."

And what he played was what Bedrich himself had sent to the great man when, in the depths of depression, he had sent off a plea for money!

"You see," Liszt said, "there was the beginning of genius, and, my God, how it has flowered!"

Bedrich was sitting with his eyes averted from Liszt's face, and the next thing he knew was that Franz was sitting beside him.

"Why do you look so downcast now, my friend?" Liszt asked.

Bedrich smiled. "No, I'm not downcast, Franz, I'm embarrassed."

"It's time you outgrew your embarrassment! Your modesty is charming, but we musicians have to appear assured, confident. We must sound our own trumpets long before anyone will begin to sound them for us. I'll tell you something—as soon as I first played that music you sent me from Prague I had a feeling in here"—he touched his heart—"that the man who wrote it was born to become one of the world's greatest composers."

Three nights later Liszt held a special house-concert in honour of Bedrich's visit, and among the guests were the famous conductor von Bülow and Fräulein Genes (widely known as a great music sponsor and powerful ally). Of the many Smetana compositions played, it was the Piano Trio in G minor which won the most applause, and at the end of it Liszt embraced Bedrich, then asked everyone to lift their glasses to toast the guest of honour.

"Von Bülow, what was it about the trio that made you applaud?" Liszt asked abruptly.

The answer came back promptly, "Its greatness."

Liszt inclined his head towards Bedrich. The 'I-told-you-so' intention was clear.

Someone said, "Speech! Speech!"

Bedrich's face above his beard was beet-red.

"Speech! Speech! Speech!" the others chorused.

He shuffled his feet and coughed, and, when they kept up the chorus of demands, at last held up his hand and, looking at the floor, said, "You are too kind . . ."

N

"Nonsense!" they shouted.

"Yes, you are...I...I have only one regret..." He swallowed. "I wish my wife could have been here—she loved the trio."

A silence enveloped them all, and then Princess Wittgenstein detached herself and came to his side. "You loved your wife," she said, "we all know that. But, Bedrich, you can *prove* your love by fighting hard to overcome your grief and looking for fresh happiness. It is what she would have wanted."

"It is not easy," he said. "Not when you have loved as I have loved."

When a respectable pause had elapsed Liszt asked if Bedrich intended returning to Göteborg. He said he didn't know. He might have to, to take up teaching again. "But I feel that my real place is in Prague. It's where I belong, and it is where I want to live and work."

"Teaching?" It was von Bülow.

"It is not what I would want to do, maestro," Bedrich answered. "But I might have to do it."

"Would you mind telling me what your main ambition is?"

"I have two ambitions. To instil into my countrymen an understanding of the majesty and beauty of music."

"And?"

"And to compose something for my people which would be truly Czech, truly great, something they could call their very own and be proud of."

"Well said," von Bülow commented. "I have little doubt but that you will achieve both. By the way, Franz has praised your *Richard III* and *Wallenstein's Camp* so highly that I am impatient to hear them."

Bedrich cast a grateful look at Liszt and said to von Bülow, "I tried to follow my friend in what I did."

"He is talking rubbish!" Liszt retorted. "They are genuine Smetana and owe nothing to me. And further, let me say that if you were ever to draw anything from what little I have to offer, you would certainly not *follow* me, my friend, you would walk *beside* or *ahead* of me."

Of all the things that had been spoken about and said during the five days at Liszt's home in Weimar, that which had the deepest impact on Bedrich was what Princess Wittgenstein had said about looking for new happiness in life. He began to entertain her advice with increasing belief that what she had advised was right.

Besides, little Zofie was now without a mother, and the child was clearly in need of maternal affection and care. As a man he could only provide one part of the love that a growing girl demanded. He didn't want to lose her, wouldn't dream of letting her go to Katerina's mother, or to the members of his own family, all of whom offered and would have been delighted to look after her and bring her up. Neither did he want her personality to be moulded by a nurse-housekeeper. He wanted her to be a reflection of himself, not of some stranger.

And again, there was the consideration that, if he were to have any hopes at all of once more getting down to serious composition, he would have to have a clear mind and heart and unlimited time to spend at his piano and desk. He would have none of these if he also had to try to give as much attention to the child as he would feel inclined.

It was with these thoughts pressing him that he visited his brother and sister-in-law in Chlomky, and afterwards went with them on holiday to Lamberk. There he met again Barbora Ferdinand, who was the sister of his brother's wife. The last time he had seen her she had been a young slip of a child. Now she was a buxom, attractive young woman of nineteen who had a fine coloratura singing voice, a talent for verse-writing, and was a very promising amateur artist who had received painting-lessons from Antonin Waldhauser.

Playing chess with her one evening, Bedrich became aware of her attractiveness and her sense of humour. Her laughter reminded him strongly of Katerina's, and the longer he remained in her company, the more attracted to her he became. At first his thoughts were mainly concerned with the idea that perhaps here was the person who would make an ideal mother for Zofie. He couldn't speak of such things to her though, for she was far younger than he and it would be difficult to broach the matter. She might well reject him, or laugh at him.

He didn't feel he could cope with either reaction, so he endeavoured to put the thoughts out of his head.

He concentrated on staying out of Barbora's company, took Zofie for walks, showed her the various flowers whose names he knew, told her folk-tales, related incidents to her from his own childhood, described the games he had played as a boy. But there was always something missing; there was an indefinable but undeniable sadness about his little girl. She missed her mother, and all Papa's efforts couldn't make up for the loss.

And so he began to think again about Barbora. He allowed himself to be thrown into her company again, asked her if he could call her by the pet name of Betty that everyone else used, admired her paintings, listened to and praised her verses, accompanied her at the piano when she sang, and fell deeper and deeper into the spell she cast on him.

She looked upon him as a chivalrous man, attractive in a quaint way, but definitely 'old' in comparison with herself. She was surprised at the increasing amount of attention he paid her, tried to shy off when he became positively ardent.

Her sister and brother-in-law, Karel, saw what was going on, talked among themselves, agreed it might be a good thing if the pair considered matrimony ("it would be so good for Zofie"), and fostered the relationship as only solicitous members of a family know how.

When Bedrich and Betty became engaged on September 7th, 1859, it was as much the doing of Karel and his wife as as any natural development of an emotional situation.

Although a little happier now, he knew he could not marry Betty in his present circumstances. As Proksch had told him by letter, nothing very much had changed in Bohemia, which meant that he would find it next to impossible to earn a living. And he could not expect the girl to become his wife without being able to offer her a life free of anxiety. He would never be able to do that if he remained in Prague. So, though he had left Göteborg intending never to return, September 16th saw him leaving once again for the Swedish city.

Capek being engaged elsewhere when he arrived, it was young Jan Rys, a devoted follower and helper of the Czech musician, who met him at the dockside.

Honzik, as Bedrich called him, saw the change in his teacher and was disturbed. The eyes were incredibly sad, there was no laugh in the voice, lines of sorrow were indelibly drawn down and across the face, and the mouth had tightened perceptibly. Honzik was too young to know much about tact, and he immediately offered his condolences over the bereavement. As soon as he saw what effect his sympathy had, the distress the newly revived memories brought, he regretted having spoken. They travelled the remainder of the journey to Bedrich's home in silence, and Honzik stood nervously by when they entered the grave-silent rooms, dark with the curtains drawn, dead with the furniture covered with drapes.

"The heavy atmosphere hit us," Honzik remembered later. "The pianos were covered with white sheets, the carpets rolled up. Smetana stood there, almost motionless, and no word passed between us. Then slowly he moved about the rooms, touching things, looking about him. Everywhere he went, everything he touched, brought back memories, and he was moved, very moved. It seemed to me that only with the greatest difficulty was he managing to hold back his tears."

But life had to go on. Mourning for the past would earn no money. The old threads had to be picked up. So he steeled himself to start afresh. He shut his ears to the sympathy he was offered, but accepted it with the right words of gratitude, and on October 1st he started giving music-lessons again.

The music circles welcomed him back with open arms, and invitations poured in on him to attend musical evenings and to perform. The Philharmonic Society pleaded with him to conduct a series of concerts they were about to embark on, and he was thankful for the chance to sink himself in work. But one person out of whose way he deliberately kept was Fröjda Benecke. It wasn't that he didn't want to meet her, but he distrusted himself as to how he would behave with her. Being back in Göteborg awakened his old feelings for her, and every day that he walked in the streets the old longing for her coursed through him.

She came to his home one evening, and no sooner did he set eyes on her than emotional turmoil gripped him. He loved her more than ever, and despite the fact that he was engaged to

Betty, the gap left in his life by the death of Katerina cried out to be filled by this woman. And though he knew in his heart it was the wrong thing to do, he told her in full.

Her face was a mask of tenderness and regret as she listened to him, and she did not once interrupt him. She waited until he had finished and was standing before her, mute, helpless, confused, weak with love and the craving he had talked of. Then she sat down and took both his hands in hers and drew him on to the couch beside her.

"My poor Bedrich," she began. "What am I to say?"

He had no answer.

"I can't do what you want me to do," she went on. "I can't marry you. In one way I would love to say yes. But in another ... " She tried to get her thoughts into order so that she could put it without hurting him. She didn't want him to suffer. She loved him. She had told him so before. "You must try to understand that our ways were marked out for us before we ever met, my dear. No matter what our hearts tell us we should do, we can't."

The look in his eyes reminded her of the dumb pleading of animals wanting to be put out of their misery.

"I understand how you feel," she said. "I know it only too well. I know it perhaps far better than you think. But there is nothing we can do. I have my husband. I am married to him. He loves me very much, and I love him, as I love you. But marriage is not a thing to be broken. And you—you have your daughter Zofie, and she needs a mother, Bedrich."

"I know," he said miserably. "I was hoping it could be you."

She shook her head. "No," she said, "it can never be me."

"Never?" he said.

"Never."

He leant forward and put his head against her shoulder. She let it rest there for a moment, then softly but firmly pushed it away and said, "You must marry Betty."

He looked at her, then dropped his eyes and bit at his lower lip.

"We can still go on feeling our love for each other," she said. "I'll never relinquish that. You'll never be far from my thoughts."

"We can still see each other?"

"Of course. But I think it would be better if we tried as often as possible to make sure it is in the company of others."

"Why?"

"You must know why. It would be courting disaster if we spent too much time alone."

"I understand," he said. "I understand, even if it is hard to accept."

"But you *must* accept it, Bedrich. There is no other way." When she saw how downcast he was she added, "But remember, I am always at hand if you need help of any sort."

The fact that Fröjda's uncle, a man named Nissen, was a respected music-teacher in Göteborg made it easier for the couple to see each other frequently, and though the meetings were invariably public affairs, Bedrich nevertheless drew great strength and inspiration from them. Just to see Fröjda Benecke, to gaze upon her face, and to know that beneath the cool exterior there was a burning love and admiration gave him the strength to hold on to normality when otherwise he might have let go.

But the difference in the man himself, the intense sobriety of expression and behaviour which Honzik had noticed on the very first day of his arrival back from Bohemia, were quickly noted by the rest of Göteborg's music-lovers. Magnus talked to Capek about it; Capek discussed it with Nissen; Nissen spoke of it to his niece Fröjda Benecke, and she had to remain silent because so much of it was bound up with herself.

The members of the various societies with which Bedrich was connected held official and unofficial meetings to express their concern and to seek ways of brightening the gloom of this man they loved. They invited him to their homes, held soirées in his honour, insisted that he attend balls. They watched anxiously to see if there were any signs that he was emerging from his personal darkness, but mostly they watched in vain. There were certain boundaries beyond which propriety would not let them venture, and when he would not divulge the inner thoughts that were keeping him chained, they left him alone.

He didn't tell them of the permanent sensation of loneliness that accompanied him in all his waking hours, the loneliness that had to do with home-sickness, death, yearning, Katerina, Zofie, Betty, Prague, Bohemia's rivers and fields and woods—and Fröjda Benecke.

Where he had once felt himself to be a part of Göteborg, he now felt like a stranger.

He remembered the way he had regained his balance through composition after Bedriska's death, and he made the decision to try the same method again. There was this vague idea he had had about a scene from *Macbeth*, the disturbing influence of the witches' appearance; there was also the memory of Proksch sitting for hours telling him how overwhelming emotional thoughts could be channelled into musical compositions.

The problem, as always, was where to begin. He roamed about the empty apartment, with its pictures and furniture, all the time reminding him of Katerina, and the running, laughing, inquisitive Zofie. Eventually he sat down, and as he had done with the trio, he translated his loneliness and heartbreak into musical terms and wrote them down without restraint. It was his own confession of sadness, created for no other reason than to help him overcome a strain that was threatening to drive him insane. And when he had finished it he wrapped it up carefully and put it away. The effort had been enormous, and he was drained out; but within twenty-four hours he felt the benefit.

The change in him was fantastic, and the societies held more official and unofficial meetings to express their relief that "Mr Smetana is again the dear Mr Smetana he was before the tragedy of his wife's death struck him down."

He approached his concerts with fresh vigour, played with verve as well as technical brilliance, won glowing praise from Press and public alike. Instead of the stilted letters he had been writing to Betty, he sent off long, newsy screeds which were interspersed with declarations of his love for her, and his impatience over the delay in their marriage. He wrote a polka for her which he entitled *Bettina Polka*, and sent it off, filled with delight at this expression of his affection.

It is simple in structure and form, he wrote, *and it can be played easily, and danced to. Of course, whether or not you will like it I don't know. Only you can answer that for me.*

She did answer, and what she wrote wounded him, because there was something distinctly lukewarm about her acceptance. There was a petulance in the manner in which she complained that the piece was by no means as simple as he had made out.

He swallowed his disappointment. Instead of becoming angry and bellowing his rage at her ungraciousness (which is what his father, old Frantisek, would have done), he accepted the rebuff humbly, and in his answering letter wrote: *I am sorry that you didn't much like your* Bettina Polka, *but don't worry, I shall write you something more to your liking later on. Just cross your name off the score, as I should not want your name to be connected with something you do not like.*

From time to time he received letters from Proksch and a few other friends who kept him in touch with what was happening in Prague. Never far from the surface of his mind was the yearning to return there to work. It was becoming a dream, something far off in the future, and yet likely to happen at any time if only the political and artistic climate would change.

The first ray of real hope came in a letter he received from one of his former pupils, Ludevit Prochazka, who, in March 1860, wrote to Bedrich and told him he was hoping to publish a collection of vocal quartets and wondered if Bedrich would be interested in writing one.

But the aspect of the letter that hit Bedrich most forcibly was that it was written in the *Czech* language.

What a letter written in Czech meant to Bedrich was that in Prague the nationalistic pride must have begun to grow once more. In its growth lay his own hopes of going home. So, though he had not written in Czech for many years, he sat down in his flat to summon his sketchy knowledge of grammar so that he could reply to Ludevit Prochazka in his native language.

Please forgive all my mistakes of grammar and syntax, he begged Prochazka. *You will understand that since I was a boy and went to school I have become accustomed to using the German language in speech as well as in writing. But surely I do not have to repeat to you what I have often told you in the past—that I am a Czech in body and soul. The glory that is our people's birthright is something I am most proud of, and of which I shall always attempt to be worthy. That is why I am now attempting to write to you in your own tongue, and why this letter, full of mistakes though it may be, will be sent to you in its present form. My homeland means the world to me...."*

He then went on to accept the invitation to write the quartet.

He was hesitant, however, to begin the composition in Sweden. He wanted to work on it in the proper surroundings, and that meant at home in Bohemia. So he postponed starting until he went to Bohemia for his summer holidays in 1860.

At his brother's home in June he got down to work on the composition. He chose as text words by the Ukrainian poet Ambrosius Metlynsky.

He also made another choice—the date on which he and Betty would be married. It was to be July 10th.

Jan Rys travelled from Sweden to be in Obristvi on the great day, and he described the transformation that took place in in his beloved mentor.

"He radiated happiness and good humour, and was so excited by the happenings of the day that he ran hither and thither, never still for an instant, laughing and joking, asking people if they were enjoying themselves, at times giggling like a schoolboy. Even when he danced he was in this excited condition, and I, who had seen him dance with considerable grace of movement at many of the great balls in Göteborg, was astounded by the energy and speed, and comparative *lack* of grace, he demonstrated. It was as if he wanted to be everywhere in the room at once, and in the end the floor was cleared for him and everyone stood around the edges applauding and laughing. It was the happiest I had ever seen him."

The happiness was somewhat lessened by Betty's reluctance to leave Bohemia. She finally agreed to go to Göteborg only on condition that if she didn't like the place they would return to Bohemia. He promised, though he knew full well that unless the changes that were taking place at home accelerated rapidly, he would still be unable to make ends meet in Prague.

He wrote in his diary: *It is really sad that I am forced to earn my living so far away from my homeland, the homeland that I love so dearly and where I want very much to live. But pray God I won't have to stay away too long this time. Live in blessings, my fatherland! Your soil is sacred to me. I want to rest my head in your lap. You have given me many riches, but above all, you have given me Katerina, and now Betty, both children of my own dear country.*

The earlier doubts he had had about how Zofie would take to Betty had long since been proved groundless. Their warm relationship grew with every passing day and, seeing it thus blossom, Bedrich himself was content.

In Göteborg he introduced his new wife to the Magnuses, the Nissens, the Beneckes, Capek, all the people in the musical societies, and he was flattered by the remarks he overheard about her beauty and behaviour.

Fröjda Benecke, whose opinion he valued above any other, took him aside and said, "My congratulations, Bedrich, she is lovely. She is very lucky, but you must know that you too are lucky."

"Yes, I know I am," he said. "Thank you."

In Göteborg Betty saw a side of Bedrich Smetana she had never known at home. In Bohemia he had been an ambitious but struggling nobody. Certainly she had heard of the high esteem in which Liszt held him, and she was sufficiently accomplished musically to appreciate that his compositions were far above the ordinary. But she had not seen him receiving acclaim, had never seen an audience rising to its feet and shouting his name, had never heard eminent people in crowded concert halls delivering speeches in his praise, had never read newspaper accounts which were devoted entirely, and favourably, to his abilities.

Now for the first time she experienced all of this, and, because she was his wife and thus captured part of the reflected glory, she looked upon him with new awe and pride. Because she was young she found it astonishing that he could accept it all simply and with no evidence of pretension. In Göteborg he was a famous man, and she, who had been no more than an attractive but obscure girl, was now the famous wife of this famous man.

But also because she was young and immature, she was jealous. Jealous of Fröjda Benecke, jealous of the other attractive women and girls who, at parties, came to Bedrich's side and hung on his every word, looking adoringly at him, happy just to be close to him.

There were any number of little scenes in the home when she pouted and accused him of encouraging other women. At first he denied it all vehemently, but his denials only seemed to implicate him further. So, after a while, he just accepted it philosophically and hoped she would grow out of her tantrums. He didn't love her any the less for her outbursts. Indeed, it somehow made his marriage feel more secure, because he had been in the habit of wondering whether she would not grow tired of him on account of the difference in their ages. But as long as other women found him attractive, and showed it, he would still have a hold on Betty. It wasn't the ideal foundation for marriage, he knew that, but it gave him some small sense of security.

He continued to receive letters from Prague, and there were continued references in them to the plans for establishing a Czech Opera House in the capital. His friends passed on to him all the gossip they picked up in the salons and at the concerts, and his hopes rose wildly when one of them wrote that he had heard it whispered that Bedrich Smetana was to be asked to come back from Sweden to become the Opera House's first musical director.

Then came later news that first there would be built a Provisional Czech Theatre, a plan that was causing uproar among those who bitterly resented and criticized the lack of a cultural centre for Czech music and drama. He followed all the reported rows with close attention, argued about them with Betty and Capek, ranted against those in political power for their half-measures.

But, as Capek pointed out, "The fact that they are at least thinking of doing *something* concrete about giving our people even a temporary theatre indicates that events are moving in the right direction. Czech culture is bursting out of its cocoon, Bedrich."

A further sign that this was indeed happening came with the news from Prague that Count Harrach was offering a prize of six hundred sovereigns for an original Czech opera—an opera based on a theme from Czech history. It was a project that further inflamed Bedrich's ambitions. It represented a challenge, a call to him, it seemed, to do something positive about creating the great Czech work he felt sure was inside him.

As the months dragged by, his conversations with Betty concentrated more and more on the prospect of returning to Bohemia, and much as she liked the limelight in Göteborg, she too wanted to go home. She was beginning to understand his impatience, could see why he was fretting that, though he was accepted as a teacher and soloist, little recognition was forthcoming for his abilities as a composer, the field in which he longed to become a force.

I must get out of here, he wrote. *I must get out into the world and not remain buried here in Göteborg. I must strive more strongly to have my compositions published so that I can tackle new activities, more far-reaching work with my pen.*

The newspapers got wind of his intentions, and at the end of a concert review on March 11th, 1861, came the words:

It must be assumed that these concerts will not go on for much longer, because the main figure behind them, Mr Smetana, will soon be leaving our city. Musicians and music-lovers will miss him sorely. All that we shall have left will be our memories of his particular brilliance. For these we thank him.

A little over a week later he made his farewell appearance before the Göteborg public, who showered him with flowers.

After a concert tour which took him to Stockholm, Norr-köping, and Norsholm—and inaccurate reports which described him as a pupil of Alexander Dreyschock and a true product of the Prague Conservatoire—he wrote to Betty from

Stockholm, and told her: *I have managed to give my name wider publicity and some little extra weight, and by accomplishing this I have gone some way towards making a good beginning for the coming autumn. Now I am hurrying home to you, my angel, and then, with you—to Bohemia.*

This time there was no panic rush away from Göteborg. They took their time about packing, and ensured that all the furniture was carefully crated to withstand the long journey. They went round to all their friends and said their goodbyes. There were some tears shed, and many complimentary things said.

On the afternoon of May 11th, 1861, Nissen and his niece, Fröjda Benecke, Bedrich and Betty Smetana, and little Zofie walked out of the apartment for the last time. As they drove down the street on the way to the dockside Bedrich sat looking behind him, keeping the house in sight for as long as possible. He felt little regret at leaving, and yet there was an almost physical wrenching when the carriage turned the corner and the house disappeared.

On the dockside Nissen embraced Betty and Bedrich, wished them the greatest of good fortune, and stood back, his face cast in seriousness. Then it was Fröjda Benecke's turn, and she kissed Zofie, pressing some coins into her hand; then she held Betty close to her, and whispered to her, "Goodbye, my dear. Take very good care of him."

She came to Bedrich, held his hand very tightly, and then exerted an even greater pressure. She couldn't say anything. Her eyes were full, as was her heart.

"Thank you for everything," he said, and returned the squeeze she had given his hand.

They went up the gangway then, and he turned once at the top and waved.

BOOK

[3]

CHAPTER

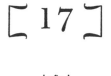

IT WAS A QUIET HOMECOMING.

On the surface his arrival back in Prague seemed to have gone unnoticed. Betty looked anxiously at him, searching his face to catch the disappointment, but she saw no evidence of it. He didn't feel any. He was glad to be back, excited in a way because he felt he was embarking on a crusade. It would be tough, he knew that, and therefore he expected to face coolness from the outset. The best way to face coolness was to meet it coolly, and he knew that the months, the years, ahead were going to call for all his strength. So the fact that he had arrived to a singular absence of welcome was a minor matter.

The only thing that annoyed him was that the paper *Dalibor* referred to him as a piano virtuoso, and made no mention of his being a composer as well. It was going to make the battle all the harder.

However, there was much to occupy his mind. Once again the craving of the people for independence of the country, and thought, and language, and art was coming out into the open. He saw a city that was alive and throbbing with hopes of marching forward.

Papers were being written and speeches being made exhorting everyone to do something about resurrecting their ambitions to have a national life and culture of their own. The prospect of their own national theatre was taken up and publicized by the poets and writers. They were passionate in their desire to make good the lethargy of uncounted years, impatient to shake off the shackles. The young provided the spur, the actors and the writers became the voices. They were intent on reawakening the hopes that had been trampled down. They wanted all Bohemia to hear and take notice.

It was a slow and painful process, but it was happening.

Bedrich set about adding his own voice to the clamour. He spoke for the art of music.

He had been back in Prague only two days when he paid a visit to Katerina's uncle, the actor-writer J. J. Kolar, and asked him to write a libretto for an opera. He wanted to start on a work to be submitted for Count Harrach's prize. But to his hurt amazement Kolar said he was sorry but he couldn't see his way to undertaking to write such a libretto. Kolar made many excuses, all of them vague. No entreaties could induce him to change his mind, and Bedrich left, a disappointed man. But whereas in other times he would have been rendered helpless and moody by such a turn of events, now he was merely angry. He would look around, find another writer.

In the meantime he had to earn money on which to live and keep a home. Inevitably he was forced back upon his abilities as a pianist, and, though he loathed the chore, he undertook to give a series of recitals at Prague Castle for the Emperor Ferdinand V.

It was after one o'clock in the morning when he returned from the first of these recitals, and Betty heard him clumping up the stairs. When he came into the darkness of the bedroom she asked, "What was it like, my dear?"

He sat on the edge of the bed and pulled off his boots before answering. "All right, I suppose," he said at last.

"Did the Emperor like the way you played?"

"He said he did."

"Was that all?"

"I'm very tired, Betty; I don't want to talk about it just now."

He slept late in the morning. After breakfast Betty said, "Now, tell me about last night."

He rubbed his hand over his eyes and said, "I'm sorry I was grumpy last night, but I was feeling very depressed."

"Why?"

"Well, he's such an old fool."

"Did he criticize?"

"Oh, no, he was full of praise, but he can't concentrate for more than five minutes at a time. I would just be in the middle of something he'd asked me to play when he'd interrupt and ask me to play something else. And you never heard such requests. His taste in music is appalling. Everything that I hate he loves. And he doesn't seem to like any of the composers I like. It was all very trying. I suppose I should be grateful that he says I'm a wonderful pianist, and that I'm getting paid well for it, but it is depressing."

Every time he went to the palace he came home late, angry and frustrated.

He could not afford to give up playing for the Emperor, and he swallowed his reluctance about performing, seeing it as at least preferable to going back to teaching.

Talk in the circles in which he moved gave him great hope that he would be appointed conductor of the new Provisional Theatre, but even before the theatre was opened the news came out that the position had been given to Jan N. Mayr. The announcement came as a great blow to Bedrich. He knew Mayr, a desiccated man who, though a good musician and organizer, was unimaginative, bitter, self-centred, and unpleasant to work with. What caused Bedrich the greatest distress was that he knew Mayr's new job was one which could have a decisive influence on the progress or otherwise of the nationalistic movement in music, and he was certain that Mayr would apply all the wrong pressure in the wong directions. This grieved Bedrich. It was galling to know that his own cause had been hindered because his reputation in Prague was centred on his work as a soloist and nothing much else.

Betty was pregnant, and there could be no diminution in concert-giving. Through June, July, and August he earned what he could at home, and after the birth of a daughter, Zdenka, he left on a concert tour.

His heart was not in public playing. He hated the travelling, the rushing about to keep to schedules, the impersonality of promoters who sought to force their wills on him, the coldness of audiences who couldn't understand him or the music he played.

A letter posted in Holland on November 21st said to Betty: *What would Nissen say if he could see me now, unhappy? I know what he would say. He would say: "And you left Göteborg where you were so much appreciated and held in such high esteem! It serves you right!"*

Thinking of Göteborg brought Fröjda Benecke back into his thoughts, and in the end he sat down and wrote to her at length about all his problems. She would understand. She had always understood.

Back in Prague, he set about establishing a reputation as a composer, and February 1862 saw him arranging his first public concert at which would be performed only works he himself had written. He hired the Zofin Hall, advertised that he would be performing *Wallenstein's Camp*, and worked himself into a fever of anticipation.

It was a bitterly cold day with an easterly wind whipping through the streets as he rehearsed the orchestra. He had a quick snack before the performance was due to start, then sat in his dressing-room, waiting.

In the box-office a bored clerk read a book. The only people who passed in were those friends of the composer who had been given free tickets. The streets were deserted. Everyone was indoors, huddling around stoves trying to keep warm. The clerk raised his head once as two street urchins ran along the pavement screaming. Then he went back to his book, pulling his scarf tighter round his neck against the cold.

At half-past seven he heard music coming from inside the auditorium, strange, unfamiliar music. He wondered why this Smetana person was bothering. There couldn't be more than a dozen in the audience, and none of them had paid.

After about ten minutes the man pushed the neat stacks of tickets away from the window and pulled down the shutter. Nobody would be coming. He was about to come out of the office and lock it up when he heard footsteps outside, and he raised the shutter. A man in a fur-collared coat was standing in the foyer, straining to hear the music. He turned to the box-office window and asked, "What's on? Who's performing?"

The box-office clerk said, "Some fellow called Smetana."

"Who's he?"

"I don't know. He came from Sweden or some place earlier in the year. You may as well go in if you want to. There's nobody there, and hardly likely to be."

The stranger stood for a few seconds longer, listening. Then he pulled his collar up and said, "I'm not surprised. I think I'll go home and go to bed."

So Bedrich played to an empty hall, and the music that had been received with rapture by Liszt and his friends at Weimar echoed among the rows of unoccupied seats.

The twelve people clapped.

Next day Bedrich Smetana spent the last of his money to pay for the hire of the Zofin Hall and the orchestra's wages. The bill came to 280 crowns.

Disappointed he certainly was, but not dispirited. This, he knew, was the rough stuff of conflict, and he had entered the conflict heart and soul. He was determined to fight with every fibre.

What was disquieting was that invidious rumours were put about that he, "as a disciple of Liszt, was attempting to infiltrate into Prague abominable imperialistic trends". Nobody said as much to his face, but he got wind of the whispers, and found himself in the dilemna of not knowing whether to deny publicly what had only been passed on at second-hand or to ignore the rumours. He elected to remain silent for the time being, but, refusing to be thwarted by the lack of response to the first concert, he set about preparing a second. This time he had to borrow money Betty had saved, and he hired the Konvikt Hall. There could be no orchestra—the available money was not enough.

His diary entry tells what took place: *The hall was full, but the net profit was a mere twenty-four crowns.*

But if the monetary reward was inconsequential, what happened in his dressing-room after the concert outstripped his wildest dreams. The tall man who came to the door and asked to speak to him plunged into praise almost as soon as they had shaken hands. Bedrich already knew Prince Rudolf Taxis by sight. He was a member of the Committee for the new Czech National Theatre, and he made his intentions clear immediately.

"I am only one voice," he said, "but I give you my solemn promise that I shall do my utmost to have you appointed musical director of the new theatre. What I heard tonight sent chills along my spine. You opened up new visions of Czech culture to me. I could never imagine Mayr accomplishing that. You can count on my support, Mr Smetana."

Bedrich left the Konvikt Hall buoyant. When he reached home the upsurge of hope inside him caused his words to spill out and trip over themselves as he related to Betty what the Prince had said.

The days that followed saw the buoyancy diminish, and the full import of Prince Rudolf Taxis' phrase "I am only one voice" was borne home to him. A lone voice on a committee was a forlorn weapon in the face of concentrated opposition, and the Superintendent of the Provisional Theatre, Dr Rieger, a man to whom had been given all the powers of general manager, was firmly in favour of Mayr. Mayr would do what he was told, and Dr Rieger liked that. Bedrich had the hallmark of a rebel, someone who had a mind of his own and a tongue which would never hesitate to voice his dislikes and his ideas. So, for the time being at least, Mayr was secure in his position, while Bedrich Smetana was slipping more and more into the depths of poverty.

He was seething with ideas, but his family had to be fed, and when Nissen wrote him a letter begging him to return to Göteborg, even if only for a short time, he gave the matter long and agonized thought. Betty was against it. His friends said he should not quit the scene. But he took the most realistic view of all. "I shall have to go. It will be the only chance I'll get to straighten out my financial tangles."

On March 8th, 1862, he left Prague, and in Göteborg he was welcomed back with open arms. Everywhere he went in the city they fêted him. Parties were held in his honour, concerts arranged for him, gifts showered on him.

Fröjda Benecke put her arms about his neck and kissed him openly in front of the onlookers—and, strangely, nobody seemed to mind. Not even Capek, who embraced him without speaking and was content just to look at him through misty eyes.

The music-lovers turned out in their hundreds for his concerts, and he spent many happy hours in the company of Fröjda Benecke, who listened avidly to everything he told her about Prague, the conditions he had found when he got back, the furore over the theatre appointments, his plans to write an opera for Count Harrach's prize.

Physically he found her more attractive than ever. Their desire for each other could no longer be concealed; they admitted it to each other over and over again. But always the final barrier remained uncrossed, and each respected the other for refraining from forcing the issue.

Capek recognized that the relationship was all-important to Bedrich, and consoled himself for not chiding his friend with the satisfaction of knowing that Fröjda's contribution to Bedrich's life was enriching beyond words. He listened without comment when Bedrich said, "It is heaven for me to be with her. I know that in your heart you do not approve, Jan, but ... what can I say?"

When the time came for him to return to Prague in May, Bedrich had earned and put by over a thousand crowns, and at a party on the night prior to his departure a prominent merchant and music-lover, a Jew named Valentin, came up to him and handed him "a token of friendship to keep you free of financial worries until you secure a proper position in Prague". The token of friendship was a gift of two thousand crowns.

All Bedrich could do was gape and say, "How can I accept this?"

But Valentin was walking away, laughing, saying, "If you don't, my friend, it will be left for the cleaners."

He had more money now than he had ever possessed in his life, and he was eager to reach Prague to restart the search for a librettist. He would no longer have to go to the palace to play for the Emperor. He was independent now—at least, for as long as the money lasted.

The day he arrived he didn't go straight home, but instructed the cab-driver to take him out of Prague, along the course of the river and through the villages that nestled on the bends. Then he alighted at a quiet place and walked among some trees and across the corner of a meadow to a spot where he could see along a good stretch of the Vltava. He looked at it with fierce concentration, described the little segments of scenery his eyes took in with each separate glance and spoke them aloud. He wanted them to remain with him in perfect clarity in case he ever again had to leave Bohemia. You are my river, he thought, the river of my country. I love you dearly, and one day I shall immortalize you.

After nearly half an hour he left the spot and walked back to the waiting cab, his jaw jutting forward and his shoulders squared in challenge, if not to the whole world, then to Prague and Rieger and Mayr.

For weeks on end he sought someone who could provide him with the kind of libretto he wanted. He received many promises of help, but they came from men who either failed to keep their promises or were found wanting by Bedrich himself when he saw samples of their efforts.

He had just about given up hope and had begun reading on a broad scale in the effort to find a worthwhile theme that he himself could build on, when a slim man about the same age as himself, but with an emaciated white face, came to his door one evening with a parcel under his arm.

Betty let him in and led him to the door of the room where Bedrich was sitting.

Bedrich looked up and smiled—despite the disappointment of being unable to find a librettist, he had been wonderfully free of tension since his return from Göteborg.

"There is a gentleman here to see you, my dear."

Bedrich closed his book and stood up. The thin man bowed awkwardly as he stepped past Betty into the room. His eyes were dark and deep-set, and there was something almost furtive about the way he looked at people. The appearance was one of fright, or vulnerability. But there was an intelligence to the face that made Bedrich want to know more about his visitor.

"Excuse me coming unannounced, and so late," the stranger said hesitantly. "My name is Karel Sabina."

"Can I help you?" Bedrich asked. He felt an instant compassion for Karel Sabina. It was as if he were looking at himself a dozen years earlier. Was this another young musician burning with ambition and consumed by despair?

Sabina had a peculiar way of holding his head so that the face was not straight up and down, but at an angle, a defensive-looking angle, the chin drawn in near to the top of the chest, the eyes half hidden under brows that were pulled down. "You are searching for a libretto?" he said.

"Yes, I am, or at least I was."

"Have you stopped looking? Have you found one?"

"No, I haven't found one, so I'm thinking about attempting to write my own. Why?"

Sabina thrust the parcel at him. His expression had changed to a mixture of surliness, defiance, triumph, and uncertainty. "I've brought you this," he said. "I've worked hard on it, and it is as good as I can make it."

Bedrich felt the weight of the paper, fingered it, explored the thickness, wondered about opening it there and then. "Thank you," he said. "I shall read it with interest."

"I'd like you to read it soon," Sabina said.

"I will, I can assure you."

"Tonight?"

"Well, I don't know about tonight—"

"I should be grateful if you could at least start on it. It means a lot to me to have your reaction as soon as possible. I've hardly slept during the last week while I was trying to finish it."

Echoes of familiarity with the situation sounded again in Bedrich's head. This Sabina looked as if fever was not far from him. But the head was straightening, the chin coming off the chest, the eyes being revealed by the brows which were receding to their normal positions.

"Very well, Mr Sabina, I shall start reading the script as soon as you've gone."

Sabina backed towards the door immediately, but was arrested by Bedrich's question.

"You are aware of *why* I was searching for a script?"

"Yes—so that you can enter the opera competition for Count Harrach's prize."

"And you know the kind of works the adjudicating committee are looking for?"

"I studied the rules carefully."

"Would you tell me what they are?"

Sabina took a step forward and, for the first time since he had entered the room, pride became part of his demeanour. And even before the words came out of Sabina's mouth Bedrich was remembering a certain day in Jungmann's study when he himself had suddenly blazed.

"Mr Smetana, I didn't come here for an examination. You're a musician, I'm a writer. I admire you. I hope that one day you may come to admire me. But for the moment . . ."

In the split second of hesitation while Sabina sought the appropriate phrase Bedrich interrupted and said, "I'm sorry. I apologize." He went to Sabina's side and continued, "It is just that among the many writers I have spoken with and whose attempts I have seen, there were many people who were totally inexperienced. We've all got to make a start somewhere, somehow, I know that. But for me time is running out. Do you understand?"

"Of course. Let me put your mind at rest. I have written for a number of years. I've had several works published, but this is my first libretto. I made a study of the technique before starting on it, and I think, with respect, that it is a good bit of work. It may frighten you off, though, I should warn you about that."

"Frighten me off? For what reason?"

"I'd prefer you to decide that for yourself."

The metamorphosis was complete. From being shy and unsure when he had come in Sabina had changed so much that by the time he left he was speaking man-to-man with Bedrich.

Bedrich began reading the libretto straight away, intending to read through the opening only, and to complete it in the morning. But the script held his attention so much that he sat up long after Betty had retired for the night, and finished it.

He ran up the stairs and shook Betty's shoulder until she awoke.

"What's wrong?" she asked sleepily.

"Sit up, I must talk to you."

"Why? What for?"

"I've got it! I've found what I was looking for!"

She was still not fully awake. "What are you talking about Bedrich?"

"The libretto for the opera. Isn't that marvellous?"

She sank back into her pillow and pulled the eiderdown up to shield her eyes.

"Isn't it?" he asked again.

"Yes," she mumbled.

He bent low over her, gripped her shoulders, and spoke softly and earnestly, "The search is *over!* I can go *ahead!* That Karel Sabina has brought me exactly the kind of libretto I was hoping to find."

With her eyes closed tight, Betty said, "Good, I'm delighted, darling. Now let me get back to sleep, please. You can tell me about it in the morning."

She was sound asleep again within seconds.

He went downstairs, into the room where he had been reading, took up the script, turned to the title-page, and read the printing there. "*The Brandenburgers in Bohemia*", it said, "by Karel Sabina".

Unlike many ideas that at night can give the impression of fulfilling every ideal, but by morning will have paled, the theme of *The Brandenburgers in Bohemia* seemed even stronger to Bedrich on the following day.

What Sabina had done was to lay bare the cause of the ache in the hearts of his fellow-countrymen—their subjugation by the Germans—and then brazenly develop his libretto around it. The only concession he made to political expediency was to place the action of his story in the eighteenth century. But there was no mistaking the depth of feeling, nor the intention behind *The Brandenburgers in Bohemia*. Even the name itself was a thin disguise for "The Germans in Bohemia".

Was it any wonder Sabina's dark, deep-set eyes seemed to

burn? The man was a cauldron. Every line that he had written was evidence of the crying out in his soul, the voice that was turned westwards to Germany and saying: "You've brought your armies to our land, your guns and your soldiers; you've shown us suffering and caused us death; you have conquered our land. But you have never conquered my people. You will never destroy us, because justice is on our side, and while we believe in the truth of this, we are indestructible as a people."

Late in the afternoon Sabina came to the house, and before he could open his mouth to ask the question he was given the answer.

Bedrich's eyes were shining as he jumped up from his chair and strode across the room to meet him, saying, "It's marvellous! Tremendous!"

Sabina's sombre face cracked into a smile. "You've read it?"

"I devoured it, every last line of it."

Sabina's face now relaxed completely, but so too did his legs, and he looked around hurriedly for the nearest chair, on which he sat down heavily. His head was lowered and he twisted his hat nervously. Then he looked up at Bedrich and said simply, "You have made me very happy, Mr Smetana."

In the beginning Bedrich spent most of every day and much of every night composing. The process of selection and rejection was employed with the most rigorous standards, and inside a fortnight he looked so worn-out that Betty became alarmed and advised him to slow down the pace. He tried flippancy in casting aside her objections, but she was very serious and he was reluctant to cause her undue worry. Besides which, his own body began to rebel against the fierce punishment. So he stopped working at night, put everything into his daylight spells, dug into his heart to tear out the finest things in his being and incorporate them in this, his first opera.

Apart from writing his first opera, he also took an active part in the Czech cultural awakening. What the poets and journalists were doing in another field he decided to do for music—to bellow for its cause, to whip up the feelings of the people, to make loud demands that the ideals he felt certain were the correct ones be recognized and understood and acted upon.

He wrote his views in a white heat of fervour, and they appeared in the paper *Slavoj*.

> If we look with keen and honest eyes at the present state of the art of music in our beloved Prague, and compare it with the conditions obtaining in the cities of other countries, we can only come to one conclusion, and a painful and shameful one it is: Music in Prague is in a lamentable state. ... The rot will continue unless we arrest it now. ...

He went on to say that Prague should act immediately to rectify the position. He gave an outline of what the programme should be; it should include the finest works written by recognized master composers, regardless of nationality (and he hit hard at the bigotry which classed 'foreign' music as unacceptable), as well as paying close attention, and giving encouragement, to composers whose work concentrated on the Slavonic idiom. "It is the duty of an artist to look with love on the country of his birth. ... Our composers have been discouraged. Let us encourage them. ..."

The article quickly came to the notice of Rieger and Mayr, and its sentiments stung them to the quick. Rieger raged and fumed; Mayr added his own poison. They held a meeting to discuss what should be done. Bedrich Smetana's name was used with bitterness and anger. But in the end they decided to remain quiet. Why give him more publicity? Better to ignore his outburst and hope it would be forgotten. The man was despicable and dangerous, they said, a fomentor of trouble. They tabled a resolution to pass on to official circles the advice to ignore the appeal, treat it as though it had never been made.

But the progressive young writers whose cause Bedrich had vigorously espoused took notice, made the article the main topic of their discussions, sent their congratulations to its writer, invited him to come and talk at their meetings. Here was a man after their own heart, a fearless fighter.

At a soirée held by Prince Rudolf Taxis, a gathering of intellectuals made Bedrich's article the main topic of analysis, and Bedrich was asked to join in and expand his ideas about the development of Czech national music. He explained at length that there was an erroneous belief that Czech composers could express the musical culture of their people only by basing their compositions on the relatively small field of so-called national songs, and stressed the real need for originality, for a breaking away from narrow confines.

"We must look into ourselves and experiment. We must *create*," he said. "We must not only adapt but build anew. One of the dangers of the old school of thought is that much of what is looked upon as intrinsically Czech in folk-music is in fact derived from the folk-music of other countries. I would go further and say that many folk-songs classed as Czech are actually foreign songs brought into Bohemia long ago, given new words, absorbed into the currency of our own folk-music, and, when the origins are forgotten, mistakenly looked upon as having originated here. And if we are to base our music on such false foundations, how can we hope to succeed in creating anything which is primarily and purely Czech?"

They applauded for long minutes after he sat down. His words and his passion had stirred them all, and each went away to spread wider the thoughts he had given them.

All over Bohemia new vocal societies were being organized, and in Prague Bedrich was invited to take over directorship of the Hlahol. Here he had an informed body of enthusiasts who followed his every step. As well as working on the score of *The Brandenburgers in Bohemia*, he took the words of J. Jahn and wrote a choral composition around the great Czech Christian reformer, Jan Hus. It was performed by Hlahol in February 1863 with Bedrich's friend, Ferdinand Heller, conducting.

But in the meantime his creativity was soaring. Even though there was much going on all around him—he was attending rallies all over Prague, giving lectures, conducting rehearsals of the vocal society, and Betty was expecting their second child—he was still able to compose with a facility that at times astonished him. His pen was unable to keep pace with ideas and emotions, and by January 8th, 1863, he had completed the first act of the opera. A little over five weeks later he finished the second act; and by April 23rd (despite the excitement of the new baby's arrival on February 19th) *The Brandenburgers in Bohemia* was ready. Its completion gave him an enormous sense of achievement. He had reached a very significant milestone, his first opera between covers, and all set for the scrutiny of the adjudicating board.

He read it over very carefully, made adjustments here and there, and then tried to make a balanced assessment of its chances of winning the prize. He was pleased by the fact that it was entirely original in the context of Czech opera. He had broken fresh ground in his choice of subject and musical method. No Czech composer before him had ever attempted to set down the great currents of feeling running beneath the surface of their people. No-one had tried to capture their desires and demands for a new life. He had done so, and was greatly satisfied by having made the effort.

He recognized that he owed much to Sabina's libretto, for Sabina had synthesized his own feelings about nationalism, and during the time Bedrich had been working on the music he had grown to know a lot about Sabina's character. He had asked the writer for his earlier writings, and in the poems written as far back as 1848, and even before, Bedrich had seen the radicalism of Sabina struggling for expression. His librettist was a man whose being screamed out for a social liberation for his people. He wanted the Czechs to be culturally, economically, and politically freed, and would never rest until that freedom was achieved. That would be his fulfillment.

And so it was that *The Brandenburgers in Bohemia* glorified in its way the struggling and the downtrodden. It was an opera with a social message. Smetana, right at the start, had to find his own direction, to quarry out his style. "Of course, Wagner had experimented brilliantly," he said at the time, "but I could not dream of following. I knew that I could not afford to. I had to strike out on my own path, or else I might be in danger of blocking off my progress for ever."

When he examined what he had created he decided that he had accomplished as much as his talents would encompass at that period of time; he had shunned slavishly copying anyone else; he had eschewed the (to him) shoddy process of disregarding true drama and treating an opera as merely a series of ensembles for vocal fireworks interspersed with throat-cracking arias for prima donnas and temperamental tenors; and he had expanded the role of the orchestra from being no more than a joint accompaniment to the singers to that of being an important dramatic partner in the opera as a whole.

He was as moved on the final reading as he had been when composing. It was with tears in his eyes that Sabina's words and his own music came to him in that part of the opera describing the feelings of the poor people who wandered and scavenged for scraps in the market-place at St Valentine's Gate. They had lost the dignity of man, but retained all instincts to live, and this was something he knew and felt about so strongly. He had built the music into a great hymn, the hymn of the suffering under-privileged.

He knew he had treated the rich savagely. He knew he had let his sympathies sway him to cry out about injustices. He knew that what he had written would disturb and jar and prove abrasive. And he knew he had not a single regret about a solitary line of any of it.

CHAPTER
[18]

JAN MAYR, THIN-LIPPED AND FROWNING, knocked on the door of Dr Rieger's office and entered immediately, without waiting to be called. He walked straight to Rieger's desk and dropped the folio. Rieger looked at it, but didn't touch it.

"The nerve of that man!" Mayr said.

"What man?"

"Smetana. This is his entry for the Harrach prize."

Rieger lifted the folio, opened the cover, and looked at the title-page. *The Brandenburgers in Bohemia* he read. "So this is Mr Smetana's entry, eh? Well, well, well." He began to thumb through the pages, made many little grunts and whistles of disbelief at things that caught his eye, eventually replaced the folio on the desk-top. "Well, the clever Mr Smetana has played straight into our hands. We shall just ignore it."

"You mean we are not going to turn it down?"

"No, no, Mayr. To do that would be to hand him a stick with which to beat us."

"I don't see what you are getting at."

"Of course you don't, my dear Mayr. That is because subtlety is not a part of your make-up. No, no, you see, Smetana will be anxiously waiting for a reaction from us, so we shall just let him sweat and wait. If we were to reject the opera he would use the rejection to gain himself sympathy. He is not without friends, and, as we both know, many of these friends are writers and journalists. If we wrote him a rejection, said that his work did not come up to our standards,

P

he would feel hurt, certainly, but he would use his influence to get his writer friends to build it up into a story, to colour it, and that could be very uncomfortable, could it not?"

Mayr could see the cleverness of Rieger's reasoning. "And what should we write to him?"

"Nothing."

"Not even an acknowledgment?"

"Not until he comes pestering us for one. Then we shall merely say that the opera has been received and will be considered in due course. But naturally we shall not consider it at all. We shall let things drift."

Mayr was smiling now, the evil smile of connivance. "Just one other question, Doctor. Supposing he demands his copy back?"

"He won't," Rieger said. "Not if I know Smetana. He will wait and wait and wait. And the waiting will drive him mad, might even disrupt his work and make him nervous, make him lose his cocksureness, force him into further nervousness, cause him to find composing impossible."

Neither of them, however, had reckoned with Bedrich's spirit. There was no disguising his impatience at the slowness of the Provisional Theatre to give him a decision about his opera, and he was annoyed. But he was not downhearted. He still nursed to himself the satisfaction that he had done his best, and the knowledge that that best amounted to something worthwhile. And besides, he was able to draw sustenance from his friends and from his new work—for already he was sketching out a new opera.

This time he was going to make a clean break from the heavy and the dramatic, and he had had long discussions with Karel Sabina about the type of libretto he wanted. Less than a year earlier, in October 1862, he had interrupted work to write the sketched outline of a light piece for voices which he had marked *Choir in Joyful Play*, and it was around this music that the shape of a comic opera had began to grow.

Within a couple of months of *The Brandenburgers in Bohemia* being completed Sabina brought his first draft of the new opera to Smetana. They had talked a great deal about the story, and it was one which Smetana himself was much drawn to, because it was based on the people and the life he loved so much, the village folk and their simple, rustic existence. He wanted to call it *The Bartered Bride*.

He was disappointed, therefore, when he found that Sabina's script was only of one-act length, scarcely sufficient material on which to build an operetta. Tactfully he asked Karel to expand the script.

He had learnt by now that, apart from *The Brandenburgers in Bohemia*, two other works had been submitted for Count Harrach's prize. One was by Mayr himself! The other was by Adolf Pozdeny. He resigned himself to a long wrangle before he would worm a decision on *The Brandenburgers in Bohemia* out of the Provisional Theatre. While Mayr was in a position to block the opera from being performed, it would never see the light of day. Not, that was, unless the adjudicating committee for the prize made it the winner. The committee was composed of three members—the head of the Prague Conservatoire, J. B. Kittl, himself a composer; the Director of the Organ School, Josef Krejci; and a well-known expert on music matters, A. W. Ambros. As a group, they seemed singularly reluctant about coming to a decision. So the two copies of the score were in places where Bedrich could not touch them.

Throughout the remainder of the year he split his time between composing, campaigning for the freedom of the theatre, making speeches, and running the sort of establishment he had sworn he would never again have anything to do with—a teaching academy. The work strained his patience to bursting point.

By now the young freedom fighters were citing England as the country on which their own should model itself. They lauded its independence, referred to it as the guiding star which should lead them into the bright place they wanted to reach. On April 23rd, 1864, the Artistic Society held a festival to celebrate the tercentenary of Shakespeare's birth, gave praise to him as the greatest dramatist of all times. The grand finale of the celebrations was a march past of costumed actors each dressed as a character from one of the great master's plays. And as they filed past the bust placed on a pedestal in the centre of the stage of the Old Town Theatre it was to the music of a march written specially for the occasion by Smetana.

The tide was starting to turn against Jan Mayr.

The operas he had been presenting at the Provisional Theatre had been not only artistically disappointing, they had conspicuously failed to draw audiences. Discontent was mounting, and the Press recognized where its duty lay.

A group of progressive writers, headed by Neruda and Halek, found a vehicle for their opinions in the paper *Narodni Listy*, and the suggestion was made, and accepted, that Bedrich Smetana should do a series of articles on musical matters for the paper. He was given *carte blanche* to present his uncensored views.

"How far should I go?" he asked Betty.

"Say exactly what you think, my love," she said.

"It is bound to hurt someone," he said.

"Of course it is. But you must take the risk of hurting whoever you intend to criticize."

"But I'm not really a writer."

"You have views. Express them."

"The trouble is to know where to begin."

"At the beginning," she said. "It's the only way."

Without another word he turned back to his desk and picked up a pen. The article was published in *Narodni Listy* on June 24th.

> The reason for these lines is to look at our national art in the field of music, to which opera belongs as its foremost exponent. Our attention must be centred in the first place on Czech opera as it exists at present. Once we have analysed its state, perhaps we can compare that state with things as they should be if our opera is to stand any chance of fulfilling the demands of true art and to meet the requirements of our nation. . . .

He went on to say that Czech opera fell far short of these requirements, that it came nowhere near depicting true Czech musical abilities and ambitions.

> Is our opera aware of the tasks before it? Can we believe in it? Does it know where it is going, or what it should be?

The answers, as he saw them, had to be 'No' on every count. The opera of his country, he said, was exactly as it had been many years earlier. The exciting steps forward had never been taken, and the only difference was that it now had a home of its own—the Provisional National Theatre.

Of the entire repertoire only a minute fraction is of any real value.... The tragedy is that while we have the necessary raw material, the aim of putting our own opera on its feet is not being realized.

In an article on July 15th he pointed out that there were in fact numbers of native works available, enough to build an entirely new repertoire.

However, if our National Theatre administrators produce *two* native operas in a whole year, they consider that they have carried out their duties. More, they expect to be praised for their efforts!

By now his blood was up, and he entered the battle wholeheartedly, firing salvoes of criticism on every musical front. He did not write for the sake of sensationalism. He wrote what he believed, and when part of what he believed was that Mayr was prostituting his position as musical director by haphazardly cutting out parts of standard works and presenting them in "shortened and spoilt versions", he did not hesitate to heap derision on Mayr's head.

If there was a chink in his make-up it was that he became oblivious to his own future in as much as he made enemies of those who could effectively blight his career. But his only consideration was to try to stop Czech musical art from rotting into the final decay.

For a while the subscription concerts that he was organizing were an outstanding success, financially and artistically. He was losing the virtuoso tag, gaining a reputation as a conductor and musical educator. He cast his net wide, presented such works as Beethoven's *Leonora* Overtures, Mozart's Piano Concerto in B flat (he played the solo himself), a symphony by Kittl, several compositions by Gluck, Berlioz's *Roman Carnival*, Loewe's oratorio *Hus*, Beethoven's Fifth Symphony, Albert's "Kolumbus" Symphony, and excerpts from his own *The Brandenburgers in Bohemia*.

But he miscalculated Prague's appetite for "the music of a higher order". The result was that audiences dropped off, and he was left with the problem of finding an amount of over six hundred crowns to clear the debts. The last resort was teaching. Once again he had to fall back on it, and once again the toll on his patience was enormous.

In a letter to the kindly Jew of Göteborg, Valentin, he wrote: *As long as Dr Rieger is Superintendent of the Provisional Theatre, there is not the slightest chance that I shall ever get the post of musical director, because Rieger looks upon Mayr as the ideal man for the job.* What he had not told Valentin was that at a recent soirée in the home of Prince Rudolf Taxis he and Rieger had crossed swords.

The talk had been of music, and the future of the Czech theatre, and Bedrich had stood silent for a long time, listening to the complacent and boastful Rieger giving forth in his loud voice about what he and Mayr had accomplished to date. But Bedrich was loath to cause a scene in the home of a man he respected as a friend. However, when he could bear it no longer he pressed forward to the front of the listening crowd. Rieger saw the movement, looked at Bedrich, and his lip curled.

"Who have we here?" he said to the front row of people, though he knew full well who Bedrich was.

Nobody answered. All eyes switched to Bedrich. Bedrich's problem was to figure out how to tackle Rieger without being humiliated from the very outset. He decided to jump in feet first, and, looking Rieger straight in the eyes, he said with as much arrogance as he could summon, "Dr Rieger, rarely have I heard a man talk so much and say so little."

There was an instant reaction from the crowd, a sort of communal gasp breaking from them as they fell back a little to let the two protagonists face each other. Rieger glanced around to make sure that everyone was ready for the annihilation he was going to bring about. Then he said, "Of course, you are an authority on all things musical. You are the great attacker. You are the voice of the people who presumes to level authority, to mend the ills of everybody and everything, the saviour of Czech art, the almighty oracle."

"If you think you are going to put me on the defensive, Dr

Rieger, you are wasting your time," Bedrich said quietly. "I haven't come here to defend myself. I don't need to."

"No? You think yourself above it, perhaps?"

"I don't."

"You look upon yourself as some form of deity, perhaps?"

"That, coming from you, Dr Rieger, is ironic."

Rieger looked uneasy. "I will ignore that comment," he said.

"Perfectly in character," Bedrich said. "Now, suppose we leave personalities out of it and return to music?"

"But I didn't think anyone could *discuss* music with you," Rieger said, trying to retrieve the situation. "I thought you were the ultimate authority."

"I only have beliefs," said Bedrich. "You're the one in authority. And you, let me remind you, are the one who has been holding court here this evening, speaking *ad infinitum*, and, if you want my own personal opinion, *ad nauseam*, about what you have accomplished. I happen to believe that you were talking rubbish."

"I have no intention of exchanging invective with you, Smetana."

"You have made a pretty formidable start."

There was a small titter of laughter, and Rieger made as if to walk away.

"Then you don't feel up to justifying your claims?" Bedrich said.

Rieger whirled around. "Just because you have been given space to expound your ridiculous ideas, do you think you can stand here and insult me?" he stormed.

"The insults began with you," Bedrich reminded him. "And furthermore, while we are in an inquisitive strain, do you happen to think that just because of your position you are above criticism?"

"Of course not! I don't mind criticism provided it comes from an informed source and not from a fool."

There were shouts and murmurings of "Unfair."

But Bedrich held up his hands placatingly and said, "No, don't stop him. If you want to see the sort of man he really is, let him have his say."

"I'm sorry," Rieger said hastily. "I didn't mean that. My

tongue ran away with me. Seriously, Smetana, the things you have been writing have got under my skin, I admit it. They annoyed me because I think they were unjustified."

"Well, prove that they were," Bedrich said. "I am here now to be convinced. You've been making the most outrageous claims about what you and Mayr have done. What *have* you done? Two domestic operas in a year, what kind of national programme is that? Where are the new Czech composers? Where are the old ones? And if you wanted to give the people *real* foreign operas, why haven't we seen Mozart's *Marriage of Figaro*, which was translated into our language many years ago? Where is *Don Juan*? Where is *Fidelio*? Why haven't we heard Wagner? Give us some facts about those, Dr Rieger."

Rieger was now shifting his eyes from face to face, looking for some sign of support, seeing none. "Everything takes time, my dear Smetana," he said.

"Time doesn't have to mean years ahead," Bedrich said. "Even if you and your administrators had the *intention* of rectifying matters, things would not be so bad. But we get nothing but silence. Silence and complacency and no adequate explanations. All I have been trying to do is to hurry up matters, and it seems that you resent this. As I have said a thousand times, Dr Rieger, I love my country, and I am proud of it, and I want to see it take its place in the world of art, not always to be a pale imitator. And when it comes to resentment I have a lot of it burning inside me, resentment of the time-wasting indulged in by you and your colleagues."

Several people in the listening group clapped, and Rieger looked more uneasy than ever. He had been bested, and he knew it.

Shifting direction, he said, "Mr Smetana, I think it is a pity that you should be spending so much time campaigning—"

Bedrich cut in, "I don't consider the time wasted!"

"It's a shame that you don't spend more time in composition," Rieger said, ignoring the interruption. "You may not believe me, but I admire your work."

Bedrich laughed.

"Yes, I do."

"I can see that from the speed with which you put on my *Brandenburgers in Bohemia.*"

Another burst of clapping from the crowd.

"Ah, so there is the crux of the matter!" Rieger said, grasping it for the God-given lifeline it seemed to him. "So that is what makes you bitter, is it?"

"Dr Rieger, don't try to slip out of this with a cheap jibe. It does you no credit. It is lowering your stock even further among these people."

"You are trying to tell me you are unconcerned about the fact that we have not yet put on your opera?"

"Nothing of the kind. Of course I am annoyed. I spent a long time writing that opera. It contains a large part of my being. I *must* be concerned. But if you are implying that your reluctance to produce it is the sole cause of what you called my campaigning for Czech music, then you are even less intelligent than I had supposed."

"My dear Smetana, if there is one piece of advice I can give you it is this: for goodness sake forget all your musical experimenting. Stick to our good Czech folk-tunes and work on them as a background to your composition. That way you will fare far better, and do immeasurably more for our national music."

Bedrich shrugged. "Dr Rieger," he said, "if that is the best you can contribute, then all I can say is that you don't even *understand* what I am speaking about, or what I stand for." He went for his coat and hat at that point, and left behind a Rieger who was boiling at the snub. Rieger was an avowed enemy from that moment.

Bedrich returned to work on *The Bartered Bride* with renewed intensity. Composing for this opera brought him great contentment of mind. He knew well the people around whom this opera was being formed, the rustic folk of the villages and farms. He had experienced their joys and their sadnesses, knew the highlights and tragedies of their lives, the wild happiness that overtook them when fairs visited the villages, the dances they joined in with abandon. In the overture he set out to create the atmosphere that pervaded their lives.

He tried out the composition publicly on November 18th,

1864, when it was performed at one of his concerts for the Artistic Society. There was no doubting its success when he looked at the faces of the audience and listened to their loud applause at the end. *The Bartered Bride* was coming along famously. *I tried to give it an entirely national character,* he wrote, *because the subject is taken from country life, and the story tells of a bridegroom who sells his sweetheart. For this kind of story only national music would suffice.*

CHAPTER

[19]

THE SCORE OF *The Brandenburgers in Bohemia* lay gathering dust in the office of the Provisional Theatre. But the knowledge of its existence was already widely known, both from the writings of Halek and Neruda and from the talk that circulated after the various excerpts had been publicly performed.

The Press was now firmly on Smetana's side, and, by repeated references to the opera, they endeavoured to force the Provisional Theatre to make a definite decision on its future. Finally Liegert, the theatre's *supremo* (he was managing director as distinct from Rieger's post of general-manager), announced that the opera was in the planning stages. But time passed, and nothing more was said. It was clear that Liegert was as much a stumbling-block to Smetana as were Mayr and Rieger.

It wasn't until a new managing director was appointed that anything was done. His name was Thomé, and the first thing he did upon taking office was to ask for the score, which he spent the next three days examining. Its possibilities excited him, and he sat down straight away and wrote a letter to Bedrich.

Having ascertained that Your Honour's opera, The Brandenburgers in Bohemia, *is already copied out in full, I am hastening to inquire whether now, under my direction of this theatre, you are willing that the opera be produced?*

The date was October 20th, 1865—well over two years since the score had been submitted.

Bedrich, of course, replied immediately in the affirmative.

Thomé sent for Mayr and gave his musical director the news. "I want you to begin getting *The Brandenburgers* ready as soon as possible," he said.

Mayr's face went white.

"Is there something you wish to say?" asked Thomé.

"I think you are making a mistake," Mayr answered.

"In what way?"

"Putting on Smetana's opera. Your predecessor—"

"What my predecessor did or did not do does not concern me. I am managing director of this theatre now, and I decide what we should put on."

"Very well," Mayr said, and walked towards the door

"Mayr!"

Mayr stopped and turned. "Yes?"

"I will thank you to show more respect."

"I'm sorry."

"Empty words won't satisfy me. And standing there with a hangdog expression on your face isn't going to do anything to foster good relations between us. I would advise you to tread carefully, Mayr."

Mayr walked back until he was standing within inches of Thomé's desk. He said, "You are making a mistake, as I have told you. If you decide to go ahead and put on this Smetana person's so-called opera you will call down ridicule upon yourself and everyone else connected with this theatre. And as for the expression on my face, we are all born as God made us."

Thomé stood up and walked around the desk to Mayr. "When I want your advice about anything, Mayr, I shall ask for it. And don't address me as if you were talking to some unfortunate second-violin player who depends on your every whim. There is only one person in charge here, and it would be as well if you recognized that. I know you have friends in high places, but it doesn't frighten me. I have been appointed to this job, and I intend to do it my way, not the way you think it should be done. Is that understood? And I do not intend to waste my time trying to soothe you and your infantile sulking fits. Now, I have given you an order. Go away and get

The Brandenburgers in Bohemia ready as quickly as you know how."

"I shan't do it," Mayr replied. "I'll have nothing to do with it."

"You are refusing?"

"I am."

Thomé pursed his lips and went back and sat behind the desk. When he had composed himself he looked up and said, "You may leave." Mayr went to the door, a little sneer of triumph already creeping across his mouth. He was about to let himself out when Thomé added, "And consider yourself under suspension until you are told otherwise."

Mayr took a shocked step back into the room and began, "You can't—"

"Good day, Mayr," Thomé said, and busied himself with papers on his desk. It was as if Mayr had ceased to exist.

Mayr left the office with murder in his heart. Within minutes Thomé came out of the office and walked past Mayr, who was standing in the passageway talking in an angry undertone to the company's leading soprano, Eleonora von Ehrenberg. The talk stopped as Thomé approached and passed without any sign of recognition. Thomé found one of the theatre staff, handed him a letter addressed to Smetana, and asked him to deliver it by hand and to wait for an answer.

Bedrich had no idea why Thomé wanted to see him, but he put his paper and pens away and accompanied the messenger back to the theatre. Thomé greeted him cordially and came to the point at once.

"Are you prepared to take the rehearsals yourself?" he asked. He saw the look of surprise and added, "There has been a difference of opinion between Mayr and myself."

"Oh!" Bedrich said. "Well, I am not at all surprised at that. But the answer is yes, I am at your service."

"How soon could you start?"

"As soon as you like."

"Good. I shall call the first orchestra rehearsal for tomorrow morning. You can meet the rest of the company in the afternoon. Will that suit you?"

"Perfectly."

Thomé stood up and shook hands. "I believe I am going to enjoy working with you, Mr Smetana. You have much to offer us, and I shall do my best to carry out your wishes. And I'd like to wish you all the luck in the world."

That night Bedrich sought out Sabina, Neruda, Halek, all his friends, broke the good news to them, joined their party, and went all over the city celebrating.

But neither he nor Thomé had made allowance for Mayr's mischief-making, and the first signs of trouble came when he met the principal singers. He handed out the parts, then sat straddled on a chair as he explained the opera's story to them. A surly silence greeted him when he asked if there were any questions.

"Very well then, let us run through the music, shall we?" he said, going to the rehearsal piano.

The first discordant voice was that of the prima donna, von Ehrenberg, who had been going through her copy of the score making derisive sounds which constantly interrupted Bedrich's explanations. Finally she stood up, held the score at arm's length as though it were a contaminated object, and let it drop with a clatter. "Do you expect me to sing *that*?" she said haughtily. "Why, there isn't a single coloratura aria in the whole opera, and I am *engaged* as a coloratura soprano." Before Bedrich could reply she turned on her heel and walked out, every eye following her, an atmosphere of unbearable tenseness behind her.

Bedrich, his face burning with humiliation, cancelled the rehearsal on the spot and went to see Thomé, told him what had happened. The managing director was extremely apologetic.

"I should have known Mayr would have tried sabotage," he said. "I never dreamt he would have stooped this low. I think the best thing would be to hold back a while, wait until I sort matters out so that nothing like this can happen again."

The result was that Thomé called a meeting of the entire company and addressed them from the stage of the theatre.

"If anything like that which happened during Mr Smetana's first rehearsal occurs again," he warned, "I shall have no hesitation in dispensing with the services of anyone in any way involved. There isn't one of you who is indispensable, and believe me, if I sack anyone, they will never again be employed in this company while I am in charge. Furthermore, I will circulate every impressario to ensure that they get no other engagements either. I expect, and *demand*, the fullest co-operation from every one of you, and I want the same co-operation given to the composer. You are professional singers, and I want professionalism of the highest order from you. That's all."

Thomé waited until tempers had cooled down. He then waited a little longer, keeping the company in the dark as to his intentions. When uncertainty had made everyone eager to start work once more he informed Bedrich that he could now begin again. By this time December had already come in, cold and dark.

A freezing wind was whipping the snow into horizontal spears on the night of January 5th, 1866, but the Provisional Theatre was filled to overflowing for the opening night of *The Brandenburgers in Bohemia*.

Bedrich walked to the conductor's podium sick with nervousness. The great, heavy curtains of the stage loomed above him, rising in folds to the top of the proscenium arch. He looked upward and asked for strength. Then his eyes slid down to that magic area above the ground where the curtains were illuminated by the most exciting light in the world. At last he turned to the audience, and for the first time became aware that they were applauding him, giving him the traditional conductor's welcome. He searched for a face, Betty's, found it, managed a smile, and bowed low. He turned back to the orchestra then, tapped his baton, held his arms out wide until everyone was ready, and launched into the first public performance of *The Brandenburgers in Bohemia*.

As the sound hit him he forgot his nervousness. Now he was the master, and the music was his own, every last note of it. He brought in the strings, the woodwind, the brass. He hushed the violins, brought in the horns, whipped them into the attack he had envisaged in his head before ever writing a line on paper, set the tempi, brought his creation to life. He mouthed the lines with the singers, smiled his encouragement up to them, caressed the notes from their throats, held them stirringly on the upper registers, moulded a masterpiece, and in the process lived an entire lifetime.

And when it was all over, his humility poured down over him and rendered him limp and weak. But the audience wanted him, and they stamped and shouted and roared time after time, so that he was called back to receive their applause on nine separate occasions.

He couldn't even talk. He could only say, "Thank you ... thank you ... thank you ... " And those two words, endlessly repeated, expressed everything he felt at that moment of time.

The opera was performed again the next night, and again the reception was overwhelming.

On January 7th he wrote to Fröjda Benecke in far-away Göteborg: *I have delayed writing to you, my dear, because I wanted to see what would happen to my opera. ... It was a wonderful success, and I am overjoyed to be able to write good news of myself instead of having to burden you with my disappointments.*

One group of men to whom the acclaim for Smetana's opera meant uneasiness and much discussion was the adjudicating committee appointed to award Count Harrach's prize of six hundred sovereigns. All this time had passed, and still they had not made a public announcement. Now the pressure was on them, and they were afraid to make a decision. By the end of February *The Brandenburgers in Bohemia* had been performed an unprecedented eleven times, and was the talk of the country. The committee were being pressed to make an announcement, and in March they felt they could remain silent no longer. The public clamour was growing, and newspaper articles attacking the committee as incompetents were proliferating.

But the activity did nothing to assuage their fears. Indivually and as a group they were afraid that the opera's frank hostility towards the Germans might shock Bohemia's Austrian rulers, so they put out a very carefully prepared statement which said:

Mr Bedrich Smetana's opera *The Brandenburgers in*

Bohemia was among three works submitted for Count Harrach's competition. In the view of the committee, it is the best of the three works and, as far as the music is concerned, it deserves favourable consideration for the prize. However, the committee feels that certain Wagnerian trends are in evidence in the composer's work, and, this being so, there is doubt as to whether *The Brandenburgers in Bohemia* fully complies with the rules of the composition which stipulate that the submitted works should be entirely national in character.

Bedrich read the statement with a mixture of anger and incredulity. "What do they mean by Wagnerian trends?" he asked his friends. "Why don't they quote specific instances so that I can defend or repudiate? Do they accuse me of copying? What am I to do?" Having worked so long and with such sincerity of purpose on the opera, he felt depressed, cheated, hurt.

"Don't take any notice," Neruda counselled.

"Ignore it," Halek advised.

He tried to take the advice, on the surface pretended not to be affected by the libel. But he could not quell his inner feelings, feelings of injustice and unfairness; and he lost sleep. The statement was a direct negation of all his frequently repeated ideals, a public attack on his integrity, a wounding assault on all the hours and weeks of effort spent living with the sole purpose of creating music that owed nothing to any source other than his love of country.

It was a statement that played straight into the hands of the Rieger-Mayr clique. If the accusations were believed, what chance would Smetana have of ever being recognized as a purely *Czech* composer? Would the public not come to look upon him as no more than a second-rate copyist? In middle age was he about to find that his whole musical life had been in vain? And how would they react to *The Bartered Bride*, which Thomé had already signed a contract to secure?

An unexpected ally appeared on the scene in the person of Frantisek Pivoda. Pivoda was the director of a private school of opera, a powerful and respected voice in Prague's musical circles. After Jan Neruda had written in *Narodni Listy*: "It is difficult to give credence to the fact that there are people

Q

among us who are opposed to Smetana's opera just because the Artistic Society, which admittedly has enemies, has accepted him as our foremost composer." Pivoda added strength to Bedrich's cause with an opinion he wrote in the newspaper *Politik*. It said: "After this magnificent work [*The Brandenburgers in Bohemia*] there can be no doubt that we have discovered in Bedrich Smetana the man who is to lay the foundations of what will become known as Czech opera." Whatever accusations of bias could be laid against Neruda as a friend of Smetana, none could be levelled at Pivoda. His was an independent voice.

Then Count Harrach himself intervened. He called a meeting of the adjudicating committee, was brief and to the point.

"Gentlemen, you have had more than enough time to deliberate. You have put off announcing your decision for far too long. From what you yourselves have said to me, and from what I have seen for myself, I have no doubts whatever but that Bedrich Smetana's opera is the one that should be awarded the prize. I do not want to enter into any further discussion on the matter, except to say that in my opinion the views you expressed about foreign influences are unwarranted. I want it to be abundantly clear to you that Smetana will be awarded the prize without any further reservations."

On March 27th he wrote personally to Bedrich and, in part, his letter said: *Your score complied in every way with the rules of the competition.... The judges were unanimous in their decision to award you the prize. My heartiest congratulations.*

So Bedrich was vindicated.

The two other entries for the prize—Mayr's *Horymir*, and *Treasure*, by Pozdeny—were never produced.

Twelve days before Count Harrach wrote his letter Bedrich had completed the score of *The Bartered Bride*.

May 30th was a day on which the sun roasted the people of Prague, beat down on the pavements and cobblestones so that they threw off a fierce heat, unsettled the horses so that they became mad, and several of them bolted through the streets, scattering frightened people on every side. Old people collapsed, work stopped, and even the children lay down in the patches of shade. The evening brought no coolness with it, and most of the city's inhabitants stayed indoors, lying half dressed on sofas and beds.

At the Provisional National Theatre musicians sat around perspiring, and Bedrich Smetana paced anxiously up and down Thomé's office. In the dressing-rooms the cast put off donning their costumes until the last moment. How could they be expected to cavort around a stage on such a night?

"There is nothing we can do," Thomé was saying. "We can't postpone at this late stage."

"But there will be nobody here," Bedrich said. "They won't come into a theatre in this heat."

"We shall have to go ahead," Thomé replied. "My dear Smetana, I understand how you feel. But some seats have been sold, the critics will come, they have been talking of nothing else but *The Bartered Bride* for weeks now. We can't just say the performance has been called off."

"So my opera will have its première before an empty house?"

"It won't be that bad," Thomé said, wishing that he believed what he was saying.

When the overture began the hall was less than half full. Bedrich had felt despair and disappointment gnawing at his belly when he took his place in front of the orchestra. My opera is doomed, he thought; how can it be a success if nobody sees it?

Then the professional in him took over, and he gathered his thoughts, all his energies, to wring a superb performance from all those who had come together under his direction during the past few weeks. With that priceless ability of his to empty his mind of everything but the task in hand, he slipped immediately into the spirit of his opera, and when they heard the opening notes of the overture the audience sat up as though on cue. The sparkling gaiety of the music, the fresh, bouncing rhythms, arrested them, and they forgot their discomfort. Couples nudged each other. Critics fiddled with pieces of paper and notebooks and began to scribble in the darkness. Heads nodded in time to the tempo, looks of boredom disappeared and were replaced by happy smiles. This promised to be a wonderful evening. Happiness was clearly to be the mood, and even before the curtain went up an air of festivity had pervaded the Provisional Theatre.

A village came to life on the stage before them. A village of happy people singing "Why shouldn't we be joyful?" The sentiments were grasped, and a people who had been living with the hourly worry of imminent war between Austria and Prussia were lost in the fantasy world on the stage. They watched with starry eyes the two lovers, Marenka and Jenik, revelled in their ecstasy, shared the sweet agony of their love duet, ceased to be citizens of a coldly practical city, and became involved instead in the story that was unfolding before them.

At intervals the applause interrupted both music and action as men and women stood up and clapped until their hands were tingling and sore. The cast and orchestra smiled with happiness.

Narodni Listy reported the occasion as follows:

> Mr Bedrich Smetana's new opera, *The Bartered Bride*, was performed last night for the first time and met with extraordinary scenes of enthusiasm. The joyful melodies, the glorious choruses and solos and dances, often had the audience thundering out its applause. The opening chorus, which is full of genuine national spirit, had to be repeated before they would let the production continue. That established the pattern of what happened continuously throughout the evening. After each separate scene the composer was applauded until the roof rang with the tumult.

A day later the same paper published a full review, and concluded by saying that *The Bartered Bride* was "truly a Czech national opera whose music is most beautiful".

Bedrich should have been happy, but he was not, for the second performance was watched by an even smaller audience than had attended on the first night.

He sat at home all day after the second performance, and Betty could not get him to talk. She spoke quietly and consolingly to him, but he made no answer to anything she said. He sat staring into space, dispirited, his whole world seeming to be in ruins about him. The only move he made was to push a chair to the window where he sat down, gazing out. She left him for an hour, and when she came back he was still in the same position. His shoulders were heaving with unrestrained sobs.

Several people came to the front door—musicians and writers who wanted to converse with him. He would see none of them.

It was very late and very dark when he got up from his chair, wrapped a scarf round his neck, and went out into the deserted, sleeping city. He roamed through the streets, touching walls as he went along unlit alleys, ignoring a small group of soldiers who were noisily wending their way back to their barracks, belching and shouting in the night.

It was four o'clock in the morning before he found his way home again. He didn't know where he had been.

The Bartered Bride—what is it worth? he asked himself. It is useless. It was a disaster. I am a failure. I have let everyone down—Thomé, Sabina, Betty, my family, my children, my country, myself. What am I? Who am I?

Even sleep would not come.

The clip-clop of horses in the streets was coming up to him in the room before he fell into exhausted slumber.

CHAPTER

[20]

BEDRICH WAS LIVING in a twilight world, the emotional limbo from which, once again, he was finding it almost impossible to extricate himself. The old enemy, depression, had him firmly in its clutches. On occasion he had the eerie sensation of being able to stand outside himself and see the grey man he had become—a doubled-up human being, bent under an unbearable weight, dry, incapable of creative work. When he saw this picture he feared for his sanity. He sweated coldly with the thought that the man he was seeing was the man he would remain.

He tried to do something about it. He forced himself to meet his friends, to enter into their discussions, to argue, to be interested in the war between Austria and Prussia. And little by little he hauled himself back to normality. His oddness tapered off gradually. He began to take up music again—not his own, but others' compositions. He studied the newest works of Liszt, played them, made notes, rehearsed. And one magic day he became vehement once more about Bohemia.

It was only then that he became aware that the Provisional Theatre had been closed down for weeks while the Austro-Prussian War was on. Now the talk was of the impending visit to the capital of Emperor Franz Josef I. There was an atmosphere like no other this time, because it was widely believed that the Emperor would make a declaration about full political and national freedom for the Czechs. So the visit would be an occasion for celebrations, not least of which would be a special performance of a Czech opera at the reopened Provisional Theatre.

Only two operas really qualified for consideration, and both were Smetana's. But this time he decided to stay out of the inevitable bickering. He had too recently come out of the abyss, and he didn't want to risk a hasty return. He let the controversy rage round him, and did not express any opinions at all.

The Bartered Bride was looked upon as a commercial failure. That was the main objection to its choice. On the other hand, *The Brandenburgers in Bohemia,* with its inflammatory theme, was a risky proposition. But here again the Reception Committee were of the opinion that there was an equal risk about putting on an opera of an admittedly comic nature. What if the Emperor wasn't amused? Would they not incur his displeasure? Could they afford to?

But a decision had to be made soon. In the end it was decided to take the lesser of the two risks, and they opted for *The Bartered Bride.* What astonished Bedrich was that Rieger raised his voice in support of the opera "because of its national character". Wonders would never cease!

To the relief of everyone concerned, Emperor Franz Josef I said after the performance on the night of October 27th that he had enjoyed the opera immensely.

It was then that praise showered down on Bedrich Smetana. Those who had spoken against the opera earlier, talking of it as being of a low standard, now performed a complete about-face and said they had believed in it all along. But Bedrich himself just smiled philosophically. Something else had occurred which fortified him, from which he was drawing new courage.

It had happened some little time before when he received a summons to attend a meeting of the Czech Society, which had taken over the administration of the Provisional Theatre. He had gone to the meeting with a certain amount of trepidation, not having any idea why they should want to see him. The assembled body of men had greeted him stiffly and formally, and he wondered whether some new barrage of criticism was to be flung at him. Mentally he began to go over the answers he should make, and he was lost in thought when the chairman spoke.

"Mr Smetana, we have a suggestion to make, a proposition to put to you, but in the light of what has taken place recently we are ... unsure of how you will react to it."

Bedrich didn't know whether he was expected to reply or not, but there was nothing he could think of to say, so he maintained his silence.

"As you know, I'm sure, only too well, Jan Mayr is the musical director of the Provisional Theatre," the chairman continued. "I should say he *was* the musical director. He no longer is. We have terminated his contract. We want to offer you the position."

Bedrich gasped, rubbed a hand across his beard, looked away, then back at the chairman. "Do you mean it?" he asked at last.

The chairman looked at his colleagues. "I believe we are all agreed?"

"Unanimously," two of them answered simultaneously.

Bedrich got up and walked away from the gathering, across to a window that looked out on to the square outside. He could hardly believe his ears. He came back and sat down again. "Would you please say it again?" he asked.

The chairman laughed. "You look positively shocked, Mr Smetana."

"I am. I'm wondering whether this isn't a dream."

"It is no dream, Mr Smetana. Will you accept?"

Bedrich was beaming. "It is a great honour ... I am very grateful ... thank you very much ... I never thought this could happen ... "

"Gentlemen," the chairman said, "I believe I speak for all of us when I say how glad we are to have Mr Smetana as our new musical director." There was a chorus of "Ayes" and "Indeeds", and the chairman turned again to Bedrich and said, "There you are. I needn't tell you that you are undertaking a tremendous responsibility."

So now, when the Emperor had conferred the accolade on *The Bartered Bride,* and the former bitter critics had renounced their earlier views, he was able to accept the situation with a calmness that was most reassuring.

His mind was now filled with the glories that lay within his reach, all of them to do with fulfilling his ambitions of establishing the native opera of his beloved land. Betty was away from Prague on holiday, and he sat down to write and tell her of his good news.

"It has happened at last—*I am musical director!*" he wrote.

He also told her that the position had certain drawbacks, most of them financial, for the funds of the theatre were very low. He would be unable to mount any productions that might involve anything resembling a large outlay. And his own salary would amount to no more than a mere 1200 ducats per year, with the possibility of one bonus of two hundred ducats.

It was a tiny remuneration on which to sustain a family for a whole year, and the job would be so time-consuming that there would be precious little chance of earning any extra through outside activities. In any event, he knew from the outset that perfection only would be his goal, and he could never afford to prejudice that by sacrificing anything of his efforts and time by turning in other directions.

His friends, of course, were overjoyed. Frantisek Pivoda called on him, said how delighted he was with the news, and left Bedrich in no doubt as to the part he had played in pressing his claims.

But becoming the new musical director meant a whole lot of new problems. For a start several of the theatre's principal singers, Mayr's friends, showed no inclination to carry on. Soprano Eleonora von Ehrenberg proved herself to be the ringleader, and when she announced that she was leaving, a number of her friends sided with her and left as well. There was no money to attract established singers as replacements. And Mayr had neglected to establish any reserve of artists. The basic requirement of an opera school had been ignored. Bedrich made plans to set one up at the earliest opportunity. In the meantime he had to fill the gaps left by von Ehrenberg and the others who had walked out.

It was then that Frantisek Pivoda turned up again. "I can help you," he said.

Pivoda was director-owner of the School of Instrumental Music and Singing, and Bedrich gratefully accepted the offer of help. However, when they got down to discussing facts Bedrich was immediately alerted to the danger of interference, for Pivoda was taking for granted that every suggestion he made would be accepted without question. This was not the way Bedrich intended to work. He had no wish to be dictated to, and he said so.

Pivoda showed his annoyance. "I do not appear to have made myself clear," he said. "It was thanks in great measure to my efforts that you were appointed."

"I am not ungrateful," Bedrich said, "but I must do things my way, and I could not possibly accept your suggestion that every year you should provide me with an entirely new cast of principals. Can't you see the necessity for continuity? Surely you must know that the whole basis of building a company is to establish a permanent group."

"I am merely saying that we could both help each other if you were to renew your principals every year," Pivoda said. "There would be no problem. I should make sure that your new yearly crop of singers would be up to standard. I do have a certain reputation, you know." The edge in his voice was unmistakable.

"You say there would be no problem," Bedrich said. "I can foresee nothing but problems, and after all I shall be the one who will be answerable."

"So you are not going to co-operate?"

"If co-operating means falling in with your every wish, no."

"I see I have made a serious mistake," Pivoda said, rising. He stumped away, halted at the door, and said, "You are an obstructionist, Smetana. You will regret this conversation." The door slammed, and he was gone, intent on mischief.

On taking over as musical director Bedrich found to his horror what he had long suspected—that the orchestra was pitifully weak. Sections which should have been strong were depleted; it was packed with mediocre or poor instrumentalists in sections which should long ago have been weeded out. The entire structure needed a thorough overhaul and rebuilding. But there was no money available to him.

Should he accept the situation as it was? Be content with the ready and justifiable consolation that the faults were not his, and that there was not the financial wherewithal to rectify the situation? It took him next to no time to reach a decision. Acceptance would have meant compromise. He wanted no part of compromise.

He summoned the members of the orchestra and spent an entire morning and afternoon making them play test-pieces that examined closely their ensemble and solo playing. By the end of the day he had a complete picture of what needed to be done with the orchestra. After the members had gone home he went to the records kept in the theatre's office, wrote down a list of names and addresses of the people he would have to ask to leave. Then, after a quick supper, he went to every home on his list, and explained delicately to each individual that unfortunately the theatre orchestra could no longer employ him. And he did it with such tact and sincerity that he left no rancour behind him anywhere he went. He promised each one that he would do his utmost to secure him an alternative job. It was a promise he kept.

He was now left with a group of musicians much smaller in number than could possibly suit his purpose, but at least he had the nucleus of a musically accomplished orchestra.

His next visit was to the Military School of Music, and he left it with a date fixed for auditions. He could have the best musicians there, and it would not cost the theatre a single crown.

From the Prague Hlahol he recruited new singers. Inside a month he had a full orchestra and chorus with which to begin his new programme.

He went through the repertoire, cast out the substandard operas Mayr had chosen, retained only those he considered to be of the highest class, made a new selection from the works of international composers who had already proved themselves, and laid plans for the encouragement of Czech composers.

Word went out that he was open to suggestions and would give careful consideration to any new works submitted. Men who had stifled their ambitions to compose because of lack of encouragement now took up their pens again and made fresh starts.

The members of the orchestra, so long discontented under the pedagogical rule of Mayr, smiled and warmed to their new musical director. They hadn't known that a conductor could be so thoughtful, so learned, so interested, so appreciative, so erudite. He took immense pains over everything he did with them, explained every passage and the reason for it, told them how it should be played and why, gave them fascinating little dissertations on what had been in the mind of the composer. He was critical, but never hurtful. He coaxed where Mayr had attempted to force. Where Mayr had been said to "rule his orchestra with a corporal's stick", Smetana, they said, "leads with a marshal's baton".

One of the musicians, Josef Jiranek (he had once been a pupil of Bedrich's), summed up his colleagues' feelings when he said, "It wasn't at all surprising that he very quickly became loved and admired by the whole orchestra. He treated all of us as artists, addressed us as though each one of us was his equal, was full of consideration for everyone. He never missed a wrong note, but was gentle in pointing it out, and he created a tremendous enthusiasm all round him. After Mayr's domineering manner and cruelty, the change when a great artist and considerate man took over was amazing."

A system of fines for 'mistakes' made during public performances was in operation in the theatre, and Bedrich had no jurisdiction over it. But these days, more often than not, the 'offenders' did not have to pay the fines—Bedrich himself preferred to do so out of his own pocket. A musician, he felt, knew well enough when he had made a mistake, and the knowledge was its own punishment.

Prague heard operas it had never heard before, and there was almost universal praise for the new musical director. Almost, but not quite, for already his enemies were massing their forces and beginning a subterranean tide of abuse that was gathering momentum and forcing itself to the surface.

It began with accusations that he was too soft, that he should rule more firmly, that the orchestra was running him. Even some of his friends came to him and said he should be more authoritarian. But he had his own way of working—he could not run against the grain of his character.

He had the total loyalty of those who worked with him, and on the night of October 18th, 1867, when he came to the rostrum to conduct his own *Brandenburgers in Bohemia*, it was to find the little platform overflowing with garlands of flowers placed there by the orchestra. It was several minutes before he could trust himself to begin.

He went home that night and told Betty what the orchestra members had done, and as he spoke his heart was full of warmth. It seemed a wonderful thing to him that at a time when the sniping against him had broken out anew he had friends who thought so much of him. There was magnificent consolation in knowing that he was appreciated by people from whom he demanded so much.

CHAPTER

[21]

HAVING SUCCESSFULLY COMPLETED two operas, Bedrich found that the nervousness and uncertainty about his ability which had afflicted him before commencing them had diminished altogether when he came to make a start on his new opera, *Dalibor*, even though the only time available to him was during the late hours of the night, and on certain weekends.

The libretto he chose was one written by Josef Wenzig on a semi-legendary theme, and offered Bedrich the opportunity to express his own feelings. It also had the merit of being Czech in thought and theme. But mainly there was the fact that its primary character, Dalibor, was a person of great bravery, a man who stood up fearlessly for his beliefs, who hated oppression, was an enemy of it, loved people. Dalibor was a man who was prepared to, and did, lay down his life for his ideals.

Wenzig's conception of the character stuck close to the historical, but Bedrich wasn't entirely in favour of depicting Dalibor as no more than a sad, captive figure rotting away in a prison cell, playing his violin to people who listened tearfully to the sounds as they gathered outside the prison window. He wanted a more heroic figure, and so he shaped the story to fit his concept. When formulating his ideas he looked back through his diaries, because he remembered vaguely that many years earlier he had written down some ideas concerning the kind of figure about whom he would like to compose an opera.

At last he found the entry he had been seeking. It had been written back in April 1858, when he had been in Göteborg. It was very short, and was to the effect that he wanted a people's hero, a man who fought doggedly for rights, freedom, humble folk; a man who would be without fear of death or imprisonment.

Reassured that his present conception was backed up by feelings he had expressed before he had ever thought of Dalibor, he went back to the construction of his character; then, once he felt he was on the right track, he put his notes aside and started his preliminary musical sketches.

The orchestral introduction he wrote to the opera was short and full of foreboding. He had in his mind's eye the assembled people—always the people, the downtrodden—waiting before the palace, singing of the man whose life hung by a slender thread, Dalibor, who had fought on their behalf and whose trial was about to begin.

The night Bedrich wrote the fanfare for the entry of the king and his courtiers, he sat for a long time in semi-darkness, the lamp burning on a table at the far end of the room. He tugged his imagination away out of the present, sent it back over the years to the times when, as a child, he had gone wandering alone around the castles at Litomysl and Jindrichuv Hradec, his mind a mass of pictures and fantasies of times gone by when grandeur held sway, when kings and courtiers had walked in worlds of pomp, and ordinary mortals had bowed in awe and subservience.

Then, with the impressions sharp in his mind, he sat and wrote. He had to project his conviction as perfectly as his knowledge and technique would permit. He experimented, rejected, often spent whole nights working, ending up with no more than a solitary line that satisfied him. He struggled against despair and tiredness. He threw hundreds of sheets of music in crumpled balls into the stove, saw hours of effort burnt to thin grey ash. He wanted this opera to be perfection itself, not only in its musical composition, but in the roundness of its characters. They had to be true to life, human beings who reacted *as* human beings to situations in which they found themselves, whose actions were true actions, whose emotions were true emotions. He had to stay in touch with reality, and at the same time create from fantasy a world which would be acceptable.

He had a great spur in knowing that, after years of campaigning, years of talk and collections from the people of Bohemia, the foundation-stone of the new National Theatre was to be laid in a few months time, in May 1868. He would have to have his opera ready in time, and on the night of the great day he would present it to the people of Prague. By the new year the opera was completed.

On March 2nd, his forty-fourth birthday, he made his way as usual to the theatre to take a rehearsal. When he reached it he found Sklenar, the secretary, waiting just inside the door, said, "Good morning," and was about to go to his office when the secretary said, "Please, will you come with me? I've been requested to take you into the auditorium as soon as you arrived." Bedrich shrugged and went along with him.

The secretary led the way through the foyer, and in through the main entrance which opened on to the centre aisle. As soon as they were inside, Sklenar stood back, and Bedrich's eyes were attracted to the stage, where the main curtains were opening, to reveal the entire company assembled there. The theatre's opera producer, Sak, was standing in the front and to one side, and as Bedrich walked slowly down the aisle, puzzled, Sak raised an arm in signal, and great shouts of *"Slava!"* ("Hail and congratulations!") rang out. Then, on another signal, the assembled company broke out into a carefully rehearsed song in his honour.

Bedrich stood rooted to the spot, blinking back his surprise.

Nor was it all over yet. When the song came to an end with three rousing cheers the leading tenor, Arnost Grund, stepped forward, unfolded an illuminated parchment, and read an address of love and devotion from the company.

The words came to Bedrich in snatches. He was incapable of listening closely. " . . . prejudice and jealousy have put all sorts of obstacles in your path . . . you have emerged victorious, and we have become your faithful followers and fighters . . . your kindness and your behaviour have secured our hearts for you . . . "

When Grund finished, the secretary, Sklenar, came out of
the wings and beckoned Bedrich up on to the stage, where
Grund handed over the parchment amid loud clapping, and
before he could murmur his thanks the company sang the
chorus from *The Bartered Bride*, "Why shouldn't we be
happy?"

One simple sentence in his diary told its own story: *I was
more than moved.*

The Habsburg Emperor Franz Josef curtly refused to make
a donation towards the new National Theatre, but if he expected this sign of his official disapproval to impede the project he was wildly wrong, for it was merely taken as a signal
for renewed efforts on the part of those who organized the
collections all over the land. In remote country villages poor
labouring folk who would never see the outside, let alone the
inside, of the theatre dug deep in their pockets and gave gladly
of whatever few coins they could afford.

The site had been procured, and it was an ideal one in every
way. Upon it would rise an imposing structure, one side of
which would look out over the Vltava towards Hradcany, the
ancient seat of the Czech kings, the other side commanding a
view of the Vysehrad. The date fixed for the laying of the
foundation-stone was May 16th.

The crowds began to assemble hours before the little cere-
mony was due to begin. Dignitaries and would-be dignitaries
came, as well as a great mass of anonymous people who just
wanted to be there and see what was going on. Ropes and
planks formed a small enclosure into which those who had
received invitations packed themselves.

In many of the city streets gay flags and posters were on
display. Taverns which had laid in extra stocks prepared for
the influx, the stall-holders opened for only a few hours in
the morning, and the shops gave their workers a half-holiday.
The roads leading in from the countryside were jammed by
streams of people coming by horse and cart and on foot. On
street corners the beggars and tricksters positioned themselves,
and flourished. In hundreds of houses clean white blouses were
ironed glass-flat, knife-edged at the creases; itinerant musicians

R

and entertainers sought out their pitches. Prague was *en fête* for this momentous day.

At the appointed hour the ceremonial trowel and mallet were produced, the heavy foundation-stone swung into place and was lowered down on to its bed of wet concrete, and, one by one, the chosen ones stepped forward to take part in the ritual.

The proudest man to do so was a forty-four-years old brewer's son from Litomysl, proud not because he was taking part, but because of what this day meant to him and to his country. And when all the speeches were over, and the invited retired to a civic reception, Bedrich Smetana slipped away by himself to the Provisional Theatre where, later in the evening, his new opera, *Dalibor*, would be presented for the first time.

As he went through the building he passed the wardrobe mistress hurrying along a corridor with a bundle of costumes, freshly ironed, over her arms. "Good luck for tonight, maestro," she said shyly, and rustled on.

He sat in his office going back over tiny details. The rehearsals had gone well. One of the critics, a friend of his, Ludevit Prochazka, had come in one day during the previous week and heard part of the rehearsals, and in an article in *Narodni Listy* had written:

> *Dalibor* is undoubtedly Smetana's most individual work to date. His very heart-beat seems to pulse through it. I see this as a victorious step forward for Czech opera if only because it is bold in conception, does not shirk the introduction of new principles, and explores the expression of high drama.

Bedrich read over the words again. *Dalibor,* he felt, was the best thing he had ever done; but still he was unable to control his nervousness.

Fifteen minutes before the curtain went up he walked on to the stage and peeped out to see the hall already full to capacity. He saw row upon row of happy faces, an audience in a state of elation, many of them laughing and talking among themselves. He went back to his office and got himself ready, and at half-past seven precisely he was on the conductor's podium taking his bow.

The audience were not prepared for what they were offered, and with a frightful sinking feeling Smetana began to sense that the seriousness of the opera was causing the festive atmosphere to disappear, until by the end of the first act the audience were sitting woodenly, barely applauding.

During the interval he would speak to nobody, sat locked in his office, on edge, worried. When he came out for the second act it was to see a number of the front-row seats empty.

The richness of the music, its grandeur, the tragedy, all were too much for them to imbibe. But one face that seemed to leap at him was that of Frantisek Pivoda, who was sitting in the third row from the front, a slight smile of what looked like disdain puckering his mouth.

Broken-hearted that the work was apparently being coolly received, Smetana tapped his baton and launched the orchestra into the second act of the opera in which he felt he had dug straight to the roots of human feelings, and into which he had poured his whole soul, all his love for his people. The very force of what he had created tore a reaction from the audience, but he felt in his bones that it had come too late, that it did not so much represent real acclaim as an awe at the might of the sound that thundered in the theatre. And at the end, when the clapping erupted again, he was convinced that it expressed relief that the evening's seriousness was over and that merrymaking could now begin at the balls and in the taverns.

The reviews, though appearing at first reading to be enthusiastic, were guarded. Prochazka's opinions were full of qualifications. His earlier enthusiasm had clearly waned. He hinted that Smetana had obviously been too influenced by Wagner, and that the orchestrations were overloud.

The anti-Smetana clique—led now by Pivoda, embittered by Bedrich's refusal to accept all his suggestions piecemeal—spread the word that the opera was a failure, that the music was anything but Czech in spirit, that Smetana had proved himself to be more Wagnerian than Wagner himself.

Numbed by disappointment and shock, sickened at the attacks on his integrity, Bedrich left Prague for a few days, took a score of *Dalibor* with him, and went to see Franz Liszt. Liszt listened sympathetically to what his friend told him, shook his head many times in disbelief, and when the sorry tale was over stood up with the score in his hands and said, "Your people, whom you love so much, are among the world's greatest fools. They don't deserve a man like you."

He took the score to the piano and played parts of it, marvelling aloud at the music. "What monumental ignorance to reject this!" he said. "God in heaven! To say it is Wagnerian and dismiss it like that is lunacy. I tell you, Wagner himself will turn green with envy at what you have accomplished. I don't believe he has it in him to create harmonies like this."

He played and talked until sunrise. "You must not give in," he said as he saw Bedrich to his room. "You must never give up. The world will always have its quota of charlatans, and it is your misfortune that Prague seems to have enough of them for three whole countries."

The second performance of *Dalibor* took place on May 29th. This time more than half the theatre was empty, and the impression Bedrich had had about the applause on the first night (that it had been born out of the high spirits of the day of the laying of the foundation-stone, or else out of relief and awe) was confirmed. A flat silence greeted everything.

On June 28th the Emperor graced the theatre with his presence. This time only the *first act* of *Dalibor* was put on. The remainder of the programme consisted of the second act of Seborov's *Drahomir* and the second act of an opera called *Lejla* by Bendl.

Bedrich now became convinced that only repeated performances of his opera would give it a chance of being appreciated. But the public's attitude had already been influenced by the rumours, the ceaseless whisperings, the deliberate slanders; the four performances in October and December all fell flat. He was embittered as well as saddened.

Pivoda, who had remained silent in the beginning, lurking like a predator until the right moment arrived, now came more into the open and attacked venomously. He started by decrying the new trends of which Smetana was an advocate. The man's hatred of Wagner transcended any musical appreciation of what the German was doing. "Wagner had pioneered a trend in which the orchestra in opera has ceased to perform its function of accompanying the singers," he said, "but our Germanic-minded Mr Smetana places his feet slavishly in the footsteps of Wagner and is ruining our chances of having our own truly Czech opera. He is dangerous because in his present position he can introduce as many foreign influences as he sees fit, unless he is stopped. He is acting like a traitor." He accused Bedrich of being and behaving like a dictator. "He thinks he knows everything. He shuts his ears to advice because he believes he knows better than anyone else."

He disregarded the encouragement the Provisional Theatre musical director gave to every would-be composer who came to him; he disregarded the burgeoning success of one of the orchestra, a young violinst named Antonin Dvorak, who had come shyly with his composition to Smetana, had received help, and who was already on his way to becoming one of the country's most brilliant new composers, and who, on Bedrich's recommendation, had been awarded a State scholarship at the Music Academy of Vienna.

When Smetana launched a series of symphony concerts in the theatre Pivoda castigated him for putting on too much Berlioz, Liszt, and Wagner, "unwelcome foreigners" as he called them. Mayr joined in, as did Krejci, the new director of the Prague Conservatoire.

They continuously attacked the whole construction and conception of *Dalibor,* then unbelievably turned on *The Bartered Bride,* referred to the role of Marenka as being unimportant and lightweight, and scoffed at Kecal as being a pitiful idiot. They publicly advised singers to refuse to take part in the opera.

Throughout 1869 and 1870 Pivoda and his followers attacked relentlessly, even resorting to having a vicious cartoon likeness of Smetana inserted in *Humoristicke Listy.* It showed Bedrich as a mercenary in Wagner's employ. Smetana, they advocated, should be replaced as musical director of the Provisional Theatre because his talent was negligible and he had betrayed the cause of Czech music.

Twice Bedrich answered Pivoda's attacks by articles in which he stated clearly the real reasons behind Pivoda's vicious sniping. But after the second he felt ashamed at the way he was descending to Pivoda's gutter level, and he retired from the dirty fight.

But others, men who admired him, were outraged, men like Ludevit Prochazka—the same Prochazka who could not find it in himself to praise *Dalibor* unreservedly—and Otakar Hostinsky. Brilliant intellectuals both of them, they decided the time had come to leap to Smetana's defence.

Prochazka lashed Pivoda in *Narodni Listy* for undertaking a smear campaign against a man of unimpeachable integrity. Hostinsky appeared in print in *Hudebni Listy*, and, after pledging his unstinted support for Smetana, caustically commented that Pivoda was a marksman of quite extraordinary consistency because "no matter what target he shoots at, all he ever hits is Wagner, and what he calls 'Czech Wagners'."

Another whose loyalty to the composer never wavered was Wenzig, the librettist of *Dalibor*. He failed to understand the blindness of people who had written off the opera, and put it down to what he called "the hatred campaign of a bunch of low clowns". His admiration for Bedrich grew. He was eager to work again, to enter into a new collaboration with the man he considered to be one of the world's greatest composers. He talked to Bedrich about a new libretto he had almost completed, was overjoyed when Smetana showed interest in the project. Called *Libuse*, it was the story of a mythical Czech princess who had foretold much of the suffering of her race, but who had seen ultimate victory and immortal glory as the fruits of bitter centuries.

Bedrich saw the story as a good framework on which to build a new work for the opening production of the new National Theatre. When he started on it in the autumn of 1870 his agony over *Dalibor*'s failure was eating into him, but it was lessened to some extent by the excitement over the turn of political events, for there were plans afoot to crown Emperor Franz Josef as King of Bohemia. This would mean that Bohemia would emerge as an independent Czech state. But then the Hohenwart Cabinet resigned in 1871, and with its going there vanished the hopes of independence. Downhearted, Bedrich faltered, became wide open again to the hurts of his attackers, and found it an enormous effort to concentrate. Instead of rushing headlong into composition, he worked only sporadically. His nerves were permanently taut.

Meanwhile he had been making alterations to *The Bartered Bride,* changing it to conform with his new and advanced theories on opera, and when the Provisional Theatre's leading bass, Josef Palecek, was offered a contract with the St Petersburg Opera Company (at that time looked upon as one of the most important operatic companies in the world) he begged to be allowed to take a copy of the revised score with him.

"I shall do my best to get them to put it on there, maestro," he said. "It is a glorious work, and the Russians, I feel sure, would fall in love with it."

Bedrich gladly gave him the score. "I hold out no hope, Josef," he said. "I was excited at the prospect of its going on in Paris last year, but for some reasons which were never explained to me the plan fell through."

"Leave it in my hands. I'll win them over."

And Palecek had been as good as his word. The summer months of 1871 were ending when the letter came from St Petersburg asking for permission to stage the opera. On its heels came a triumphant letter from Palecek: *It will take some little time yet, because it has to be translated, but I expect it to be ready for production some time in January.*

The Prague papers announced the forthcoming Russian production, and there was a great deal of congratulatory talk from those who believed in Smetana. Pivoda and his clique burnt with jealousy, and remained silent. They couldn't scoff in case they were made to look fools, but if ill wishes could influence the Russian reception *The Bartered Bride* would be a total failure before it even went into rehearsal.

On January 12th, 1872, a telegram was delivered at Bedrich's home. He ripped open the envelope and read the message. It said: GLORIOUS SUCCESS FOR BARTERED BRIDE STOP OVERTURE AND EVERY NUMBER APPLAUDED STOP POLKA ENCORED STOP GRAND DUKES PRESENT FULL HOUSE STOP REPEAT FRIDAY STOP MY OWN REWARD FLOWERS STOP GLORY TO YOU—PALECEK

Bedrich let out a whoop of delight, gave the delivery-boy

a florin, and ran into the room where Betty was preparing a meal. He thrust the piece of paper at her, and when she turned smiling to him he grabbed her hands and whirled her into the polka from the opera.

"Let Mr Pivoda swallow that!" he cried.

But his joy was short-lived, for two days later the St Petersburg critics' views were published in Prague. They tore the opera to shreds. The most important critic, Kjuj, summed up *The Bartered Bride* as "just about worthy of a gifted fourteen-year-old".

Bedrich might have been able to swallow his humiliation but for the fact that Pivoda and all who surrounded him used the comments with crippling sarcasm. They quoted and requoted what Kjuj had said, used "gifted fourteen-year-old" as a mocking catch-phrase, drove their victim into a condition of extreme mental pain in which he questioned everything he had taken for granted about himself. For a number of weeks it became so serious that each day before he met the opera company he had to stand, fists clenched, in the privacy of his office, forcing himself to walk out there and stand in front of them. It was not that he had any doubts about their loyalty, but he had this frightful fear again.

Surely, he thought, some of what is being said about me will be believed. Can those musicians and singers who look to me to give them direction and inspiration continue to respect a man who is the object of such sarcasm, fun-making, attack? How should I walk? Should I try to appear unconcerned? But *how* does one look unconcerned? Or might I not appear to them as being the very soul of arrogance? How can I be *anything* ever again? Perhaps all those things they say against me are true. Perhaps I have no real talent. Perhaps the things my friends say about me are said just because they *are* friends. How can I know? How can I walk out there now and take a rehearsal, and do it with authority, and do it well?

At home Betty felt that she might as well be living with a stranger. Bedrich showed no affection to her. He was permanently preoccupied, gloomy, lacking patience, or working ridiculously long hours into the early morning on his opera *Libuse*.

*   *   *

Jan Neruda had grown in fame and influence. As a writer he commanded big fees and vast respect. He still had all his fire, and was able to harness it in such a fashion that editors were always eager to publish his articles. He was provocative and brilliant.

He was also sensitive and capable of great fury, and both of these qualities were flowing in full strength over the treatment his friend Smetana was receiving. He could see Smetana growing old before his eyes. What was appalling was to see the man apparently on the brink of capitulation, not far from a state of collapse.

He was trying to evolve some way of countering more effectively the Pivoda-Mayr-Rieger campaign. He had read the St Petersburg critiques, had mentally wept for poor Smetana at the cruelty contained in them. He had become quite sick with anger.

In the ensuing weeks he had elicited from St Petersburg that in fact the translation into Russian of *The Bartered Bride* had been poorly done. The essence of the story had been lost, and, worse still, the production had made use of a number of clowns, and had developed into a cheap harlequinade which baffled those critics who saw it. Their verdicts had therefore been accurate enough about the production they had witnessed, but had very little to do with *The Bartered Bride* as it should have been produced; and in the confusion they had witlessly ignored the true quality of the music.

This Neruda made clear to Prague. But the damage had been done, and Smetana became a man without spirit, not utterly broken, but in dire danger.

Now it was September 1872, and Neruda had come from Smetana's home, where he had had the unique treat of hearing a piano transcription of *Libuse*—the only man other than librettist Wenzig who had heard a single note of it. He was lying in bed, wide awake. His brain was whirling. An article was formulating in his mind.

On September 8th it was published in *Narodni Listy*. It started off with a profile of Smetana as he, Neruda, knew him. Then he went on to write of the man's compositions:

God alone could explain the inexplicable magic in his

music. Tears shoot into the eyes at the tenderness of it; and at other times you will find yourself standing up from your seat, not having been aware that you had stood up. This happened to me at the finale of the second act of *Dalibor*. It happened at the dress rehearsal, and again on the first night.

The finale is tremendous. It rises like a mighty tower, like the steeples of a splendid Gothic cathedral. It carries you up with it to the peak reached by a great genius. As the last notes rang out I found myself out of my seat, standing in my box, my whole body tense. I came to with my eyes fixed unseeingly on some far-distance place. Every nerve had been affected by a rare and indescribable beauty.

In a later article, another tribute, he wrote:

No receptacle has yet been designed which could contain the stupidity of some of our alleged intellectuals in this city of Prague. True talent is ignored, or vilified, be it in the field of literature, pictorial art, or music. Let us take the case of Bedrich Smetana. Anyone with a smattering of intelligence can see that whatever and whenever he lifts his baton to conduct, or his pen to write, real art flows out and enriches. But there are among us those who seek to destroy him and who do their utmost to entice others to join in this artistic assassination.

And what is the object of it all? To replace Bedrich Smetana and reinstate Jan Mayr. As a musician Mr Mayr will never come within miles of Bedrich Smetana.

On December 12th, 1872, Smetana at last finished *Libuse*. It had taken him two years. On the last page he wrote: *Completed after many interruptions and castings aside.*

His hopes were that it would be produced on the opening night of the National Theatre, but the building wasn't even near completion yet, and Smetana hid his score away. He wouldn't dream of trying to put the opera on in the Provisional Theatre. The malice of the attacks against him had grown so virulent that he had become a shadow of the man he had been. He was a gaunt figure with a hunted look about him. If *Dalibor* had called down such crude accusations upon him, what would be the effect of *Libuse*? He could only imagine the answer, and it horrified him. He would wait until the opening of the National Theatre. Perhaps by then his attackers would have tired of their campaign. Perhaps by then the musical appreciation of Prague's citizens would have advanced enough to enable them to understand what he had attempted.

But Pivoda was as ruthless and brutal as ever.

There were no funds available, and when it was impossible to stage certain operas because of shortage of money, and when others that were put on lacked grandeur of presentation, Pivoda laid all the blame at the feet of the musical director. He accused Smetana of not having artistic sense. In the journal *Osveta* he wrote that "The Czech opera is still waiting impatiently for its creator to come along. We are being served shabbily by the present claimant."

Finally, dispirited, on the verge of a breakdown, Bedrich felt he could carry on no longer, and towards the end of 1872 talked of resigning. His friends crowded into his home, beseeched him not to give in. He was tired, he said. He felt unwell. He was afraid for his health. He had his family to consider. They would be in dire straits if he collapsed.

But his friends persuaded, cajoled, begged him to hold on. "If you resign," they said, "it will be just what Pivoda and Mayr and their followers want."

"What have I got to look forward to?" Bedrich asked. "More slanders, more lies, more ridicule, more worry. Gentlemen, I am not made of stone. I am weary of it all."

"Think of the ideals you had when you started."

"They have become swamped," he answered.

"Think of the people who believe in you."

"Are there any left?"

"More than you could ever count."

"At times I wonder."

"Have you lost your beliefs, all of them?"

"I believed in *Dalibor*."

"So do we. But was Dalibor the man just a lie? A theatrical device?"

He bristled. "How could you suggest that?"

"It was deliberate—to sting you into awareness."

He hung his head.

"We believe in you."

"I am touched," he said, and they could see he meant it.

"So you will carry on?"

"I shall try," he replied.

"Just one other thing—do not mention to anyone that you had considered resigning."

But a hint of his feelings had reached the ears of Pivoda, and in no time the rumour that Smetana had actually resigned was sweeping Bohemia and beyond. In the restaurants and taverns and meeting-places it was discussed, and knowing ones added to it at every telling. A group of composers who did not know the real story became so alarmed that they drew up a memorandum which they had published.

"Should the moment come when Mr Smetana is replaced as musical director of the Provisional Theatre," they wrote, "we, the undersigned, shall refuse to entrust our works to the new occupier of his position." The names at the bottom included such well-known figures in the Czech musical world as Antonin Dvorak, Frantisek Skuhersky, Karel Bendl, and Zdenek Fibich.

The public reaction was immediate. The outcry and demands for explanations grew, and the Theatre Society did the only thing they could do in the circumstances—they renewed Bedrich's contract and granted him better working conditions.

Smetana's enemies met in fearful anger, planned their next move, and then went into action. A letter signed by sixty-eight season-ticket holders was sent to the theatre administration demanding the sacking of Smetana. It ended with the statement: *The Czech Opera can be resurrected only by the man to whom it should be grateful for its origin.* They didn't name him, but it was obvious they were referring to Mayr.

Pivoda began to criticize Smetana on the score of age, said he was "too old" for the position, questioned his real age, implied he was in his dotage!

Those who stood behind Smetana refuted every charge that was made, tried to ensure that Bedrich was sheltered from the main force of the attack. They saw full well that there was no depth to which the attackers would not descend. And they hit upon a scheme to counter the sixty-eight-signature letter. They had special forms printed which were put on display in the windows of the publishing firms of Stybl and Greger-

Dattl. The public were invited to come inside and take them, read them, and, if they agreed with the sentiments contained in them (to the effect that the signatories were behind Smetana's retention as musical director), to sign and return them.

By the end of the first day over two hundred signatures had been handed in.

But the theatre administrators had already been swayed by the letter signed by the season-ticket holders, and on December 15th made an announcement that they had approached Jan Mayr to see whether he would be willing to take up his old post once again, and that Mr Mayr had graciously accepted. "This move has been made to allow Mr Smetana to devote more time to composition," the statement ended. It was a cunning ploy.

Neruda and his fellow Smetana supporters were furious. They went out into the streets of Prague, stopped passers-by, asked them their opinions, and found them to be over-whelmingly against Smetana's replacement. Within six days over nineteen hundred people had signed the forms in Stybl's and Greger-Dattl's offices.

The forms were delivered to the theatre administrators. The evidence in favour of Smetana's retention was too strong to ignore. So, for a while at least, his enemies had to retire and lick their wounds, while Bedrich himself began to pull up mentally and physically to something closer to his norm.

[22]

MIDWAY THROUGH 1873 BEDRICH settled on a subject for a new opera. Hints were dropped that he should write another *Bartered Bride*, but he was not interested. He wanted, as always, to try something new, and it was some months before he struck on the idea of *The Two Widows*. He had seen Mallefille's comedy on the stage in 1868, and now, when he looked back to it, it seemed perfectly suited to what he had in mind.

He mentioned it to Emanuel Züngel, who enthused, and they met on several occasions, talked around the proposition, compared notes, found something concrete taking shape on which they were both agreed. Finally Züngel went away to produce a libretto, and on July 16th Bedrich felt confident enough, sure enough in his own mind, to embark on the new work.

There was little he shared now with Betty. Her interest in his doings had slackened off so that their home life amounted to little more than a mutual toleration. He made no demands on her. She made few on him. But with the passing years he had grown ever closer to Zofie, the daughter who looked so very much like her mother, Katerina.

She was a gentle girl, a young woman now of unquestionable attraction who occasionally came and sat in his room when he was composing, as she had come to hear him rehearse when she was a child. And there had developed in her an intense love for Bedrich. She felt terribly for him in the vulnerability he still displayed when exposed to harshness of any kind. She wasn't yet old enough to mother him, but she did as many acts of kindness for him as she could. She knew instinctively that he liked her presence in the room when he was composing. He would occasionally turn round and look at her, smile in that shy, grateful way of his, and, though only silence filled the space between them, it was a silence full of eloquence.

In her bedroom at night she often lay in the dark, listening for sounds from the room where he was working, thinking of the loneliness in which he must exist in trying to create beauty. Sometimes she took a book into her bedroom and forced herself to sit up reading, so that she would be awake when he stirred and got ready for bed. Then she would slip into the kitchen and warm some coffee, bring it to him, cuddle him, and whisper, "Always remember, Papa, I love you." He rarely replied in words. His eyes talked for him, as did the hand-pressure on the backs of her fingers.

Although she had been no more than a child, she recognized in those eyes the same look he had given her after her mother had died. It had disturbed her then. Now it filled her heart with compassion. She didn't know what it was to hate, but she intensely disliked the men who were always, it seemed, seeking to ruin this man who would not willingly hurt anything or anyone.

Her big worry was that he would be like a ship cast adrift when she married in February. She had seen the expression of sadness that had mingled with the happiness when she told him she wanted to marry Josef Schwarz. He had held both her hands, still sitting down. Then he had stood up and looked at her, his eyebrows high in questioning arcs, as though saying, "So soon?" But he had not spoken those words. He had had to turn away from her for a moment, pretending to blow his nose. But she hadn't been fooled. His eyes were glistening when he turned around again and took up her hands.

"My little Zofie. So recently you were a baby, and now you are going to be married. It makes me feel old."

She had come to him, tearing her hands loose and holding him tightly. After a while he whispered, "Will the link be broken for ever?"

And it was by that sentence she had learnt how precious she had become to him as a reflection of what her mother had been.

"Never, Papa, never while I have my health," she answered.

"I knew it," he said. "God make you happy, my little Zofie."

She was married on February 3rd, 1874, and as a wedding-present Bedrich gave her a piano, the most beautiful gift he knew.

A week later someone knocked on the door of his office in the Provisional Theatre, and he looked up to see Edmund Chvalovsky, the stage director, coming in.

"I see exactly what you mean," Chvalovsky opened. "I'd love to do it. I'm sick and tired of the old clichéd ways we are expected to use every time."

"And you think *The Two Widows* will lend itself to the new treatment?"

"No shadow of doubt about it."

"They won't like it, you know."

"The public?"

"No," Bedrich said, "the administrators."

"To hell with them!"

"You may find yourself in an awkward position if the experiment doesn't come off."

"I'm prepared to risk that," Chvalovsky said. "Prague isn't the only city in the world. I can always go elsewhere. But let's cross that particular bridge if and when we come to it."

"Very well. I'm delighted that you're going to go ahead with it, but we must keep it absolutely quiet. I want to spring it as a surprise on the public."

"And the critics?"

"And the critics."

"What about the dress rehearsal—they'll see it then."

"They won't. We'll make the dress rehearsal private, and I'll swear the company and the theatre staff to secrecy."

The two men shook hands on it and then sat down to plan an opera production that would kick over the traces of the accepted traditions of Prague. For Bedrich had suggested to Edmund Chvalovsky that he used his undoubted skills as a drama director on *The Two Widows*, and to forget all the theatre's laid-down rules about set pieces. In other words, Bedrich wanted real acting in *The Two Widows*.

For the next six weeks the rehearsals were carried on behind closed doors, with an elaborate system of look-outs ready to warn if it was found impossible to head off any unwanted intruders.

Pivoda and Mayr were stepping up their campaign once more, but on March 9th, at a performance of *Faust*, Bedrich was the centre of noisy scenes of acclamation. He came out to find the conductor's podium garlanded, and at the end of the opera there were repeated shouts of "Conductor! Conductor!" until he went up on the stage to take his applause and be hit by cascades of flowers.

On the night of the 27th he was about to leave his room in the theatre to conduct the first performance of *The Two Widows* when he turned and knelt down, something he had not done for a long time, covered his eyes with his right hand, and said, half aloud, "Dear God, if it is Your will, make this night good." Then he stood up, tugged the wrinkles out of his jacket which had ridden up round his neck, and went out to take his place before the orchestra.

On the podium were two huge garlands. Each was bound by cream-coloured, broad satin ribbon which shone like mother-of-pearl. After bowing to the roaring, clapping audience he turned left and right, smiled to the members of the orchestra. Suddenly they stood up and joined in the applause, and, embarrassed by this show of affection, he dropped his eyes, and for the first time saw that there were inscriptions on the satin ribbons. He bent down to the first one and read: "To our famous maestro, Bedrich Smetana—from the members of his orchestra." The other one said: "To our beloved musical director, Bedrich Smetana—from the members of the opera." And, lying across the garlands, glinting among the flowers, was a solid-silver baton. When he saw it he looked away, almost guiltily, and caught the eye of the leading violinist, who nodded and pointed at the baton, then at Bedrich.

s

He picked it up. He could just make out the engraving: "27th March 1874—*The Two Widows.*"

The people in the front two rows of seats saw the white handkerchief he took from his pocket to dab at his face, saw the little head-shake as he put the handkerchief away, saw the tightly compressed lips as he looked from face to face in the orchestra. . . .

The first act took the theatre by storm.

At the end of the performance even the critics were on their feet screaming their "Bravo's!" with everybody else. They had never known a night like this with so much emotion running wild, such dramatic happenings on the stage, such love for a man spontaneously bursting from throats both young and old.

He was hauled on to the stage, had his hand pumped, his back thumped, was loaded with flowers from the Prague newspapermen, from the members of the Academy of the Readers' Society, from the administration of the Academic Society. Then the members of the company gave him an ovation, and a deputation of soloists came to him bearing a magnificent wreath wrought from silver, on the leaves of which were inscribed the names of his operas.

The audience refused to leave the theatre until he had taken countless curtain calls, and after they had gone he stood in the centre of the stage for twenty minutes while the company toasted him, made speeches about and to him, and nearly broke his back and mangled his hands with congratulations.

The sour note had to come. He saw the administrators in the wings glaring in his direction; a stage-hand bustled his way through the throng and told Bedrich that they wanted to see him. They walked to the main office, and when the door was shut behind him they turned on him with cold fury.

"By whose authority were the accepted patterns of production ignored?"

"Mine," he said.

"You are the *musical* director, you had no right to countermand our instructions."

He said nothing.

Each of them in turn upbraided him. He did not reply.

They spent ten minutes abusing him. Not one word of praise crossed their lips. They dismissed him curtly with the warning that *The Two Widows* should be produced the following night "with none of these dramatic tricks". It was to go on in the old style, or not at all.

But when they saw the morning papers, when they read the glowing opinions about the new production methods, they were forced to relent, and word was sent to Bedrich that the opera could be produced as on the first night.

It was, all in all, a triumph that gave him quiet and intense pleasure, a pleasure that lasted the whole of that day, and he indulged it to the full because he knew that of a certainty the accusations, the undermining, the attacks, would start again on the morrow.

They did, with renewed intensity.

CHAPTER

JULY 4TH WAS ONE OF THOSE golden days of summer when
God seems to smile on the world, happy at what he has created. The sun had risen into a sky in which not a fleck of
cloud was visible; the birds' dawn chorus sounded as though
it had been specially orchestrated for this day and no other,
and the colours were richer and more vivid than Bedrich had
noticed for a long time. It was the beginning of his holiday,
and he moved about the rooms humming happily to himself,
for soon he would be on his way to Zofie's house at Ovcarny
to stay with her and her husband, Josef Schwarz.

He had already visited them once before, in April. Josef, a
forest inspector, a quiet, round-faced man whose head, apart
from the sides and back, was one huge area of glistening, pink
skin, had made Bedrich very welcome. With his slow, deliberate voice, his love of birds and animals and the countryside,
Josef was the kind of man Bedrich would have liked to have
been had he not been a musician.

The cab arrived early, and the driver, a cheerful, whistling
fellow, carried Bedrich's bags out and swung them high up
on to the driver's seat.

"It's a good day to be alive, Mr Smetana," he roared.

"It is indeed," Bedrich agreed.

"Here you are, sir, let me give you a hand up. The old legs
aren't what they used to be, eh?"

Bedrich pulled away from him, laughing, and said, "Good
Lord man, do I look that ancient?"

The driver scratched his head. "Only trying to be helpful, sir. No, sir, you don't look all that old, come to think of it. In fact, I hope that when I'm your age I'll be—er—as fit-looking as you are."

"How old *are* you?" Bedrich asked.

"Fifty-seven, sir. Fifty-eight in October."

"I see," Bedrich said, then abruptly stepped up into the cab. He was fifty years of age...! But it was a day on which sadness could not live, and within half an hour his good humour was back with him again, raising his spirits, making him look forward to the warm days ahead.

His mind was locked against worry, for the time being at any rate, and on his journey through Prague his heart leapt with a rush of love for the familiar sights that had been part of his life for so long. The river, wide, silver, and slow-moving, reflected all the glory of the day. And when he glimpsed the Vysehrad history seemed to crowd into the tiny compartment with him.

Soon Prague was behind and he was travelling through countryside painted with rich, lush greens and warm, golden yellows. "My country," he said aloud. "This is my country."

He would be alone with Zofie and Josef, because Betty had already gone to Pecice with the two younger children, Zdenka and Bozena. They were stopping with Bedrich's brother Karel. One of the reasons he had decided to go to Zofie's rather than Karel's was because Karel had no piano, and at the back of Bedrich's mind when he was arranging his holidays was the thought that one day sooner than anyone near him seemed to imagine he might have to take up virtuoso work again. His position as musical director of the Provisional Theatre felt anything but secure, and the administrators were looking for a convenient reason to get rid of him. The accumulated criticism from Dr Rieger, Mayr, and Pivoda had had its desired effect.

Zofie was on her own when he arrived, and she clung to him for a long time before they went indoors. When Josef came home later he stood by the door beaming his welcome, then came over and held Bedrich's hand. "You are welcome, Papa," he said. He never spoke much, but what he said he meant.

For the first two days Bedrich did nothing. Sometimes he sat on a chair in the sun at the rear of the house, dozing peacefully in the heat, soothed by the humming of the bees. In the evening Zofie asked him to play for them, and, fitting in with his mood of relaxation, he played softly and with great feeling.

On the third day of his stay he rose early, and when he came into the room for his breakfast Zofie said, "Why are you out of bed at this hour?"

"I've got work to do," he said.

"But you're on holiday, Papa. You are here for a rest."

"It's all right," he said. "I shan't overdo it."

"You are going to compose something here?"

"No, Zofie, I am going to practise the piano."

"But you played perfectly last night."

"I played passably well, but not well enough to please a concert audience."

"But, Papa, you don't have to please a concert audience by *playing* any more. All that's behind you now. You please them by *composing*.

"I may soon have to play for them again, my dear. I may not be musical director for very much longer."

"Oh, Papa!" she cried, and ran across to him and put her arms about his neck. "They are so cruel!"

Five days a week for the next three weeks he practised for as long as nine hours a day, punishing himself in the process. Zofie was by the window one day, working on some embroidery, when the music stopped and she looked up to see if he was about to pick up a new sheet of music. But he was sitting shaking his head. She said nothing. Then she saw him putting his hands up and covering his ears. She put her embroidery on the windowsill, wondering what the matter was. Her father stood up, and now he was hitting his ears with the palms of his hands. She was about to go to him when he turned, took a step towards her, and suddenly fell face down on the floor. She was beside him in an instant, panic making her eyes bulge like those of a frightened faun.

"What's wrong, Papa? Are you all right?"

His head was cradled in the crook of her arm, and he was blinking.

"Are you all right?" she asked again.

He became a little impatient now and tried to get to his feet. "Yes, I'm all right, Zofie, don't fuss me," he said. "Help me to get up."

By holding on to her and levering himself up with the other hand on the piano-stool, he was able to get to his feet. He was still blinking his eyes, and he put a hand to his right ear.

"What happened?" Zofie asked.

He walked shakily to the sofa and sat down heavily. "I'm frightened," he said quietly.

She sat alongside him and asked, "What made you fall down?"

His eyes wide, he looked at her. "I became dizzy and lost my balance."

"And your ears—what's wrong with your ears? Why were you hitting them?"

His face had gone ashen grey. "That's what frightens me," he said. "The noise in them, it was unbearable."

"What kind of noise?"

"A humming first, but suddenly it grew so loud that I thought my head was going to burst open."

"How is it now?"

"There's just the humming. I think it's going away."

She put her hand on his brow, felt the clamminess of sweat there, pressed his forehead firmly but gently until his head was resting on the back of the sofa.

"Don't talk," she said. "Lie back there and rest. You've been working far too hard. I'll leave you alone for a while, and you try to get a little sleep. I'll fetch a rug to put over your legs in case you catch a chill."

She got the rug and draped it across his knees, then stood watching him anxiously for a few minutes until she was sure he was asleep. Then she ran out of the room, and when Josef came in he found her weeping on their bed.

Dr Zoufal was baffled. He had noted down all the symptoms Bedrich Smetana had told him, had listened to Josef Schwarz who had come to Prague with his father-in-law, had examined the ears, and could find nothing organically wrong.

"I must admit I don't know what could have brought this on," he said. "The humming sound is still there, you say?"

Bedrich nodded.

"But you can hear all right?"

"Yes, it's as though you are talking over the sound of far-away thunder. I have to strain to catch your words, and watch your lips very carefully."

"And at night?"

"It stays there all night. It takes me hours to get to sleep, and when I wake up it is still there."

Zoufal shook his head in bewilderment. "All I can think is that it is something developing, some infection. I'll get a second opinion, if necessary. But if, in the meantime, you have any pain, come back immediately."

They returned on August 8th, the humming having stayed with Bedrich all the while, but the loud noises coming only intermittently. This time when Zoufal examined the ears, he detected inflammation of the middle ear.

"Ah," he said, "now we have something to work on. Let me see." He picked up a heavy book from his desk, looked up a reference, thumbed through the pages until he found what he was looking for, read it in silence, then closed the book and stood up again. "Yes, as I suspected, you are suffering from catarrh. I'll give you an inhaler, and in a little while I think you'll find it will give you relief."

But now pain came as companion to the humming, and a few days later a high, piercing whistle came into Smetana's right ear, and no sound, no treatment, could drown it.

Betty returned to Prague, and Bedrich visited Dr Zoufal every day. Between visits he sat vacantly, sometimes hitting his ears fiercely in a blind hope that one pain would relieve the other.

In a little publication founded by his friends and named *Dalibor* in his honour a small item was published which said that he had fallen ill "because of the continued mental upheavals caused by the activities of a certain section of the musical community. It is with regret therefore that we have to announce that Mr Smetana will have to give up all his musical interests for a short time."

On September 7th he wrote to Dr Antonin Cizek, one of the administrators of the Theatre Society: *In my right ear I have lost all hearing and can hear but little with my left ear. I am undergoing treatment—indeed, I have been under constant treatment since July—and such is the state of my health that I am forced to ask you if you would convey my apologies to your fellow administrators and ask them if they could see their way to excusing me from my duties for the time being.... If my condition should worsen during the next three months it goes without saying that I should be forced to resign my position.*

The news spread and was received with jubilation by those who had been working towards his dismissal. Under the head-line: *"Muss gehen oder brechen!"*—"Must go or break!"— which quickly became their slogan, they began a fresh cam-paign to have him ousted. With a rare brand of viciousness they mocked and goaded the sick Smetana, their callings for his replacement becoming more strident as the pain-wracked days wore on.

Through the rest of September and into the first week of October the noises and the pains beat at him remorselessly. Sometimes he was completely deaf for days on end, had no idea of what was being said to or around him, was fearful of standing or walking without support because of the fits of dizziness which made his head reel and caused his legs to buckle beneath him. But around mid-morning on October 8th he experienced something like an explosion in his head, and a shooting pain, as if ice-cold needles were being forced straight into each ear, tore a moan of anguish from his lips.

"Bedrich!" The sound of Betty's little cry of alarm screamed at full volume through his brain, and he looked at her, an expression of stupefaction on his face.

"Say it again," he said suddenly.

"What?"

"Anything, say anything!"

"What made you cry out?"

"I can hear!" he shouted. "I can hear! *I can hear!*" Before her amazed eyes he ran to the piano, pounded indiscriminately on the keyboard, and turned to her again. "I can hear, Betty!

I played a C and a D and an E, and I *heard* them!"

Miraculously, his ears had cleared. Betty was smiling with relief. Like a mechanical man he came towards her, and then his arms were about her, clutching her to him.

"I want you to get ready immediately after supper," he said. "We're going out."

"Where?"

"To the opera," he replied.

He sent word to the theatre that he would be coming, and when he arrived there before the performance began he was led on to the stage, where the whole cast as well as the orchestra were assembled ready to greet him. Their master had come back.

He went home that night so buoyed with relief that for the first time in months he spoke to Betty about his work. He poured her a drink, went and sat on the piano-stool, and swivelled round so that he was facing her.

"During my lucid moments during the past weeks," he began, "when I was locked away in silence from you, my love, from my children and from my friends, I began thinking of a new composition. You know what Bohemia means to me, how I love this land of ours? Well, it has always been my ambition since I was a little boy to ... to enshrine that love, to enshrine my country in a musical work ... to paint pictures in sound so that anyone who heard would know what I felt ... to create pictures so that people in other countries who might never see Bohemia would know how beautiful it is."

Betty stood up, anxious, but he waved her into a sitting position again.

"No, don't say anything yet. You see, I even worked out what to do—write a series of symphonic poems, each one devoted to a subject. One I shall call *Vysehrad*, another *Vltava*, another *Bohemia's Woods and Fields*, and so on. And I shall call the whole cycle *Ma Vlast—My Country*."

"But you know what the doctor said," Betty protested. "You mustn't strain yourself."

"It's all right. I'll be careful, but don't try to stop me. I must do it. I must do something or I shall ... " He couldn't finish it, and turned away from her.

"Don't you think you should go to bed now?" Betty tried again. "You could begin tomorrow. You've had a very exciting day and you must be tired."

"I'm not tired," he answered. "I want you to listen to this. Already a theme has been running through my head, and I believe I know how *Vysehrad* should begin. I haven't been able to play it before, and I haven't written it down. I want you to hear what it will sound like."

Betty put her untouched drink on a little table beside her and linked her fingers round her knees. The bones of the knuckles showed white through her skin.

Bedrich flexed his fingers to loosen up the joints, then sat still for a few seconds as he recalled the chords that had been with him in his pain. When his mind was quite clear he raised his hands and brought them down, sending a rich sound through the room. When he stopped he threw his head back, savouring the music he had made, and said, "Yes, that's how it will begin, that will be the opening of *Vysehrad,* and it will be played on harps. Can you imagine it? Harps for the opening. I don't believe anyone has used them in this way before." He spun around. "Do you like it?"

"It sounds wonderful," Betty said.

"I mean really."

"Yes, yes, I mean it," she said.

"Good," he said, turning back to the keyboard and beginning to play again, humming as his fingers caressed the keys.

Betty leant back now and closed her eyes the better to give her attention to the music. She sat up suddenly when a loud, discordant crash of sound lashed at her. At the same moment Bedrich screamed, a high, harsh, ugly sound. She saw him raising his hands up and bringing them down with full force to send another jangle cutting through the room. She was on her feet as he bellowed, "Betty! Betty! Can you hear anything? Is there any sound? Betty! Betty! *Bett-eeee!*"

He was punching the keys now with clenched fists, and as she reached his side he wrenched his face towards her, looking like a madman.

"Oh, God! Oh, God!" he sobbed, "I'm deaf. I—am—deaf!"

She led him to his bed and saw the face of a man who felt that life was being crushed out of his body.

In twelve days' time the fiftieth performance of *The Bartered Bride* was due to be performed, and he was due to conduct it. But as sleep overcame him he knew he would not be able to hear it, let alone conduct it. He felt totally forsaken.

Dr Zoufal wouldn't let him leave the house. Sometimes he felt so isolated that he truly wanted to die. But one day he remembered what Beethoven had accomplished after his hearing had gone, and he felt so ashamed that he determined not to give in, to press on, to commit to paper at least one more work to which he would devote every ounce of knowledge, technique, and feeling he had accumulated over the years.

Vysehrad—his symphonic poem depicting the proud castle which had been the first seat of the early Czech princes—took shape rapidly, and he used the harps at the beginning to create the character of the legendary bard, Lumir, singing of the old place's past glories. From this motif he evolved a whole series of themes, and decided to incorporate them in various forms throughout the remainder of the cycle. As before, he mentally lived through the actions and times he had set out to recapture. For moments of glory he wrote music that was truly glorious. For passages telling of struggles he immersed his mind in thoughts of strife, then wrote down what he felt. And when he came to the downfall he wrote in a spirit of tragedy.

Two days after completing *Vysehrad* he began *Vltava*. The date was November 20th, 1874.

He brought the great river into his room, remembered every emotion he had felt from the first time he had seen it, the countless times he had gazed at it, the changing character of what began as a lively, sparkling stream, hopping and leaping gaily over a million rocks and stones, gaining in speed and broadening, running deep through green glades, coursing with seeming pride through ravines, meandering across the grasslands, thundering over falls, and flowing with majesty into the great city; tumbling with deep-throated authority down its weirs, passing beneath its spanning bridges, winding off into evening sunlight. He remembered with love. He wrote it down with truth and beauty. And he was as deaf as the lifeless river-bank.

He wanted to give the fullest picture of the Vltava—the Vltava in its every mood—and to do it would mean using all the brass, all the percussion, all the woodwind, all the strings. The river in a meadow was far different from the river in a cataract—he knew that better than anyone.

He had been in love with it since boyhood, had dreamt about it, talked about it, gazed at it for endless hours; had seen it in cold, grey rain and in spring sunlight; he had stood looking down into it at that time when man's spirit is said to be at its lowest and coldest, in the early hours of the morning, and had wanted to use it as an instrument of his own death. In Göteborg and in Germany and in Poland and in Holland he had yearned for it. He knew every sound it made, knew they varied from whispers to roars, from gurglings to rumblings, from the beautifully simple to the wrathfully majestic. He knew all of this.

For a hearing man to capture it, if he wanted to do it with clarity and accuracy and beauty, would be a stupendous task because it would require total recall, experiments, attempts and failures and small successes, and, above all, dependence on the ears to listen, analyse, sift, accept, and reject. Bedrich had only his love, his memories, his talent, and the ears of his mind.

The house was still, the city silent and locked in coldness on the last night of November. He stood up from the table where he had been working for close on six hours and pulled back the heavy, velvet curtain from the window. He put his face close to it, drew back sharply when his forehead touched it and the coldness struck like a pain. Even before he did the next thing he knew it would be useless, but nevertheless he tried—he knocked on the glass with his knuckles, *just in case his hearing had come back.* He felt the knocking sensations in his fingers, but heard nothing at all.

He took his diary out of the drawer. *I can't hear anything,* he wrote. *Dr Zoufal still has some hope about my condition. I have no hope at all.*

*   *   *

Josef Srb-Debrnov actually reached the Smetana front door three times in the following week, but each time turned away, unable to summon enough courage to ask to see his friend. How could he talk to a deaf man? And yet every time he walked away he despised himself. Bedrich must be in desperate need of friendship.

On December 8th Srb-Debrnov finally conquered himself by the simple device of shutting out of his head all thoughts of embarrassment and walking straight up to the door and knocking. As he waited for someone to answer he filled his mind with memories of the first time he had met Smetana. It had been in the 1860's, when Srb-Debrnov had joined the new Prague Hlahol as an ambitious twenty-five-year-old in love with music and intent on making a career as a music critic. Bedrich had befriended him, encouraged him, helped him, in a sense educated him. Since then, down through the years, as his own career had grown successful, their friendship had strengthened; Srb-Debrnov's admiration for this man of genius had mushroomed. He thought of those years, and nothing else, as he stood facing the door. When it opened he was relieved to see a child there, and not Betty Smetana. He said he wanted to see Bedrich, and the child led him to a room and ushered him in, then went away, shutting the door.

Bedrich was sitting with his back to him, and Srb-Debrnov, forgetting himself, first coughed, then said, "Maestro." But of course there was no answer, no reaction. He walked wide of the table to give the deaf man a chance to see him out of the corner of his eyes. He didn't wish to startle him. Bedrich caught sight of the movement, looked up with a little jerk, recognized his visitor, then stood up with his arms out.

"Josef! My friend! What a pleasant surprise!" The voice was unnaturally loud, the first traces of ugliness creeping into it. "You are well?"

"Yes, thank you, maestro," Srb-Debrnov answered, and realized that he himself had shouted, and that shouting meant nothing to Smetana, whose eyes were locked on his mouth. He spoke very slowly, pronouncing each word as carefully as he could, so that Bedrich could follow the movement of his lips. "How do I find you?"

"Tired, but happy and relieved now," Smetana replied. "I have just completed my *Vltava*."

"Your *Vltava*?"

"Yes. Here it is. A symphonic poem." He picked up a sheaf of paper. "Would you do me a kindness?"

"Anything, maestro."

"Would you listen?"

"It would be an honour."

Bedrich took the papers to the piano. "You may not think so when you have heard it." He looked around sharply. "I have to depend on others to be my ears now. Be honest, Josef, that is all I ask."

Bedrich played the piano transcription, and Srb-Debrnov heard the two bubbling springs joining to form into a brook, heard that grow and become a stream. He saw a picture of forests in which a hunting-horn sounded; villages took shape, and when a polka melody came in he saw a village wedding. And then, through the alchemy of Smetana's music, it was night, and somehow there was moonlight and old castles, and clearings where nymphs danced. But always there was the presence of the river, growing and widening and rushing and splashing, flowing through Prague and out and beyond, and disappearing with its air of ageless mystery, its splendour.

It was uncanny, and very moving.

Was it possible that all this had come from the pen of a man to whom the sound of a thunder-clap would be no different from the pudgy hands of a baby coming softly together, since he could hear neither? Surely deafness had to mean depression? Depression that would embitter and stifle all creative urges? And doubly so in the case of a musician who, more than anyone else, lived by his hearing?

Smetana had turned on the piano-stool and was looking at Srb-Debrnov, who, for some reason Bedrich could not understand, was bent forward in his chair with both hands covering his eyes. Why has he said nothing? Bedrich wondered. Have I failed so completely that he cannot face me? Has my pen let down my mind? Is he hiding because he is my friend and does not wish to shatter me by revealing a face carrying the shock of having heard a travesty? Is this, then, the end?

Srb-Debrnov took his hands down from his face. "I have no words, maestro," he said.

Bedrich, trying to read his friend's lips, missed the words and said, "I have failed?"

Srb-Debrnov was alongside him in three strides. He put his face close to Bedrich's and spoke clearly and slowly. "I have never heard anything like it. It made me want to cry. It is a miracle."

"You are not saying this because we are friends?"

Srb-Debrnov clasped the sloping shoulders and then, putting a hand under his friend's chin, as he would do to a child, tilted the head back until their eyes met. "Maestro," he said, "it is a miracle, a heart-breaking lovely miracle."

"And it is the river Vltava for you?"

"It is the river Vltava for everyone for all time. Anyone who hears it once will never forget it. And whenever a Czech who is away from Bohemia hears it it will break his heart and send his soul soaring with love and longing."

"Then I can breathe again, Josef?"

"You should be thinking instead of climbing to the highest tower of Hradcany Castle and screaming your name out to the whole world."

The Christmas festivities passed him by, left him a lonely, silent figure on the periphery. He was penniless. He had been unable to buy presents for the family, and the children were frightened of him because he shouted so loudly. So for the most part he sat hunched in a chair with his thoughts as his only company. He had never felt so remote.

He had not received his December salary. Mayr had been reappointed to the Provisional Theatre, and the Theatre Society announced that Mr Smetana was to be given a pension of 1200 crowns a year. The smallness of the amount terrified him now that he was cut off from all other sources of income. His friends, when they heard the figure, said it was "too little to live on, and just enough not to let him die". Nor was the pension a pension in the true sense of the word. It was not given to him free of obligations. He was still expected to compose for the theatre.

Swallowing his pride, in January he wrote a letter to Cenek Bubenicek, chairman of the theatre administrators. He asked humbly for his December salary, then went on to discuss his pension and inquired if there was any chance that it could be increased to 1500 crowns per annum. If they could see their way to granting this, he said, he would undertake to let them produce all his works in future without payment of royalties. Saying this was like cutting a lifeline.

But Bubenicek's answer was curt and hurtful: *You must surely know that the theatre is going through a period of financial crisis. You would be well advised to accept our offer without cavilling. I would point out that 1200 crowns a year for the mere right of producing your works—very few of which are commercial successes—is not an inconsiderable amount. It is my own view that the Theatre Society is treating you nobly in the circumstances.*

Bedrich hid the letter away.

Three weeks later he took out pen and paper and wrote another letter, this time to Fröjda Benecke in Göteborg.

I am completely deaf, that is, I cannot hear talk or singing, or music. Sometimes I can lip-read, but mostly those who wish to communicate with me have to write down what they want to say. I feel so cut off from the rest of humanity. I cannot teach, I cannot conduct, I cannot earn enough to feed my family. When I try to talk to children, all I see are the frightened looks on their faces as they cower away from me. From me who loves children! It is terrible. The doctor who has been treating me says that there is still some hope of my being cured if I can go to some great specialist, whose name I have forgotten, living in Würzburg. But, dear Fröjda Benecke, it is out of the question. I have not got the money. I feel lost. I cannot bear to look at myself in a mirror, because what do I see? An infirm old man with despair in his eyes. On occasions I have managed to claw my way out of despair to do some work, because I feel I still have much good work left in me. So I know that the old man who looks out at me is no part of the real me. He is just a body in which I am forced to live. Do you understand?

I feel mean about what I am going to say, but rely on your

T

great heart to forgive me. I wondered if you would approach my friend Capek and ask him if he could arrange—perhaps by holding a concert?—to raise some money to lend me. I do not want charity. I will do my utmost to repay as soon as possible.

When I re-read the last part I became confused about whether to send it or not. If it offends you please disregard it and attribute it to the state of mind into which my condition had projected me.

Before he received her reply *Vysehrad* and *Vltava* were performed by a full orchestra to an audience who echoed all Srb-Debrnov's sentiments. Josef himself came to Bedrich and told him, saw the composer's face coming to life, saw the new hope as a tangible thing building up as he realized that he was not, after all, finished as a composer of music.

In February Countess Eliska Kaunic-Thun, who as a little girl had been a pupil of the young Smetana, organized a concert in her salon, and made a collection among her guests. The proceeds, nearly 1800 ducats, were handed over to her former teacher. But the kindly action did not go unnoticed by Smetana's enemies, and the two papers which published most of their vilifications, *Politik* and *Hudebni Listy*, carried pieces which attacked Bedrich for "begging".

It was too much for Jan Neruda. He answered back powerfully in *Narodni Listy*. His article concluded by saying:

To suggest that the Theatre Society is giving him charity is both impertinent and false. Indeed, it should be considered an honour by the Society to help Smetana in any way it can at this, the worst hour in his life. It is he above anyone else who has enabled the Czech theatre to win admiration for itself. . . .

With the funds from Countess Eliska Kaunic-Thun and Fröjda Benecke (1244 sovereigns) Bedrich left Prague on April 18th on his journey to Würzburg to see the eminent specialist, Dr Troeltsch. He was accompanied by a friend, J. N. Novotny.

Troeltsch carried out a detailed examination, but even before he spoke Bedrich knew the worst. There was nothing Troeltsch could do. The only advice he could give was that Bedrich should travel to Vienna, where there was a certain

Dr Pollitzer who might be able to help. But it was clear from the way he expressed himself that he held out little hope.

Novotny offered to accompany Bedrich, and once more they set out on a long, arduous journey, this time via Munich and Salzburg to Vienna. Again the story was the same. Nothing could be done. There was complete paralysis of the hearing nerves. Bedrich Smetana was incurably deaf.

$\begin{bmatrix} 24 \end{bmatrix}$

THE JOURNEYS TO THE TWO SPECIALISTS, and the fees, had eaten into Bedrich's capital. Summer was already in, but the problems on his mind had numbed his appreciation of the sunny days which always, in the past, used to make him feel like a new man.

On scraps of paper he jotted down figures, added them up, became downhearted when the totals showed that he was on the way to being a pauper. Prague was so expensive, and Betty never lost an opportunity of telling him. About the only benefit of being deaf, he thought, was that he did not hear her voice.

In the frustration and anger that took hold of her she turned cruel. She deliberately let the stove go out so that he could not make coffee. She left nasty notes around for him to see—scribbled sentences about hungry children and doting old men who would insist out of pride in trying to live in circumstances beyond their means. She took to picking up the children's shoes, examining the heels, throwing the shoes from her, and bursting into tears. She only did it when he was present. Whenever his socks became worn out at the toes she chose to ignore them. When any of his friends came in she said pointedly in front of them that there was no wine or other drink in the house, and that she had run out of coffee.

One night when this happened he felt so humiliated that he begged to be excused, said that he had a bad headache and wanted to go to bed. When the visitor left he went in search of Betty. She flounced out of the music-room and was about to pass him when he caught her by the arm and nearly swung her off her feet.

"What are you trying to do to me?" he yelled. "Why are you tormenting me?"

"Let me go!"

He couldn't hear her, but he knew from the expression on her face that she had screamed. He propelled her ahead of him into the music-room and banged the door. His head was pounding with anger. By God he was going to get to the bottom of this. He flung her into a chair and, shaking, stood above her.

"Are you trying to make me look a fool?" he shouted. "And *look* at me when you talk!" He was boiling now. "Now, Betty," he said in a thin, tight voice, "I want some answers from you. Why have you turned against me? Haven't I got enough trouble? Why *have* you?"

"You mean you don't know?"

"I wouldn't be *asking*, woman, if I knew!"

"If you don't know, what's the use of going into it?" she said.

His anger was simmering. "That kind of answer helps neither of us."

"Well, what do you expect me to say?"

"Just *tell* me. Is it because I'm not earning?"

"You can't help that."

"Well?"

"The way we're living," she said. "We shouldn't be here in Prague at all. It's too expensive, and we can't afford it."

"And where do you suggest we go—to *your* people? Have we been asked?"

"No, we haven't, but I'm sure they would take us in."

"And give us charity?"

"Isn't it better than starving?"

"We are *not* starving!"

"We soon will be. How long do you think your little bit of money will last out? And how far will your pension go?"

"So that's it," he said. "You want to get out of Prague. Do you know what leaving Prague would do to me?"

T*

"It wouldn't make you any deafer—or older," she replied, and immediately regretted it.

He turned abruptly and went out of the room. She heard him walking up and down his bedroom through most of the night.

In the end Zofie made it easy for him. Her husband, Josef, had been promoted, they had moved to Jabkenice, and they had a fine, roomy house on the edge of the forest.

Zofie knew her father's circumstances, and ever since his deafness had felt closer to him. When she had visited him in Prague she found that her stepmother had grown cold and critical, and with a woman's intuition Zofie had been able to piece the story together.

She talked to Josef about it and said she would love to be able to do something to help her father in his last years. Would Josef object if Bedrich and his family came to share the house with them? Josef had no objections. Any man who could write a piece of music like *Vltava* (it appealed to Josef more than anything else Bedrich had composed) could have half of anything Josef possessed. And, apart from that, he was extremely fond of Bedrich as a man.

At first, of course, Bedrich wouldn't hear of it, but said he would keep a small flat in Prague and come to Jabkenice on visits. In this way he felt he was not relinquishing his link with Prague. But as time went by the cost of the journeyings to and fro, the rent, the presents he insisted on bringing each time (he was now a grandfather and very proud of his grandson Zdenek), drained away his capital.

The day he left his flat in Prague for good he shed bitter tears. He had a frightful feeling that it was the beginning of the end. He was cutting himself off from everything and everyone he knew. He was banishing himself, leaving the arena clear. He had been round to see all his friends, beseeching them not to leave him alone to vegetate in Jabkenice. They all reassured him, however, and Neruda said, "One would imagine you were going to Siberia instead of a few miles away! Of course we'll come to see you. But get on with your composing.

You have a great deal to do before you give up to become a country bumpkin."

Zofie made quite a fuss of him when he and Betty arrived, leading him to a corner room with views of cornfields and woods.

"There you are, Papa, the best room in the house, fit for the best composer in the world. And it's yours for as long as you want it."

They brought the trunks into the house, and the boxes with all his possessions—his manuscripts, notes, favourite pens, paper, pictures. Josef and he lifted in the desk that had been brought from Prague, and arranged it so that it would get the best light from the windows. When he was left alone he took out the various pictures he treasured and polished the glass.

Over the desk he put a portrait of Franz Liszt. Around the walls he hung other pictures—Katerina, himself, one of his father and his mother. Inside a week it was as if he had known this room all his life.

He took long walks alone out into the surrounding country-side, striding up hilly fields to get newer and better views; sometimes he went to a cornfield and lay in the hot sun, nibbling at the hard grains he forced out of the wheat. The feeling of the sun on his back was a sensation he hadn't had since he was a boy.

One day, when he walked back to the house, Zofie saw him coming and ran towards him with the baby in her arms. He held out his hands, and the baby immediately leant out from his mother, ready to be taken. Careful not to talk, Bedrich took the child, held him close to feel his softness. He tickled the little fellow's ribs, felt his squirm and kick, saw his face breaking into open-mouthed smiles. He handed Zdenek back, kissed Zofie, and nodded his silent thanks to her.

He went to his room and stood a little while at the window watching Josef coming across the fields towards the house. Then he took out the folio of music he was working on, a piano cycle he had called *Dreams*. The first of the pieces had the name *Lost Happiness* written across the front page. He wondered if anyone would ever know how much meaning there had been in that title for him. Or in the next one—*Consolation*.

He finished the cycle on September 14th. The last part was called *Village Festival,* and the ink was hardly dry on it before he started composing again, this time the next symphonic poem for *Ma Vlast*—to be called *From Bohemia's Woods and Fields.*

By November his appearance was frightening Zofie; his body was shrinking and hopelessness was all that was to be seen in his eyes. But on November 11th Eliska Krasnohorska's libretto for *The Kiss* arrived. The change in Bedrich was astonishing. Several years dropped away from him. The stoop straightened, the footsteps quickened, and the feet were lifted instead of being dragged. He even laughed out loud. He had a new project on which to work.

He opened the libretto with certain misgivings, because Eliska Krasnohorska was only twenty-eight, and had already sent him a libretto (*Lumir*) which he hadn't liked very much. As soon as he read *The Kiss* he wanted to make it into an opera. But receiving it like this did something else, something that was slightly alarming. It reminded him that buried somewhere among his manuscripts and scores was another libretto by Krasnohorska—indeed, one that he himself had asked her to write for him—*Viola*, based on Shakespeare's *Twelfth Night.*

What alarmed him was that he could have forgotten it. Had the deafness affected his mind in any other way? Were there other things he had forgotten? Would he be able to cope with composing a whole new opera? Was his mind bursting apart, slowly but irrevocably?

He woke up screaming that night, after dreaming that he was in a lunatic asylum. He was surrounded by crazy, lewd faces, and he was trying to tell a doctor that he was not mad. He saw himself bound in a chair, unable to move, trying to convince the doctor that he was sane, that it had all been a mistake. But the doctor suddenly opened his mouth and ran away, screaming with laughter, and then Bedrich himself had screamed. He woke up to find Zofie coming into the room with a lighted candle in her hand. All he would tell her was that he had had a nightmare.

He threw himself into his work as soon as he got up in the morning, did the same thing every day. At one period, so as to keep his thoughts occupied, he actually worked alternate days on *The Kiss* and *Viola*, attempting to write two operas simultaneously.

He was happy enough while working, but as soon as he stopped he was beset by insecurity (he had no money at all, because the theatre administrators were holding up his over-due pension) and worry about his deafness.

On the day he was fifty-two he wrote in his diary: *The fifty-second year of my life. If my disease cannot be cured I hope my life will soon end.*

He made two visits to Prague in an effort to get his money, but returned empty-handed each time. He was worrying about the strain he and his family were being on Josef and Zofie; he was unable to buy even the smallest novelty for his grandchild. He had to borrow to buy food for his wife and children. And, most disturbing of all, he still had not settled with Eliska Krasnohorska about her fee for writing the libretto of *The Kiss*.

By May, when the opera was nearing completion, he could conceal his feelings of shame no longer, and he wrote to her: *You have given me a truly wonderful libretto, and I want to repeat my thanks to you. I am, however, deeply embarrassed over the question of your fee. Although I do not want to burden you with my private affairs, let me tell you that I am waiting for the Theatre Society to pay me the money they owe me. I have not received my monthly remuneration from them for over four months. Hoping that it would arrive, I have postponed writing to you. Please accept my regrets as well as my apologies. And please let me know how much I should pay you. As soon as I receive what is due to me from the Theatre Society I shall discharge my debt to you.*

Her reply came swiftly. She wanted no fee; she deemed it an honour to work with him; she wanted no further mention of money; she had only one request—to be allowed to collaborate again.

On July 23rd, 1876, *The Kiss* was finished.

He went to the opening performance on November 7th, the first time he had attended an opera since he lost his hearing. The ordeal of sitting in the box and trying to gauge peoples' reactions by watching the expressions on their faces had just reached an unbearable point, and he was about to get up and leave, when he saw the movement—the fluttering of hundreds of pairs of hands clapping in unstinted applause. He flopped back into his seat, radiant with happiness, and from then on he sat in a state of mounting excitement. The only disappointment he felt was at the crudeness of the scenery and the make-do costumes of the cast. But the first act was no sooner over than a theatre attendant came to the box, took him by the arm, and led him down on to the stage in front of the curtain. As soon as he made his appearance the audience stood up and clapped, and he looked back at them, nervous, smiling, unsure of what to do. When he walked into the wings the principals were there waiting for him, and they turned him round and sent him back out again.

At the end of the performance the same thing happened. He was called back for three long standing ovations, and the audience, knowing that he could not hear a single "Bravo!" or any of the clapping, took out handkerchiefs, waved them together with gloves and flowers and anything that made a show. A poem in his honour fluttered down from the balcony, came to rest near his feet. A deputation came up on to the stage from the stalls and handed him a bouquet and a silver trophy, and the cast gathered round and clapped.

Seven nights later he was back in the theatre, this time as the guest of honour at a special performance, all the proceeds of which were to be handed over to him; the triumphant scenes of the first night proved to be no more than a pale shadow of what took place on this gala night.

The audience—made up in the main of representatives of every artistic and civic body in the city, as well as special deputations from Litomysl and other places in which he had lived —were on the verge of rioting, so enthusiastically did they greet the composer and his newest opera.

There were laurel-wreaths (some of them made from solid silver) from The National Club, The Society for the National Theatre, from the newspaper *Narodni Listy*, from the town fathers of Litomysl, from the district of Louny, from The Artistic Society, from The Society of Academic Readers; there were numerous bouquets from private individuals. A beautifully bound poem by Jaroslav Vrchlicky was handed to him. Altogether he was called before the audience ten times, and backstage the celebrations carried on for nearly two hours.

But, as with almost every event in his life, there was a blight. This time it was the attack in the Press on his librettist, Eliska Krasnohorska. Most of it came from the paper *Lumir*, and she was accused of writing "an impossible libretto for an opera which was saved only by the magnificent music written for it by Smetana". Sickened by this unfair criticism of such a talented young woman, he invited her to come and visit him at Jabkenice, and he sat talking with her for two undisturbed hours. He knew how she felt. He had bitter experience to draw on, and he had the proper words of encouragement to give. Later he took her for a walk along the country lanes, and by the time they returned to the house had got her to promise to work on another libretto for him.

Ever since the night in Prague when he had lost his temper with Betty, they had been drifting farther apart. Although they lived under the same roof at Zofie's house, the process of estrangement continued. They rarely conversed with each other, and when they did it was only out of sheer necessity, and was done with frigid politeness.

Over the occasional meals they ate with the family (Zofie brought most of his food in to him) he stole glances at Betty, searching her face, her eyes, forehead, hair, cheeks, mouth—seeing them objectively for the first time in years. He saw the little down-turnings at the corners of the mouth, the signs that said unhappiness, disillusionment, hardness—he couldn't make up his mind which. Whatever it was, it disturbed and irked him, as if it had no right to be there.

His room was his refuge. He was safe in it, undisturbed, secure. Nobody came uninvited. There was no distraction, save of his own making. He could sit surrounded by familiar objects—heaps of scores, notes, pictures, letters—reminders of the good times and the bad, reminders of his childhood, of Katerina and the children, of his struggles and achievements.

They were memories he knew, and, because of their familiarity, they were in an odd way reassuring.

The past became the present for him. There was a yawning emptiness that needed to be filled by a sharing of the memories and the yearnings with someone else. Zofie was too young to remember enough. Josef didn't know the times or the places or the people. And Betty was lost to him.

Rather than dwell too long on his needs (he had a realistic fear that to do so would affect his reason) he directed his emotions into creative activity, into a new musical work. He began to write it for two violins, viola, and violoncello, and gave it the name *From My Life.*

He took himself right back to his childhood, searched out the sensations he had had as a boy growing up, when romantic thought had filled his head most of the time. He remembered the soul-searching and the torture, translated it all into music. He spanned his life and came to the recent past for a certain sound of premonition, physically shook with a sort of ague when he wove into the texture of his music the appalling note of the high whistle that had heralded his deafness.

As he wrote, for days at a stretch he was lost to the present, oblivious of his surroundings. He acted like a man in a trance. Whenever he went out and saw children playing, or talked to Zofie or Josef, they somehow became figures from his past life. He transported himself backward in time to when he loved to dance, to when he went with Havlicek and Buttula to the village fairs, to when he wrote dance rhythms for his music groups to play, to his first loves, and his first *real,* lasting love, inevitably to the good times with Katerina.

And as the work grew, and the memories came closer to the time in which he was really living, the composition changed character; he wrote nobly of his pride at the recognition of music's importance in the creation of a new culture for his native land. And then, finally, he brought back that terrifying high tone, persistent and painful, the scream in his ears before his hearing died.

When he finished he felt satisfied. He had put the best of his knowledge and the truth of his experience into his work.

But they turned it down. They couldn't see it for what it

was. They criticized cruelly: "An impossible work." They found fault: "A quartet written as though for an orchestra." They rejected it and returned the manuscript to him. And by some miracle he accepted the rejection philosophically.

He had his hopes—perhaps in time they would get round to reassessing it, see it as he had seen it, put it on.

But they never did. Not in his lifetime.

He worked diligently on his new opera *The Secret* (the libretto was again by Krasnohorska) and attended its first production on October 18th, 1878. It was received with tremendous enthusiasm, and though he could not hear what they were saying, the audience stood facing his box, chanting their appreciation.

The pains in his head were becoming more frequent, more difficult to bear, and on many a morning when Zofie went in with his breakfast she found him red-eyed and pale from the agonies of the night.

He completed the cycle *Ma Vlast* with the symphonic poem *Blanik* on March 9th, 1879—having finished *Tabor* in the second week of December. But he still pressed on. There was still more work to be done. He was in constant touch with Krasnohorska, looking for a new libretto. She gave him three, none of which he found suitable.

A number of friends were beginning to put gentle pressure on him to find another librettist. Krasnohorska, they said, was written out. She could be of no more help to him. Why didn't he work with Svatopluk Cech, one of the country's best writers?

The simple truth was that he didn't want to. The campaign against Krasnohorska hardened. Public statements were issued which the girl saw and heard, became confused and bitter about. But Bedrich refused to be put off.

"Do not heed them," he told her. "Do not worry about the difficulties, we shall overcome them. But these people do not understand. They have no conception of what is entailed in creating an opera. They do not understand what it is to work with a composer who cannot hear. You understand me, and I like your work."

But his search for a new comic opera was driving the girl to an extreme level of nervousness and frustration. It was only her respect for him which compelled her to continue trying. One day, in a complete change of direction, she proposed a story to him involving a devil, and even before she expanded on the theme his eyes lit up and he grasped her hand and said, "My dear, tell me no more. Go away and write it. I think it could be the answer."

While waiting for the libretto he worked on the revision of his *Czech Dances,* and in the autumn moved back to Prague to stay for a while with Srb-Debrnov. Returning to his beloved city was like a rebirth. He found a café where he was allowed to sit at a table by the window in the evenings looking out at the passers-by, writing odd snatches of melody on the blue-veined marble of the table-top, or looking across at Hradcany Castle. Eliska Krasnohorska visited him frequently, and they discussed *The Devil's Wall,* the new libretto.

The year was drawing to a close when the first talk about a jubilee concert in his honour began circulating in Prague. But the first he heard of it was when a letter arrived asking him if he would perform one of his own polkas and a Chopin nocturne. The rest of the programme, the letter said, would consist of *Vysehrad, Czech Song,* and first performances of *Tabor* and *Blanik.* And perhaps he would like to compose something else for the occasion?

He went to the door of his room (he was back at Jabkenice) and called for Zofie. Afraid that something was wrong, she hurried from the kitchen, alarm in her eyes as she wiped her wet hands on the bottom of her apron.

"Is anything the matter, Papa?" she asked, clutching his wrist.

"No, no, child, come in here a moment; I want to show you something."

She stepped into the room. He closed the door behind her, then handed her the letter. She read it through to the end, and her eyes were alive and dancing when she looked up at him. On an impulse she kissed him.

"Oh, that's wonderful, Papa!" she said excitedly, then

stepped back from him and repeated the sentence more slowly so that he could follow the movements of her lips. "You are going to play, of course?"

"I don't know," he said.

"But you *must*."

He put out his arms, and she stepped into his embrace. "You have such simple faith in me, little one," he said. "I am very moved by it. But you know, I *am* getting old, whether I like it or not, and when a man becomes old it is not so easy to take failure. Resilience is a young person's gift."

Zofie stepped back again so that he could see her face. "You must do it, Papa. It will be good for you."

He shook his head, a look of simple tolerance on his face. "So you too think I am old?"

"No. What do you mean?"

"It is what people always say to the old and sick—'It will be good for you'. You feel I need it, don't you, now that I am both old and sick?"

It tore at her heart to hear him speaking like this. She tried to hold back the tears, but they came, brimmed over, and ran down her face.

"No, you mustn't cry, my little Zofie. You are a grown-up woman now. You mustn't cry for your Papa. You must keep your tears for your own family."

She buried her head against his chest and stayed that way for several minutes. When she eventually looked up at him she saw him looking somewhere a long way off. She squeezed his arm, and when he looked down at her she said, "Papa, I want you to do it for me, and for . . . for Mama."

He turned his head away from her abruptly. Then he looked at her. He was biting his lip, but he was nodding his head. "Very well," he said. "I shall do it."

The concert, on January 4th, 1880, was an oustanding success. And even if the great man didn't play as well as he used to do, there were no complaints. It was an emotional experience just to see him there on the stage, lost as ever to the music, not able to hear the notes his fingers played on the keyboard, but forced now to imagine them.

* * *

When Eliska Krasnohorska delivered the libretto of *The Devil's Wall* he worked on it as often as he could. But concentration was becoming ever more difficult. The periods when the ideas flowed well were becoming shorter, with longer spaces in between them. There were times when he just sat staring vacantly, though his mind was anything but a blank.

He was having to fight the pains. Days were disappearing from his calendar with nothing to show for them. There were alarming periods when he seemed to lose whole weeks, and be left with no recollection of what had taken place other than that he had been suffering, that the nights were long, that his mind was in a turmoil of agony and hopelessness.

Some of what he wrote he didn't recognize as his own work. *The Devil's Wall* couldn't have been more different from the comic opera he had intended to write. Indeed, he cast aside many of Krasnorhorska's scenes (she had written a light, amusing affair in accordance with his constant demands) and stripped the libretto of comedy. Nothing seemed funny or amusing any more.

In October Srb-Debrnov, who had come to Jabkenice and been shocked at the deterioration in his friend, tried a new ploy to shake Bedrich out of his depression. In a letter, he asked if the maestro would set one of his (Srb-Debrnov's) poems to music. Perhaps the challenge of having to tackle something new and short would have some sort of beneficial effect.

It was the kind of situation Bedrich revelled in, because it gave him the opportunity to do something for Srb-Debrnov in return for all his kindness. He put *The Devil's Wall* aside and studied the poem.

A week later he wrote to Srb-Debrnov: *The arrival of your poem was like the breath of life to me. I have read and re-read it. I have walked up and down my little room here reading it out aloud until I knew every word, every comma, and, do you know, Josef, the words somehow turned into music in my head. The day that happened I sat down and sketched out the framework, and almost before I knew that it had happened I had completed the final version. All in one day! For me at this time that is something wonderful.*

So the idea had succeeded. If it worked once, might it not

work a second time? Within a week Srb-Debrnov sent another work. The finished musical setting (called *Prayer*) arrived at Srb-Debrnov's apartment in November, and there was in it a quality of peace and tranquillity that set Srb-Debrnov's mind at rest. Bedrich had apparently retained his mental balance.

But work on *The Devil's Wall* proceeded slowly and painfully. The winter was grey and cold, the old depressions set in, he became convinced that this would be his last full opera. He confided his feelings to the pages of his diary:

My illness, the wretched state of my health, and all the other difficulties make it impossible for me to compose as I composed in the past—with freedom and speed. So often I can work for only pitifully short periods. There are days when I can do nothing. I promised Srb-Debrnov that I would have the opera completed by Christmas 1880. And here, March 1881 is with us already and I am only now coming to the end of the first act.

Zofie, passing the door of his room one afternoon, heard him talking aloud, and she stopped to listen.

"What is happening to me?" she heard him ask. "What is going wrong with my mind? Can you tell me? I want to go on, but I feel so tired. I need you to come and hold me close, but that can never again happen. If only we could be together. I feel like a lost child, alone. Very much alone...."

She opened the door, and saw him facing the picture of Katerina on the wall, talking to it. She closed the door and left him. She couldn't go in.

THE NEW CZECH NATIONAL THEATRE had risen high above the banks of the river, and when Bedrich was taken to see the almost completed building he looked at it with pride surging through him. The dream was coming true.

"Paid for by the coins of our people," he said to Srb-Debrnov. "Doesn't it make you feel proud of them?"

"I have a surprise for you," Srb-Debrnov said by way of answer.

"Yes? What is it?"

"This isn't the place to tell you. Come on, let's go back to the apartment."

Indoors, where nobody could hear them, Srb-Debrnov said, "It is now official."

Bedrich nodded. "So it is now official," he said. "Would you mind telling me *what* is official?"

"*Libuse*—your *Libuse*—it is to be put on for the opening."

Bedrich wiped a hand across his forehead, and said, "You are serious?"

"Would I joke about such a thing?"

Bedrich sat down, dropped his head in thought, then looked up, but not at Srb-Debrnov. He was gazing at a point somewhere near the corner of the ceiling. A small smile played across his lips.

"So," he said, "after ten years gathering dust in a drawer the score is to be taken out and actually used. I can scarcely believe it."

"You can take my word for it," Srb-Debrnov said. "I have seen it in writing. But I am bound to say, you are taking it very calmly."

"It hasn't sunk in, Josef, that is why."

"But you are pleased?"

"Pleased? My dear boy, what can I say? What can I say that could express what I feel?"

"Then don't try," Srb-Debrnov replied. "I think I know what you feel. Let's drink to it."

He fetched the glasses and the decanter, toasted Bedrich, and then sat back in silence to allow Bedrich to savour the pleasure of the revelation.

After a long time Josef said, "Now, there are some other things also which I must tell you."

"It couldn't be better news, whatever it is," Bedrich said.

"No, I'm afraid it isn't."

"Bad news then?"

"You may think so."

"I'm ready, Josef. I think I could accept any news at this time."

"Well, you probably know that the original intention was to have the official opening of the theatre on September 11th, and it was to be a great festive occasion. That has been changed. Crown Prince Rudolf and his wife are making a State visit to Prague in June, and our enlightened administrators have taken it upon themselves to bring the opening date forward to June 11th."

"I see," Bedrich said. "So instead of it being a tribute to the people of Bohemia who paid for the theatre, it is to be turned into a celebration for the visit of the Austrian Prince. Isn't there something typical about that, Josef?"

"Indeed there is. And I can tell you there's widespread indignation about it already."

"That is the bad news you had to give me?"

"There is more."

"Yes?"

"Your great ambition to conduct your opera for the opening of our National Theatre—"

"Oh, that would be out of the question." Bedrich cut in.

"I couldn't do it. It wouldn't be fair to the cast or the musicians or the audience."

"Then you don't mind?"

"No, no, no. I am disappointed, but at myself, at my damned ears."

Srb-Debrnov sighed with relief.

The people of Prague did not take the decisions with the same docility. They resented fiercely the official opening date being altered to accommodate the visit of the Austrian Crown Prince. It was *their* theatre, they said. The high-handed action was a disgrace, a humiliation, they said, and they would boycott June 11th.

On the night most of the seats available for sale were empty; only those reserved for invited dignitaries were filled.

Bedrich sat in a box with Srb-Debrnov, and when Josef touched his arm to attract his attention, and then pointed towards the box where the Crown Prince and his party were seated, he swivelled his head to see the occupants of the box clapping their applause.

When the curtain came down at the end of the performance Srb-Debrnov nudged his arm and said, "Stand up, the audience are calling your name. Stand up. Take a bow."

"They liked it?"

"Look at them. They're going wild!"

Indeed they were, and Bedrich stood, all shyness as usual, while the audience faced his box and waved and shouted. He was still standing when he felt his sleeve being tugged, and he turned to see an attendant beside Srb-Debrnov.

"The Crown Prince wants to meet you," Josef said. "You are to go to his box."

In his embarrassed haste Bedrich tripped over the legs of his chair and almost fell. Josef caught his arm and steadied him. In the passageway Bedrich stood waiting for Srb-Debrnov to emerge. When his friend didn't come out he went back in and asked him if he was coming.

"No, I haven't been invited. You must go quickly. This is your moment. I shall be waiting here for you."

Bedrich went out to the attendant and followed him to the

Crown Prince's box. He bowed stiffly when he entered, and shook hands with the visiting Prince.

Prince Rudolf still had the programme in his hand and was holding it by the side of his nose, obscuring his mouth, as he said, "How long did it take you to write this opera, Mr Smetana?"

Bedrich couldn't see the lips and, having no idea he was being addressed, remained silent. The rest of the time he spent in the Prince's company was full of strain, for no-one had told Rudolf that the composer was deaf. Sweating with relief, Bedrich was at last dismissed, and made his way back to Srb-Debrnov.

"Well?" Josef asked.

"I think he liked it," was all Bedrich replied.

In Jabkenice, Bedrich read about the public outcry that demanded a new official opening night. He also read the accounts of the campaign by his enemies that a work other than *Libuse* be performed for the occasion. They wanted it to be *Dimitrij*, an opera Dvorak hadn't even finished yet. They were determined to block *Libuse* any way they could, to deprive Smetana of any further honour that seemed likely to come his way. They were trying to smash the man into the ground, and in the quietness of Jabkenice he felt their vicious heels grinding into his face.

On August 12th he left Zofie's house to go to Prague to visit Srb-Debrnov. He was standing in the station waiting for the train when a porter who recognized him came up and said, "What a terrible business this is about the National Theatre, Mr Smetana! All that money and all that time, and nothing left but a heap of ashes!"

Bedrich reeled and closed his eyes. Then he looked hard at the porter, grabbed the man's arm, and said, "What are you talking about?"

"You haven't heard? It caught fire and burnt to the ground, and I'm told that—"

But Bedrich didn't wait for any more. *Burnt to the ground!*

The porter watched him staggering, legs gone to jelly, walking away from him, along by the side of the railway-line.

Shocked by the sight, he saw Bedrich stumble over one of the rails, his hands clasped across his eyes. He heard the moans that were breaking from his lips, the sounds of anguish, saw him stop about fifty yards away with his arms flung wide as he stood swaying in the centre of the tracks. It was then that the porter heard the train, realized it was making straight for the deaf man's back, heard the screaming of the whistle, the ugly shriek of steel on protesting steel. The porter began to run, threw himself the last few feet, hauled the demented man clear as the huge bulk of the engine roared past, inches away.

He had to half carry Bedrich along the line to the station, and when the train for Prague came in he settled him in a compartment by himself. Bedrich was sitting back with his eyes closed as the train pulled out.

It was a grief-stricken Bedrich that Srb-Debrnov met at the station in Prague. He led Smetana to the waiting cab, having decided not to attempt consolation in a public place, but the cab had no sooner swung away from the station concourse than Bedrich leant across to say, "Take me by the place so that I can see it, Josef."

They went along by the river-bank and saw the little knots of people, many of them openly weeping as they gazed at the ruins of the proud building. Bedrich said nothing. He took his thin-rimmed glasses off once and wiped the lenses with a handkerchief. That was all. Then he said, "Let us go now."

At Srb-Debrnov's apartment he asked to be left alone for an hour to think. When Josef returned he saw a remarkable change in Bedrich. The head was held high once more, and the shoulders were no longer drooping. There was something very business-like in the way he addressed Josef.

"Sit down now and listen to me," he began. "A terrible tragedy has befallen us, but we must not waste our time living with regrets. We must do something definite to make sure that work starts again on the building of a new and even finer theatre."

"But, Bedrich—"

Bedrich wasn't looking at Josef. He started pacing up and down the room, and interruptions went unnoticed unless he happened to be watching Srb-Debrnov's mouth.

"We must organize concerts to collect funds. If people are interested in hearing an infirm old man playing the piano I shall give some recitals. And since *Libuse* seems to be the topic of so much discussion, I think perhaps if it were put about that the composer was going to conduct a performance of the overture it might attract some people willing to pay out money. What do you think of that idea?"

He turned to Srb-Debrnov for an answer.

"I appreciate your willingness, maestro, but—"

"You have your doubts?"

"Well, yes, I'm not sure how the orchestra would react to the proposition that they be conducted by a—by someone who can't hear."

"You think they might refuse?"

"It would be most hurtful to you if they did."

"Well, as I am the one likely to be, as you say, hurt, let me do the asking, eh?"

Two days later he went along to the hall where the orchestra was rehearsing, waited until there was a break in the rehearsal when the conductor left the hall, and then made his way to the podium.

They heard him coming and turned in astonishment as he stepped up and stood before them. He picked up the baton and tapped it, then gazed at the ring of faces.

"Gentlemen," he said, "I think most of you know me. I see many familiar faces in front of me. You are probably wondering what I am doing here. I'll tell you. The burning down of our National Theatre came as a great blow to me, as I'm sure it did to every one of you. Already plans are being laid to collect funds to start building afresh. I want to do my part. Unfortunately I have nothing to offer other than my waning abilities. But what I want to suggest to you is this: to be allowed the privilege of conducting you in a performance of the overture to my opera *Libuse*. Would you consent to this?"

They stood up and clapped him, and nodded their heads.

He held up his hand to quieten them.

"I know it is an unusual request, and, indeed, those close to me tried to persuade me against asking you. But believe me, it is no fad of an old man seeking lost glories. I merely want to perform what to me is a sacred duty."

The concert was held, Smetana conducted before a full house, and those who knew about such things affirmed that the orchestra had never performed with such feeling and technical brilliance. The proceeds went straight into the fund for the new theatre.

A few days later he was sitting alone in Srb-Debrnov's apartment, trying to do some work on *The Devil's Wall*. He was finding it hard to make the ideas flow, and he rose from the table at which he had been sitting and walked about the room, forcing his brain to think. As he was passing a window he noticed a cab pulling up outside the front door, and he pulled back the lace curtain in an effort to see who might be coming. His sight was failing, but there was something familiar about the walk of the woman who paid off the driver and came to the front door.

Anticipating the knock, he went to the door and opened it.

His heart almost stopped when Fröjda Benecke stepped forward and embraced him. She was the last person in the world he had expected to see.

He led her inside, and as she followed him she had to fight hard to keep a rein on emotions that churned inside her at the sight of the frail little bearded man he had become. When they stood before each other in the room her face was composed.

"Fröjda," he said, "Fröjda—"

"No, don't talk. Don't talk, Bedrich."

"I'm not a happy sight," he said, and the way his head hung took her back to the boyish shyness she had known so many long years ago.

"It doesn't matter to me how you look," she said. "You are a great, great man. I always knew you would become one. All I can say is that I am very proud of you—"

"*Proud* of me, Fröjda? You have never lost your kindness."

"The same self-effacing Bedrich. Franz Liszt pronounces you a genius, and you think I am being kind saying I'm proud of you."

To shift the conversation from himself, he said, "What

brings you to Prague? I never thought I would see you in my city. I was so surprised to see you standing outside the door."

"How did you know I was there? I hadn't even knocked when you opened it."

"To be truthful, Fröjda, I didn't know it was you. You see, I saw the carriage pulling up, and saw a woman—a lady, pardon me—stepping out. But my eyes aren't as good as they used to be. Too much paper-work, I suppose. And in light not strong enough. It was eerie recognizing some familiarity about the walk, and yet not knowing who it was. Did I look foolish? My mouth must have dropped open in astonishment. Tell me, how does Göteborg look? How is Capek? Dear, kind Capek. Are all my friends well? Is good music being played in Göteborg these days? And yourself, dear Fröjda, how have you been keeping?"

"Oh, so many questions, Bedrich!" She had pulled off the long, black, silk gloves that reached to her elbows, and she placed the tips of the fingers of her right hand against his lips to still the flow. His own hand closed over hers for an instant, and he held the fingertips against his lips and kissed them.

"Tell me," he said, "why are you in Prague?"

"To see you," she replied.

"You've come all this way of your own accord just to see me?"

"I was sent," she replied. "Or, rather, I was asked to make the journey."

"Asked by whom?"

"By the people who will never forget you or what you did for them."

"I was only doing what I was being paid to do."

"No, no, much more than that."

"And they asked you to come, just to see me?"

"And to bring you something."

He stood up and walked away from her, turned when he was right across the room. "Whatever it is, I can't take it," he said. "I am still in their debt. I owe them too much already. It is not easy to live with the knowledge of a debt unpaid."

"Part of the reason why I have come," she said, "is to tell you that you owe them nothing."

U

"But I borrowed—"

"No. They *gave*."

"But I asked—"

"You will offend them if you do not accept."

"But, Fröjda—"

"Bedrich, your own people may not appreciate you, but in Göteborg your name is honoured."

She stood up and, taking an envelope from her purse, handed it to him.

"This is the other reason I was asked to come. To give you this with their love, their gratitude, and their hopes that it will help to lift some of your hardships from you. Two thousand sovereigns, collected in three days."

He turned from her, and she had to walk round him to press the envelope into his hands.

Eventually he looked at her. "I am torn between humiliation and ... gratitude. Thank you. Thank them for me. Tell them ... "

She could see he was not far from breaking down.

"I'll tell them," she said. "And now, Bedrich, I must go."

"Already?"

"Yes. I do not wish to meet Betty. Even in Göteborg we have heard certain things, and I could not trust myself to speak civilly."

"It is not entirely her fault," he said.

"I prefer to keep my own opinion," she replied. "I want you to remember the way things were between us. I want you to know that what I said to you once I meant. I want you to know that I shall always feel the same. It's important that you keep it in your mind and in your heart, because I do not think we shall ever meet again. This is the last time."

She put her hands up, and pulled his head down and kissed him on the forehead, and then, while he was still standing there, she picked up her gloves and left the room. She let herself out. He went to the window to watch her leaving. She didn't turn round, but he waved nevertheless.

The news that *The Two Widows* had been successfully performed in Hamburg (his first opera to be performed in

Germany) eased him a little way out of his melancholia, and he continued with the laborious business of completing *The Devil's Wall*. On April 17th, 1882, he wrote the last section of music.

Production was held up while the operatic company (under Mayr) rehearsed Dvorak's *Dimitrij*, which was put on at tremendous expense. By contrast, *The Devil's Wall* was treated shabbily, with ill-chosen costumes, badly painted scenery, amateurish direction. The audiences sat through the first three performances sullen and complaining. The sense of anti-climax was all-pervading. There were no encores. No bouquets. No applause.

Narodni Listy, in an article after the first night, said:

> For a long time there has been no opera production in Prague which did a work such scant justice as that which we witnessed last night. The direction was thoughtless and slack.... The production was without dignity. The scenery was the poorest yet seen—how could a river flow upwards? And yet that is what it was represented as doing on the stage. Into this office this morning came a stream of written protests.... In short, it was a production beyond all comprehension.

On November 5th the complete *Ma Vlast* was performed for the first time in Prague, and though the warmth of the reception was of a brand that threatened to get out of hand, Bedrich was by now so sunk in despair that the success did nothing to buoy him up.

He became bad-tempered. He couldn't think clearly. His rages consumed him. Nobody could console or cheer him.

He was hearing voices by day and by night, voices that mocked and scorned and drove with piercing pain into his brain. When friends came and handed him reviews of *Ma Vlast* after performances in Glasgow, London, and America, he ignored them, or shouted rudely at them to leave him alone. He was in the middle of a fearful, lonely battle.

His memory went. There were huge periods of time which were no more than blanks filled only by intense mental persecution and physical agony. In his lucid moments he recognized the anxious face of his doctor, always begging him, ordering him, trying to persuade him not to tax his brain.

But the voices raged at him, and he was locked in a cell of roaring sound which remorselessly beat at him. He craved sleep and couldn't sleep. Early one morning he sat up in bed, roaring at the indescribable agony. Suddenly it stopped and he fell back, exhausted and sweating. He hadn't even seen Josef and Zofie who came into the room to try to ease his pain.

But when he awoke late the following afternoon there was a composition in his head, bursting to get out—a new string quartet. And when that was finished he would, he determined, write his final opera—*Viola*.

When Josef Srb-Debrnov came to see him Zofie met him at the door, and Srb-Debrnov immediately asked, "How is he?"

"Today, all right," she said quietly.

"And on other days?"

"It is terrible to say it about your own father," she said, her lips trembling, "but he acts as if he is quite mad. Do you think he is mad?"

"He has had a hard life. He has been under frightful strain."

"But do you think he is mad?"

"The music I've seen so far from the quartet is the work of a great brain," Srb-Debrnov said, still evading the question. "Can I go in and see him?"

"Yes, of course," Zofie said. "I'll let you in."

"There's no need, I'll go in on my own."

"Wait, I'll get the key."

"Key?"

She nodded her head before she spoke. "Yes, I have to lock him in now. I'm afraid for the children. Sometimes he becomes very violent."

She was clearly horror-struck by the admission, and Srb-Debrnov thought it best not to make any comment. When Zofie opened the door for him he waved her away, then slipped into the room.

Bedrich was sitting facing the door, his face the grey-white of a corpse. He didn't get up when Srb-Debrnov entered. He held his hand out tiredly, the grip slack, and he said, "Hello, Josef."

"Hello, Bedrich."

"Has my appearance scared you so?"

"You don't look well, Bedrich."

"Don't I? I haven't seen my face in a mirror for weeks."

"Are you still working on the quartet?"

"When I can." The voice was flat and soft and lifeless.

"Why aren't you dressed?" Srb-Debrnov asked.

Bedrich looked down at his clothes. "I am dressed," he said.

"In your night-clothes—that isn't like you, Bedrich."

"Oh, I haven't been in anything else for—I don't know how long, Josef. There's no point."

It was the sort of admission of defeat which chilled Srb-Debrnov to the marrow. "There is *every* point, Bedrich. You are letting yourself go."

"You don't understand either, Josef. You see, I am a captive. In my room here. With my voices. With my screams. With my deafness. With my hallucinations. I have to snatch every moment of lucidity, no matter how brief, to write down in music what I've still got left to write. The lucid times are precious, and very short, and I can't waste time in dressing up to write music. Time is slipping away from me. I begrudge every moment lost. That is why you see me like this. I suppose I must look terrible."

"Are you eating?" Srb-Debrnov asked, noticing the thin face and bony hands, the fleshless wrists and forearms.

"Zofie is very good to me," Bedrich answered. "I have no inclination for food, but she takes such trouble and she worries so much that I try to eat some of what she brings me. You saw her as you came in, of course?"

"Yes."

"She unlocked the door for you, didn't she?"

Srb-Debrnov didn't reply.

"Oh, it's all right, I know she locks it. She has to. She has to safeguard herself and her children." He was speaking with ferocious control, but suddenly it slipped, and he was crying uncontrollably, every inch of his body heaving and trembling. "She is so kind," he said between sobs. "She tries not to show her fear ... she tried to convince me the first time that it wasn't locked at all, that it was only stuck ... she doesn't want to hurt me ... but can you imagine what it must be like for her ... living under the same roof as a maniac ... a maniac who is her own father?"

Srb-Debrnov couldn't stand it. He went to a part of the room where he didn't have to look at Bedrich, but he couldn't shut out of his ears the terrible sounds of grief. And he had no idea what to say or do. When he looked round Bedrich was wiping his nose and his eyes with the sleeve of his bed-shirt.

"Don't turn your back on me, please, Josef," the old man pleaded.

Srb-Debrnov came and sat down opposite him again.

Bedrich took a deep breath. "I feel all right now," he said. "I feel fine ... I can look at you, know who you are. I can see a fly crawling up a window, and know it is a fly, so when I am feeling like this, recognizing things, able to describe and give names, I must be sane, mustn't I? Mustn't I, Josef?"

"Yes, of course, Bedrich."

"Oh, God, if only I could hold on to these moments, prolong them instead of having them shrink on me. Will you come again soon, Josef? You won't go away and leave me here and never come back?"

"I'll come back, have no fear."

"You still think of me as a friend?"

"I'll always think of you as a friend."

"You won't let them get me?"

"No, I won't let them get you."

"Ever?"

"Ever."

"You promise?"

"Yes."

"Say: 'I promise'."

"I promise, Bedrich."

"I feel very tired. I haven't slept for nearly a week. Do you mind if I lie on my bed and rest?"

"Here, let me help you."

"No! NO! Don't put your hands on me, I can walk!" The voice was raised in anger. Bedrich walked on shaky legs to the crumpled bed, hoisted himself on to it, and lay back. He closed his eyes. In a moment he opened them and said, "Josef—I'm sorry. You see, I've got to retain *something* that I can do for myself."

He was deeply asleep inside two minutes, and Josef let himself out of the room and went back to Prague.

In early March Bedrich somehow finished the String Quartet No. 2 in C minor. Like *From My Life*, it was mainly autobiographical in that it was based on his experiences—this time during illness, telling of depressions, mental disorder, confusion, the triumph of still being able to compose, the gargantuan struggle he was going through.

With the coming of spring, his son-in-law, Josef Schwarz, took him out of doors, tried to interest him in plant life and animals, saw the improvements, and was happy. Josef loved this man, and was heartbroken at what had happened to him.

For a while a total recovery seemed possible, and Bedrich took an interest where before he had been immured from outside happenings. He somehow got the inspiration to compose again, and, miraculously, embarked upon a work of gaiety and lightness—*Prague Carnival*. It exhausted him, but he worked on, orchestrated the whole of it, and turned at last to *Viola* and Krasnohorska's libretto.

He was even well enough on November 18th to travel to Prague for the opening of the rebuilt National Theatre. He was present, but was strangely quiet and uninterested, even though the opera was *Libuse* and the scenes of enthusiasm unprecedented.

Back in Jabkenice once more, the ever-present voices in his head began their cacophonous attacks with increasing frequency, only now they had faces, and the words they screamed at him were lewd and vicious, mocking with more venom than he had ever experienced.

The violence first reappeared when he tore the pictures off his walls, smashed the frames, made a fire of manuscripts and letters. On pages of *Viola* (only part finished) he wrote sentences which no-one could decipher. The scraps of music he scribbled were jarring and discordant and possessed of an ugliness entirely foreign to his nature. He became confused, bellowed incoherent phrases while hammering on the walls of the room, attacked Zofie once when she came with his food. At night the children woke up terrified at the noises he made as he beat the door and the floors.

In March 1884, when gifts and telegrams arrived in profusion for his sixtieth birthday, he tore and smashed in frenzy.

The two doctors who now came periodically to see him were punched and kicked whenever they approached him. He thought they were enemies. He wanted to kill them. He picked up bits of furniture and hurled them, first at Dr Guth, then at Dr Sladecek. When the two men went out of the room for the last time they were white and shaking, and the imprecations behind the locked door mounted in a tirade until the voice became hoarse, and then they heard him slumping to the floor and crying like a baby.

Dr Guth turned to Zofie and shook his head. "You can no longer keep him here," he said.

"You mean—"

"I'm afraid he will have to go into the asylum at Prague, Mrs Schwarz."

Zofie shrieked and ran to her room.

Guth sat down and wrote a letter to the Chief Medical Officer of the Asylum for the Mentally Disturbed at Prague:

The patient is physically weak, though at times he becomes extremely violent. He shouts for hours without a break, and is suffering from recurring hallucinations during which he variously imagines himself to be Liszt, the Crown Prince, Wagner, and the Emperor. He does not recognize his own children or those close to him. In his calm moments he begs to be helped, but has made repeated attempts to escape from his room. He has broken windows and furniture, goes without food for several days at a time, then wolfs ravenously at anything edible. I consider him to be a danger to his family who can no longer adequately care for him, or, indeed, guard themselves against his outbursts. I recomend that he be admitted to your care at the earliest possible moment.

He signed it and dated it April 15th, 1884.

On the morning of the 22nd Josef Srb-Debrnov arrived at

the Schwarz house at Jabkenice. Zofie, her face swollen and her eyes red, let him in.

"I'm terribly sorry, Zofie, but it is best for everyone that your father goes," Srb-Debrnov said.

Zofie was incapable of making any reply.

"How is he this morning?" Srb-Debrnov asked.

Josef Schwarz came down the stairs, followed by Betty Smetana, who, Srb-Debrnov noticed, appeared to be quite unmoved.

"How is Bedrich?" Srb-Debrnov asked again.

"He's been very quiet since he had his breakfast," Schwarz answered.

"Is he dressed?"

"Yes, I helped him."

"Does he know?"

"He didn't say a word."

"He knows he's going out?"

"I said we were going for a drive."

"Did he say anything to that?"

"Nothing at all."

"Who is coming?" Srb-Debrnov wanted to know.

"Only myself and Anna—Anna Capek, the maid."

"Why is she coming?"

"Betty doesn't want to come, and Zofie says she couldn't bear to come. And as Anna has known him for years, I thought it might allay any suspicions."

"Very well, I suppose the sooner we get away the better. Zofie, do you want to say goodbye to your father?"

But Zofie ran past him, crying loudly now, and went to her bedroom, where she locked herself in.

"I'd better go in and get him," Srb-Debrnov said.

Bedrich was sitting facing the door. He looked wasted, and his eyes were very dark, with black rings beneath them. Srb-Debrnov had to clench his fists to control himself.

"Bedrich," he began.

"... and the fisherman, with the line ... don't burn it down, Mayr ... the little children will want to run, and I can't Capek, I can't ... very sad ... very sad ... very sad ..."

Bedrich had no idea who Srb-Debrnov was. He stood up

meekly when his friend took his arm, walked out of the door as docile as a gentle child. He looked straight past Betty and Josef, turned back to look at Betty when he had walked past her, gave her the smile of a simpleton.

Josef Schwarz brought out the valise. Anna Capek followed him. They all got into the waiting carriage, and then they drove away from the house.

At her bedroom window Zofie stood with tears streaming down her cheeks, and as the carriage turned away down the road she moaned, "Oh, Papa, Papa, Papa . . . "

All the way to Prague Bedrich sat quietly, occasionally smiling, glancing neither to left nor to right.

When they reached the asylum Srb-Debrnov and Anna Capek got out, and Josef Schwarz touched Bedrich's arm to get him to rise.

Bedrich's eyes opened wide with fright. He shouted, just the once, "I want to go home! Where is Viola?" But then it was over, and he got out meekly.

They took him upstairs to a room which looked out on to a garden bathed in bright spring sunshine. The bars on the window were stout and strong. The birds were singing when they said goodbye to him.

Srb-Debrnov was the last to leave the room.

You won't let them get me?

No, I won't let them get you.

Ever?

Ever.

You promise?

Yes.

Say: I promise.

I promise, Bedrich.

"Goodbye, Bedrich," he said.

Bedrich was sitting on the bed, rocking backward and forward. He was saying "Katerina, Fröjda Benecke, Viola, Katerina, Fröjda Benecke, Viola" endlessly.

The day was glorious and warm, and the sun was playing strange and beautiful tricks on the Vltava. The spires of the city were shimmering in the heat haze, and children were playing in the streets.

Antonin Vesely pushed his barrel-organ up the street. It would be a good day, he knew that, and the new tune on the roll, although it had taken the last of his ready cash, would earn him some good money today. The people in the taverns were singing this song every night, and the errand boys whistled it as they made their deliveries.

He paused for a moment to mop his brow with a dirty rag. He looked up. The asylum. He'd get no money from here. Still, he thought, maybe they'd like to hear the tune. He turned the handle, and the gay music began to jangle pleasantly in the quiet street. He was in good form, and he began to sing, "Why shouldn't we be happy?" from *The Bartered Bride*.

At about the same time as he started singing, a deaf man of sixty in a room filled with sunshine up above Antonin Vesely's head fought for breath. There was an unpleasant gurgle of sound, and then the struggle was over.

Bedrich Smetana was dead.

There was no-one in the room with him.

It was Monday, May 12th, 1884.

Bedrich Smetana's Music on Gramophone Records

Gallop in D major; Early Polkas—Luise, Georgette, Fragment in B flat minor; Gallop di Bravoura; Quadrille in F; Quadrille in B flat; Polka—Student Life; Impromptus—E flat minor, B minor, A flat; Duo Without Words. Vera Repkova, piano. Supraphon SUA 10074.

Polka—Remembering Pilsen; Waltzes—Nos. 1, 2, 3, and 4; Bagatelles et Impromptus—Innocence, Anxiety, Idyll, Desire, Joy, Fairytale, Love, Quarrel; Mazurka-Capricio in C sharp minor; Etudes—C major, A minor; Characteristic Variations on a Folk Song; Pensée Fugitive. Vera Repkova, piano. Supraphon SUA 10075.

Sonata in G minor; Polka in E flat; Six Keepsake Pieces; Polka Fragments—E minor, C major. Vera Repkova, piano. Supraphon SUA 10076.

Keepsake Pieces, Opus 2; Scherzo Polka in A; Andante in E flat; Romance in G; Composition in C sharp minor; Sketches, Opuses 4 and 5; Two Keepsake Pieces—To Robert Schumann, The Wayfarer's Song. Vera Repkova, piano. Supraphon SUA 10077.

Six Characteristic Pieces, Opus 1—In the Woods, Rising Passion, The Shepherdess, Desire, The Warrior, Despair; Romance in B flat; Caprice in G minor; Polka in A. Vera Repkova, piano. Supraphon SUA 10078.

Marches from 1848; Wedding Scenes; Polkas—E major and F minor; Characteristic Pieces in C flat; Allegro Capricioso in B minor; Polkas—G minor, F sharp, and C major. Vera Repkova, piano. Supraphon SUA 10079.

Three Drawing Room Polkas; Three Poetic Polkas; Bettina Polka; Treasury of Melodies; A Keepsake Piece in E flat minor; The Forest Sentiments and Impressions; The Curious Man; Village Girl. Vera Repkova, piano. Supraphon SUA 10080.

Ballade in E minor; Concert Etude in C; On the Seashore; Le Cid; Ximena; Macbeth and the Witches. Vera Repkova, piano. Supraphon SUA 10081.

Vision at a Ball; Remembering Bohemia in Polka form; Polkas from Czech Dances; Two Keepsake Pieces—B flat major, B minor;

Andante in F minor; Fragment of an F minor Polka; Bettina Polka (second version). Vera Repkova, piano. Supraphon SUA 10082.

Fantasy on Czech Folk Songs; Two Keepsake Pieces; Dreams—Bygone Happiness, Consolation, In the Drawing Room, In Bohemia, In Front of the Castle, Harvest-home. Vera Repkova, piano. Supraphon SUA 10083.

Czech Dances—Furiant, The Hen, The Oats, The Bear, Little Onion, Stamping Dance, The Lancer, The Astride Dance, The Neighbours' Dance, The Jump Dance. Vera Repkova, piano. Supraphon SUA 10084.

On the Seashore; Concert Etude, Opus 17; The Lancer. Rumiana Atanasova, piano. Supraphon SUA 10525.

Polkas—A minor, F major. Anatoli Katc, piano. Supraphon SUA 10526.

Luise's Polka. Played on the accordion by Milan Blaha. Supraphon SUA 11560.

VIOLIN MUSIC

From My Homeland, No. 2. Misha Elman, violin. Decca LXT 5304.

From My Homeland, No. 2. Ruggiero Ricci, violin. Decca LXT 5460.

From My Home—Duo for Violin and Piano. Josef Suk, violin, and Jan Panenka, piano. Supraphon SUA 10464.

CHAMBER MUSIC

Piano Trio in G minor, Opus 15. Suk Trio. Supraphon SUA 10277.

String Quartet No. 1 in E minor—From My Life; String Quartet No. 2 in D minor. Smetana Quartet. Supraphon SUA 10448.

Quartet No. 1 in E minor—From My Life. Edres Quartet. Decca PL 10190.

Quartet No. 1 in E minor—From My Life. The Guarneri Quartet. Decca VIC 1232.

ORCHESTRAL MUSIC

Macbeth and the Witches. Prague Symphony Orchestra, conducted by Vaclav Smetacek. Supraphon SUA 10538.

Shakespeare Festival March. Czech Philharmonic Orchestra, conducted by Jarmil Burghauser. **Supraphon SUA 10153.**

Festive Symphony. Czech Philharmonic Orchestra, conducted by Karel Sejna. Supraphon SUA 10875.

Richard III; Wallenstein's Camp; Haakon Jarl. Czech Philharmonic Orchestra, conducted by Karel Sejna. Supraphon SUA 10341.

Ma Vlast (My Country)—Vysehrad, Vltava, Sarka, From Bohemia's Meadows and Forests, Tabor, Blanik. Vienna Philharmonic Orchestra, conducted by Rafael Kubelik. Decca LXT 5474/5.

Ma Vlast (My Country)—Vysehrad, Vltava, Sarka, From Bohemia's Woods and Fields, Tabor, Blanik. Berlin Philharmonic Orchestra, conducted by Sir Malcolm Sargent. His Master's Voice HMV SXLP/XLP 20064/5.

Ma Vlast (My Country)—Vysehrad, Vltava, Sarka, From Bohemia's Woods and Fields, Tabor, Blanik. (Historical recording.) Czech Philharmonic Orchestra, conducted by Vaclav Talich. Supraphon SUA 10262/3.

Ma Vlast (My Country)—Vysehrad, Vltava, Sarka, From Bohemia's Woods and Fields, Tabor, Blanik. Czech Philharmonic Orchestra, conducted by Karel Ancerl. Supraphon SUA 10521/2.

Vltava; From Bohemia's Meadows and Forests. Bamberg Symphony Orchestra, conducted by Joseph Keilberth. Decca GMA 68.

Vltava; From Bohemia's Woods and Fields. Czech Philharmonic Orchestra, conducted by Karel Ancerl. Supraphon SUF 20135.

Vltava. Berlin Philharmonic Orchestra, conducted by Herbert von Karajan. Columbia SAX 2275 and CX 1642.

Vltava. Bamberg Symphony Orchestra, conducted by Joseph Keilberth. Decca GMA 73.

Vltava. Israel Philharmonic Orchestra, conducted by Istvan Kertesz. Decca LXT 6024.

Vltava. Los Angeles Philharmonic Orchestra, conducted by Alfred Wallenstein. Decca AXTL 1063.

Vltava. RCA Victor Symphony Orchestra, conducted by Leopold Stokowski. Decca RB 16259.

Vltava. Vienna Philharmonic Orchestra, conducted by Rafael Kubelik. Decca CEP 568.

Vltava. Czech Philharmonic Orchestra, conducted by Vaclav Talich. Supraphon SUK 30125.

OPERAS

The Brandenburgers in Bohemia (complete recording). Prague National Theatre Chorus and Orchestra, conducted by Jan Hus Tichy. Supraphon SUA 10541/3.

The Bartered Bride (complete recording). Prague National Theatre Chorus and Orchestra, conducted by Zdenek Chalabala. Supraphon SUA 10397/9.

The Bartered Bride—Overture, Polka, Furiant; Vltava. Czech Philharmonic Orchestra, conducted by Karel Ancerl. Supraphon SUA 10547.

The Bartered Bride—Overture, Polka, Furiant, Dance of the Comedians. Los Angeles Philharmonic Orchestra, conducted by Alfred Wallenstein. Decca AXTL 1063.

The Bartered Bride—Overture, Polka, Furiant. Israel Philharmonic Orchestra, conducted by Istvan Kertesz. Decca LXT 6024 and CEP 5524.

The Bartered Bride—Overture. RCA Victor Symphony Orchestra, conducted by Leopold Stokowski. Decca RB 16259.

The Bartered Bride—Overture. Royal Philharmonic Orchestra, conducted by Sir Malcolm Sargent. His Master's Voice HMV SXLP/XLP 20034.

The Bartered Bride—Overture. Czech Philharmonic Orchestra, conducted by Karel Sejna. Supraphon SUA 10179.

The Bartered Bride—Dance of the Comedians. Mantovani and his Orchestra. Decca LK 4161.

The Bartered Bride—Marenka's Aria, Act 3. Prague National Theatre Chorus and Orchestra, conducted by Zdenek Chalabala. Supraphon SUA 10414.

Dalibor (complete recording). Prague National Theatre Chorus and Orchestra, conducted by Jaroslav Krombholc. Supraphon SUA 10220/2.

Dalibor—Dalibor's Aria, Act 1. Prague National Theatre Chorus and Orchestra, conducted by Bogdan Wodiczko. Supraphon SUA 10644.

Libuse (complete recording). Prague National Theatre Chorus and Orchestra, conducted by Jaroslav Krombholc. Supraphon SUA 10701/4.

Libuse: Overture; Premysl's Aria, Act 2. Prague National Theatre Chorus and Orchestra, conducted by Zdenek Chalabala. Supraphon SUA 10413/4.

The Two Widows (complete recording). Prague National Theatre Chorus and Orchestra, conducted by Jaroslav Krombholc. Supraphon SUA 10283/5.

The Kiss (complete recording). Prague National Theatre Chorus and Orchestra, conducted by Zdenek Chalabala. Supraphon SUA 10230/2.

The Secret (complete recording). Prague National Theatre Chorus and Orchestra, conducted by Jaroslav Krombholc. Supraphon SUA 10240/2.

The Secret—Rose's Aria, Act 2. Prague National Theatre Chorus and Orchestra, conducted by Bohumil Gregor. Supraphon SUA 10589.

The Secret—Overture. Czech Philharmonic Orchestra, conducted by Rudolf Vasata. Supraphon SUA 10590.

The Devil's Wall (complete recording). Prague National Theatre Chorus and Orchestra, conducted by Zdenek Chalabala. Supraphon SUA 10361/3.

VOCAL MUSIC

Choruses for Male Voices—Festive Chorus; Sea Song; Dedication; Prayer; Two Choruses; Three Horsemen; Renegade; The Peasant Song. Moravian Teachers' Male Chorus, conducted by Jan Soupal. Supraphon SUA 10029.